CONFLICT
IN
WORLD SOCIETY

CONFLICT
IN
WORLD SOCIETY

A new perspective on international relations

Edited by

MICHAEL BANKS

Lecturer in International Relations
London School of Economics

Foreword by Professor Herbert Kelman

Richard Clarke Cabot Professor of Social Ethics
Harvard University

ST. MARTIN'S PRESS   **New York**

All rights reserved. For information, write:
St. Martin's Press, Inc., 175 Fifth Avenue, New York, NY 10010
Printed in Great Britain
First published in the United States of America in 1984

Library of Congress Cataloging in Publication Data
Main entry under title:

Conflict in world society.

Essays written in honor of John Burton.
Includes index.
1. International organization – addresses,
essays, lectures.   2. International relations –
addresses, essays, lectures.   3. Burton,
John W. (John Wear), 1915- addresses,
essays, lectures.   I. Banks, Michael.   II.
Burton, John W. (John Wear) 1915-.
JX1954.C578455 1984 341.2 84-4834
ISBN 0-312-16229-4

To
John W. Burton

Contents

List of Contributors

Chadwick F. Alger is Mershon Professor of Political Science and Public Policy at the Ohio State University.

Michael Banks is Lecturer in International Relations at the London School of Economics.

Anthony de Reuck is Senior Lecturer in Linguistic and International Studies at the University of Surrey.

A. J. R. Groom is Reader in International Relations at the University of Kent at Canterbury.

Christopher Hill is Lecturer in International Relations at the London School of Economics.

Margot Light is Lecturer in Linguistic and International Studies at the University of Surrey.

Richard Little is Lecturer in Politics at the University of Lancaster.

C. R. Mitchell is Senior Lecturer in the Department of Systems Science at the City University, London.

Robert C. North is Professor of Political Science at Stanford University.

A. N. Oppenheim is Reader in Social Psychology at the London School of Economics.

Helen Purkitt is Associate Professor of Political Science at the United States Naval Academy.

Dennis J. D. Sandole is Associate Professor of Government and Politics at George Mason University.

Matthew R. Willard is a doctoral candidate in Political Science at Stanford University.

Introduction

Michael Banks

This book deals with the 'world society' perspective on international relations, together with its associated body of conflict theory. The objective is to set out in a single volume the main sources of the approach, its principal arguments and implications, and also some of its strengths and weaknesses.

The task of explaining international relations is so demanding that any writer who claims to be offering a 'new perspective' is likely to provoke a critical response. Nevertheless, the fourteen authors of *Conflict in World Society* are agreed upon both the novelty and the importance of the world society perspective, even though we differ among ourselves in the extent of our commitment to it. And we believe that where new ideas do exist in this most difficult of scholarly fields, they should be presented and they deserve to be discussed.

The idea of writing the book came from the Centre for the Analysis of Conflict. This is a research group which meets regularly to coordinate the work of its members on applied conflict resolution. In a 1981 meeting the group considered the paradoxical state of the international relations discipline in the present decade. On the one hand, it is clearly prospering in several ways. On the other hand, its practical yield, in terms of understanding of real-world problems, shows little improvement in comparison with earlier periods. At the research frontier, there seems to be progressively less agreement about the core ideas that are supposed to hold the discipline together. In the classroom and in the learned journals, students and decision makers alike are presented with a confused picture of what the academics have to say about world politics.

There is encouragement to be found, however. For a generation now, scholars in the field have been aware of a long series of insights, findings, hunches, perspectives and partial theories that seem to hint at new ways of looking at the old problems of international politics. Known as 'islands of theory', they have arisen in the study of perception processes, systems analysis, interdependence, linkage politics, decision making, bargaining techniques and many other areas. Together they hold out the promise of forming a pattern. Many people have tried to fit them together, but found themselves unable to do so. It is clearly the case that the pattern, if it exists, is not obvious. And the search has been hindered by the fact that the behavioural movement of twenty years ago, with its emphasis on methods rather than ideas, effectively discouraged the production of generalists within the discipline.

But there have been a few generalists at work, and among them one stands out: John Burton. Over the period since 1950, the accumulated writings of this Australian diplomat-turned-scholar have gone farther than any other single body of work towards the creation of a genuine synthesis of the fragmentary islands of theory that have so teased the discipline. His work achieves this despite its flaws, and it is unfortunate that the flaws – in clarity, coherence and evidence – have occupied disproportionate attention in comparison with the overall achievement.

The Centre for the Analysis of Conflict has therefore sought the cooperation of a cross-section of Burton's colleagues, former students and friends in putting together this book. Its function is not only to mark his contribution and to honour him for making it, but also to explore some of the many questions which his work, inevitably, has left as yet unanswered:

Each author was invited to combine exposition with criticism, and also to extend the discussion of a given aspect of 'world society thinking' in an effort to develop it. The essays, in consequence, are critical interpretations. The broad franchise given to the authors has resulted in a varied set of treatments of the new perspective, with occasional overlaps between authors and in a few cases an inconsistent use of terminology between one chapter and another. Without the application of editorial discipline to an unacceptable degree, such unevenness is always a feature of multi-authored books, even where – as here – the essays are composed within an integrated plan. And at the present early stage in the development of the world society perspective, a homogenised treatment would be inappropriate.

Planning the book was an exercise, initially, in listing and trying to answer the questions that are usually asked after a first encounter with Burton's work. But it quickly became apparent that there are too many of them, ranging too widely, to treat comprehensively in a single volume. For example, how far is this approach wholly new, and how far does it merely restate the well-known idealist assumptions about world politics? How does it relate to the behavioural movement? Do human needs differ from human rights? Can there really be constructive solutions to zero-sum conflicts? How can a political society be stable without some powerful authority to keep order? Why, if the object is to explain international politics, is so much attention paid to strikes, ethnic attitudes, deviant conduct and other domestic matters? Surely violence is inevitable, and warfare permanent, in international politics?

Necessarily, the plan eventually adopted became a selective one, relying partly on the agreed framework, partly on the judgment of individual authors. The selection that emerged was a three-part arrangement: origins of the world society perspective, its substantive arguments, and its applications.

Herbert Kelman's foreword opens the discussion with a personal account of the impact of Burton's work, especially on those scholars who, like Kelman himself, have sought to make a contribution to the peaceful resolution of conflict. Then *Michael Banks* surveys the history of thought in international relations, with a focus on recent trends. His argument is that the world society perspective is not idiosyncratic, as is sometimes suggested, but is simply the logical extension of the pluralistic world-view which most scholars in the discipline now accept.

Robert North and *Matthew Willard* then assess the implications of post-behavioural thinking for research on international relations. They first employ an analysis of recent discoveries in the philosophy of science to show that the 'behaviouralist-traditionalist' confrontation between 'hard theory' and 'soft theory' has now been transcended. Then, in an argument which implicitly echoes Burton's frequent calls for the direct involvement of social scientists in ongoing, real-world conflict situations, they conclude that future progress will be possible only through the artistic creation of better theory, firmly linked to the gathering and skilful management of better data.

The first part is rounded off with *Dennis Sandole*'s presentation of the necessity for an adjustment in thought that must be made if the new perspective is to be fully appreciated. This process, usually known as a 'paradigm shift', is a feature of the world society approach that has often led to misunderstandings. Sandole begins by contrasting the world society paradigm with that of the 'realist' school. He then points out that the appropriate judgement to be made is *not* that of deciding which is right and which is wrong. Rather it is a matter of recognising how and why it is that thinkers within each paradigm belong to different mental worlds. Like the editor, he detects signs that a paradigm shift is now underway in international relations.

The second part, dealing with substance, contains four chapters. In the first, *C.R. Mitchell* analyses the single most important idea in the world society perspective: the proposition that the politics of the world is to be explained by studying relationships within systems. In the past decade, many scholars have noted that the increasingly pluralistic discipline of world politics must take account of many interaction patterns, not just intergovernmental ones. Attention is being shifted from foreign policies towards such non-governmental relationships as those of business firms, market forces, ethnic links, ideological groupings and revolutionary movements.

But the discipline as a whole has not yet taken the next step, in terms of general theory: to make the entire set of interaction patterns the main focus, instead of relegating the non-governmental ones to ancillary status while keeping the principal level of analysis fixed on governments. Burton has taken that step, but his work does contain loose ends. Noting this, Mitchell sets about the task of tying them into the general theory. He analyses the problems involved in defining the relationships, classifying them, assessing their legitimacy and tracing their effects.

The other three chapters in the 'substance' part are all devoted to the further development of the general idea of systemic, or functional, relationships within a single world society. Traditionally, political affairs in the world as a whole have not been treated as a single system, but as two systems – inter-state relations being one and the domestic politics of states the other. With two distinct political arenas to be studied, two autonomous disciplines have developed. On the one hand there is international relations, tenuously linked to history, law and philosophy. On the other hand is political science, more closely linked to the behavioural sciences but studiously avoiding global generalisations because of its concentration upon relationships which operate under the authority of a common government. Only during the 'behavioural revolution' of the 1950s did the intellectually crippling implications of this distinction undergo serious criticism, particularly by John Burton.

Richard Little, therefore, takes as his theme the problem of social stability. If it is valid for the new perspective to employ 'the domestic analogy' to examine the world as a whole, then it becomes crucially important to identify the means by which stable social relationships are established and maintained within states. Grouping the issues under the headings of social order, conflict management and mechanisms of social control, Little summarises the existing state of knowledge and Burton's contribution to it. In doing so, he notes that all forms of social order appear to rest upon ideological foundations, and if that is the case then the world society perspective must be presented and judged as an ideological interpretation.

In *Anthony de Reuck*'s chapter, the focus is moved from order to conflict. Just as stability is seen in the new perspective to be a unitary phenomenon at all societal levels, so conflict is treated as a single process wherever it occurs. There are, obviously, differences between, say, a family quarrel and a civil war, or between an ethnic riot and a superpower confrontation. But there are also similarities, and the world society approach seeks to make progress by concentrating on the similarities rather than the differences. de Reuck uses his analysis of the origins and dynamics of the conflict process to demonstrate the inherent potential for the peaceful resolution of conflicts, as opposed to fighting them to a conclusion or settling them by forcible intervention. His comments on the subjective nature of many conflict interactions are further developed in *A.N. Oppenheim*'s account of the benefits flowing from the recent introduction of social psychology into international relations studies. Psychologically oriented research has deepened the understanding of group identity, explored the cognitive maps of decision makers, and illuminated behaviour patterns in crisis situations.

The third part of the book contains applications of the world society perspective. The five chapters each give further exposition of the content of the new perspective, but also provide commentary or criticism, and in each case the author explores a different set of practical issues. *Chadwick Alger*, in an argument drawing on his extensive research on the international relations of a midwestern US city, extends and illustrates the idea of functional relationships. Analysing the multifarious networks that connect an average city to the world as a whole, he suggests that the full development and exploitation of such links would, over time and with adequate understanding of politics by ordinary people, transform the nature of international politics.

Just as Alger provides a concrete illustration of the constructive potential of systemic relationships, so *Margot Light* develops the constructive potential of conflict theory. Unlike most international relations treatments of conflict, which result in policy recommendations, the world society perspective leads to recommendations about methods. Taking as her theme John Burton's insistence that the analysis of a conflict is itself the formula for its resolution, Light

describes the problem-solving workshop. In that unique setting, she
argues, the insights of theory can be integrated with the hard realities
of policy to produce a changed political situation. A case study of the
relevance of world society thinking to one of the least manageable
forms of conflict then follows, in *Helen Purkitt*'s discussion of
terrorism. Drawing upon recent developments in organisation theory
and the study of information processing by decision makers, Purkitt
argues that political terrorism can, potentially, be controlled, but not
by deterrence alone. A more sophisticated strategy is needed,
responsive to grievances where they are legitimate and backed by a
public opinion which is kept informed of the issues.

The two closing chapters also deal with the problems faced by
decision makers, but more generally and within contrasting frameworks. *Christopher Hill*'s contribution is a sharply critical, though
sympathetic, assessment. Conscious of the tension between the
difficult issues of foreign policy and the need of authorities for a
legitimate relationship with their domestic supporters, he analyses
the merits and weaknesses of each major proposition of the new
perspective. *A.J.R. Groom* does not share Hill's image of the decision
maker as a responsible but autonomous agent, free to accept or reject
specific advice from academics or any other group. Instead he
portrays a wider social process, whereby academics and decision
makers each make distinct contributions at different stages of the
flow of policy formation.

Finally, a word is in order about the spirit of this book and the
theoretical enterprise behind it. It is best expressed in Thomas Kuhn's
The Structure of Scientific Revolutions (1970, p. 5), in a passage with
which many scholars in international relations are uneasily familiar.
Any branch of research, Kuhn reminds us, can – over time – become a
'strenuous and devoted attempt to force nature into the conceptual
boxes supplied by professional education'. This is a book by people
who are worried about their confinement in those conceptual boxes,
and are hopeful that John Burton's world society perspective may –
just possibly – have pointed to a way out.

Foreword

Herbert C. Kelman

The essays assembled in this volume were written in honour of John Burton. The authors are but a few of the many colleagues, friends, and former students – from all regions of our world society – whose lives John has touched in significant ways. The impact he has had on each of us has, no doubt, been unique, but I can best illustrate the quality of that impact by describing my own experience.

I can literally say that meeting John has changed my life – and this despite the fact that I was already in the fortieth year of that life at the time. I had been actively involved in the development of the peace research movement in the early 1950s, in the founding of the interdisciplinary *Journal of Conflict Resolution* in the later 1950s, and in the work of the Center for Research on Conflict Resolution at the University of Michigan in the 1960s. As a social psychologist, my particular interest was in identifying the points at which psychological factors – notably in the form of images and interaction processes – enter into international relations. When I first learned, in 1966, about 'controlled communication' – the approach to the analysis and resolution of international conflict developed by John – I instantly recognised it as the arena *par excellence* for exploring such points of entry. My interest in the approach deepened when I had the opportunity to participate in a controlled communication exercise on the Cyprus conflict that John conducted in London later that year.

Controlled communication (or interactive problem solving, as we now prefer to call it) attempts to produce changes at the level of political systems by inducing changes at the level of individuals – changes in the perceptions and attitudes of representatives of conflicting parties who are in a position to influence the policy process. The social scientists who, as a special third party, facilitate the process of communication and problem-solving, have an opportunity to learn about the dynamics of international and intercommunal conflict (and of the particular conflict under discussion) by observing the interaction between the conflicting parties. Thus, I realised that, with respect to both resolution and analysis of conflict, problem-solving workshops operationalise social-psychological factors in international relations (without falling into the trap of psychological reductionism). The approach I learned from John allowed me to bring together not only my various pursuits in the social psychology of international relations, but also my work on social influence and attitude change and my interest in psychotherapy and group process. Gradually, the development and application of the problem-solving approach to international conflict resolution has moved to the centre of my professional work. I like to think that I have made some contributions to our joint enterprise – particularly in the conceptualisation of a model of intervention – but whatever I have done is merely an elaboration or extension of the basic insights contained in John's model of controlled communication (as described, for example, in his *Conflict and Communication*, 1969).

As I continued my applied work in conflict resolution, I became increasingly aware that the problem-solving approach to conflict resolution implied a particular view of international conflict. Not only does a theory of international relations guide the method of intervention, but the practice of the method in turn reveals and clarifies the underlying theoretical model. Thus, this work helped me to define and integrate more systematically the theoretical and applied contributions of social psychology to international relations. In the process I came to appreciate ever more the wider ramifications of John's pioneering approach to the analysis and resolution of international conflict. From the beginning, he not only saw an intrinsic connection between theory and practice, but he sought thoroughgoing alternatives to conventional approaches at both levels. Starting with his early work on nonalignment and security (see *The Alternative: A Dynamic Approach to Australian Relations with Asia*, 1954; *Peace Theory: Preconditions of Disarmament*, 1962; and *International Relations: A General Theory*, 1965), he has been expressing criticism of the power model that underlies both traditional international relations theory and diplomatic practice, and he has been dedicated to the improvement of theoretical as well as diplomatic efforts.

Development of the problem-solving approach to conflict resolution went hand in hand with John's theoretical efforts to reconceptualise the international system and the study of international relations, making use of systems analysis (see his *Systems, States, Diplomacy and Rules*, 1968) and culminating in his view of world society (see *World Society*, 1972). Central to John's intervention technique is the introduction of theoretical ideas and empirical findings by the third party, which the conflicting parties can use as tools in the analysis of their own conflict and in the search for creative solutions. It is not surprising that John and his collaborators tend to introduce ideas that flow from his conceptual model – such as ideas for establishing functional relationships between the conflicting parties instead of bargaining over constitutional issues. But, beyond such instrumental uses of theory in the course of practice, there is an organic connection between theory and practice in John's approach. Interactive problem solving for him is not just a technique, but an alternative diplomacy appropriate to his alternative conception of the international system as a world society.

Throughout his work, John has sought to provide a scientific basis to the formulation of policy. On the assumption that a theory of international relations must be consistent with what we know about human behaviour and social organisation at all levels, he has drawn widely on the behavioural sciences in the development of a thoroughly interdisciplinary approach. Thus, his conception of world society utilises general systems theory to provide an underlying framework, sociological thinking about society to capture the entire range of overlapping and cross-cutting relationships that characterise the global system, and the psychology of perception to explain the ways in which these relationships are observed and interpreted. Though enthusiastic in his advocacy of behavioural analysis, John has always been 'post-behavioural' in his orientation: he has not been interested in the refinement of measurement tools as an end in itelf, but in the contributions of behavioural science to an analysis that is alive to the value context within which policy is formulated.

In his psychological formulations, John has shifted from an emphasis on perception in the late 1960s and early 1970s to an emphasis on human needs in his more recent work (*Deviance, Terrorism and War*, 1979; *Dear Survivors*, 1982). The concept of universal human needs is central to a paradigm shift that John notes in recent social science writings and that he calls for in policy thinking. It is a shift from a paradigm based on the exercise of power, leading to adversarial and coercive methods for enforcing legal and social norms, to a paradigm based on the analysis of relationships, leading to no-fault, interactive problem solving methods for satisfying human needs. Thus, John's latest work adds another concentric circle to his continually expanding contribution. We can see with ever increasing clarity the integral relationship between his innovative method of diplomacy, his alternative analysis of the global system, and his emerging paradigm for the study of social relations more broadly.

John's work has generated increasing interest in the United States. His influence is particularly noticeable in two organisations with which I am associated: the International Studies Association and the International Society of Political Psychology. The International Studies Association appointed John as ISA Scholar in Residence at the Byrnes International Center (University of South Carolina) for 1983. During his tenure there, he produced a proposal for a Continuing Seminar and an International Facilitating Service, which was presented to an international group of scholars at the ISA meetings in Mexico City in April 1983. This proposal represents an ambitious effort to institutionalise the problem-solving approach to conflict resolution through a non-governmental, professional agency, accessible to governments and other parties in conflict.

Thus, John continues to innovate at all levels, challenging old assumptions, modes of thinking, and decision-making models, and proposing new paradigms, methods, and institutional arrangements. In doing so, he has established a unique place for himself among scholars concerned with the understanding and improvement of international relations. His work is a living organism – an open system – which allows others to draw on, to build on, and indeed to criticise the novel insights and imaginative formulations that it contains. The essays that follow provide a sampling of the responses that this work has stimulated or provoked. I am confident that in these essays, as in the work of John Burton that they are designed to honour, the reader will find many exciting new ideas about world society – its nature, its study, and its potentialities for change.

Acknowledgements

Everything in the book was written especially for it, so my first acknowledgement as editor must be to my fellow-contributors. Though at times I urged submissiveness upon them in routine matters, our friendly disputations over issues of substance have left me not just better educated, but also more respectful of the anarchism natural to academics. Within the group, John Groom provided firm support throughout the project, and Margot Light solved some of the most difficult editorial problems.

At LSE, my students deserve a tribute. The concepts and methods seminar has been a weekly tonic, encouraging me to believe that there may be a substantial audience for the ideas presented here. My research students have offered assistance and criticism, especially Carla Garapedian and Mark J. Hoffman who helped with research and editing. Typing on successive drafts was done at several universities, and at the LSE by Elizabeth Leslie, Anna Morgan and particularly Hilary Parker, a magician when dealing with a temperamental word processor. At Wheatsheaf, Edward Elgar has been the most constructive and decisive of scholarly publishers. But at the end of the day, the views in each chapter are those of its author, and editorial responsibility for the whole is mine.

Michael Banks

Part I
THE RISE OF THE WORLD SOCIETY
PERSPECTIVE

1 The Evolution of International Relations Theory

Michael Banks

This chapter is an attempt to summarise the history of thought in the study of international relations. Its purpose is both to show the historical context of the 'world society' way of thinking, and also to establish a framework within which the more detailed arguments of the following chapters can be considered.

The theme is that the key to the understanding of international relations consists of ideas, not facts. The facts of life for the globe's five billion people are, of course, solid enough: wealth or poverty, freedom or oppression, mobility or confinement, peace or violence. These conditions exist objectively. But there is nothing necessary or permanent about them. They result from choices. The choices are made within the complicated, uneven institutions of international politics. There is no single government to allocate values for the world as a whole, but the values are allocated nevertheless. 'Who gets what, when and how' is determined by power balances, ideological movements, tyrannical or democratic regimes, foreign intervention, booms and slumps of industrial production, patterns of trade within borders and across them – and much more.

All these structures and processes are man-made. They began as schemes in the minds of statesmen and entrepreneurs, or as systems of thought in the literature of philosophy and society. To apply the ideas, power and leadership were needed. Initially, these resources came from sovereigns. Efficient institutions like diplomatic immunity therefore gained acceptance while inefficient ones like licensed privateering died away. Later, the needs and values of mass populations slowly made themselves felt. Their political energy, mobilised and directed by elites, was inspired by visions: of justice, of the good life, of right conduct, of putting down enemies and keeping faith with friends. Popular ideas like self-determination consequently became firmly established, while such barbarous practices as the slave trade or colonial empires met increasing resistance. Over time, many institutions initially devised to fit past conditions came to be valued for their own sake, sentimentally, rather than for any practical benefits that they might confer.

Effectively, then, the international political system today is a haphazard set of practices, organisations, habits and beliefs evolved over several centuries. It consists of the surviving competitors of past struggles over ideas, vested interests, and ideologies, with new ones continually being added. The 'real world' of global politics is not a naturally given state of affairs like the physical environment. Its extreme complexity does require elaborate empirical work in order to describe its condition at any one time. But the task of explaining it is not a matter of hunting down immutable laws. It is an exploration of the manner in which some political ideas have become political facts, whereas others have not. Ideas come from thinkers, and are put into practice either directly where thinking men assume power, or indirectly where the powerful interpret the world and act in it according to the lessons they have learned in their youth.

To seek an understanding of international relations, therefore, is to take part in a debate between competing sets of ideas. The debate is both ancient and modern, having been underway since at least the seventeenth century when the basic features of international politics emerged, and having been established for the past seventy years as an academic discipline in Western universities. This flowing stream of ideas shapes the explanations of international relations offered by the scholars; guides the decision makers who conduct the policies; and prescribes the blueprints for each of the periodic attempts to reform the system of world politics.

From the scholar's point of view, the function of the debate is the search for truth. But absolute truth, in international relations as in any other branch of social science, cannot be discovered and presented in any single coherent package of known-laws-plus-appropriate-methodology-plus-established-proofs. This is because each set of ideas either strengthens or weakens existing reality, and thereby alters it. So each contribution is not just an intellectual act, but ultimately a political act as well. In formal language, this means that the distinction between the positive and the normative is difficult, perhaps impossible, to sustain. Factual statements blend in with value judgements; preferences intrude despite the best efforts of scholars to maintain their objectivity (Bernstein, 1976). In consequence, the study of international relations must be regarded as part scholarly inquiry, part ideological discourse, shared among scholars, commentators and practitioners in all parts of the world.

THE CLASSICAL HERITAGE

All the conventional ideas of the international relations discipline date from European thought in the early modern period. Between the sixteenth-century Renaissance and the catastrophic world war which began the twentieth century, the system of sovereign states was invented and established in Western Europe, and began the spread to the rest of the world that it has now completed. As Martin Wight has shown (1977; 1978), the early development of the system both produced and reflected a comprehensive set of ideas about the nature of post-medieval politics. Philosophers, historians, political advisers, journalistic commentators, military theorists and, in particular, international lawyers produced in combination the framework which continues to this day to structure most thinking about international relations.

If the classical literature is viewed now as a single body of thought, incorporating both the pre-modern work of classical Greece and the middle ages, and also writings from the 1648–1914 period, several characteristics become clear. First, in comparison with twentieth-century contributions, many of the writings were masterly. The cynical but thoroughgoing policy advice of Machiavelli, the wise historical observations of Thucydides, the moral forcefulness of the medieval just-war theorists, the soaring humanity of Kantian philosophy or the dry detachment of Clausewitzian strategic theory (to mention only a few of many) have no equal in contemporary scholarship. Unfortunately, their work has been used only selectively, and the authority of those thinkers whose arguments are used to justify partisan doctrines has tended to inhibit creative thinking in our owh century – thinking that might both reflect changed conditions and also guide conduct in international politics towards goals that are now, but were not formerly, attainable.

Second, the basic framework of classical statecraft was described with compelling lucidity, producing a conceptual toolbox which continues to this day to dominate both the practice of world politics and much of its interpretation. The framework portrayed mankind as divided into separate, sovereign states, each keeping law and order within its borders by the application of force from the centre, and also using force to keep secure against other states. Relations between states were conducted by diplomacy, against a background of military preparedness and alliances, and within a limited code of international law of which states, not people, were the subjects. The whole system of states was sustained against overthrow by the balance of power. The associated terminology – national interest, reason of state, deterrence, power politics, legitimate self-defence, diplomatic necessity and the rest – has become the staple diet of most international relationists ever since.

Of course, both history and the growth of thought about it were far more complicated than any simplified extrapolation can encompass. It took several centuries of uneven development for centralised states, with stable borders and national consciousness, to emerge from the semi-anarchy of localised princedoms of the Europe of the Middle Ages. Although an early version of the principle of peaceful coexistence between states with differing ideological systems was effectively established at the Westphalia Settlement of 1648, its implications still continue to be argued today. The doctrine of sovereignty has shifted in character, from an idea describing the absolute power of a king over his own subjects but not over those of other monarchs, to a notion today of the solidarity of a people under common government, using their national independence to pursue whatever aims they might choose. In the twentieth century, much of classical theory is commonly violated, such as the norm of non-intervention, or the principle that alliances must be flexible, or the proportionality doctrine of just-war theory. But the system of ideas itself, like the pure theory of microeconomics, has both a logical attractiveness and great emotive pull, worldwide. People, clearly, like their states; and the crude appeals of power-political slogans form potent capital for national leaders everywhere.

However, the classical period also endowed the world with an intellectual heritage richer by far than the basic vocabulary of international politics. From the wars of religion onwards, there emerged the first 'great debate' in international thought, between liberals and realists. Both groups belonged to the mainstream, in that they acknowledged both the existence of separate, powerful states and the necessity of some form of continuing contact between them. But they differed on the nature of the states and on the character of inter-state relations.

For liberals, the essence of the state was its sovereignty, seen essentially as a moral claim to legitimate rights – rights to ownership of land and to an exclusive governmental system and way of life within its borders. Rights, the liberals argued, confer obligations: one state's sovereignty could be recognised as legitimate only if that state in turn recognised the reciprocal rights of others. As Grotius pointed out, international law defined that relationship. World society was therefore a club, with shared membership by civilised states and sanctions against violators. For realists, in contrast, the essence of sovereignty was that it had to be defended. In place of a pattern of mutual respect and cooperation within the society of states, the Hobbesian view emphasised the inevitability of clashing interests, the central role of coercion and the importance of fears and insecurity. Outside the mainstream, other thinkers further enriched the debate with sets of ideas that went much farther and can properly be termed radical. Rejecting the basic concept of statehood as either necessary, appropriate or even as truly real, they started from an assumption that the world contains simply people living within a variety of political systems. For them, the essential unity of mankind was the starting point. Some, like Marx, postulated social class as the significant organising principle, and like Hegel saw the arrangement of sovereign states as only a temporary phase in some grander historical progression. Others, such as Mazzini, read the lessons of the French and American revolutions and generalised them into the doctrine of national self-determination. This encouraged the potential destabilisation of virtually every state in Europe and later the world, for all states contain groups capable of thinking themselves to be a separate nation. Most revolutionary of all, perhaps, were the various religious thinkers, with their emphases on loyalties above the idols of statehood and on principles that identified people as individuals rather than as objects of state authority. In particular, the Christian theologians who dominated the early phase of international thought derived from their metaphysics of natural law the principles which were in the twentieth century to subvert the logic of statehood by introducing a universal commitment by states to the idea of basic human rights.

TRADITIONALISM: THE EARLY YEARS OF ACADEMIC INTERNATIONAL RELATIONS

When the massive irrationality of the First World War smashed the complacency of Victorian statesmen and thinkers who had believed the international system to be not only efficient, but manageable too, there was a burst of activity in the universities. As a leading classical writer, John Hobson, put it, there was general recognition that 'at the present stage it is of paramount importance to try to get the largest number of thoughtful people to form clear, general ideas of better international relations, and to desire their attainment' (1915, p. 8).

The effect was to produce an institutionalised discipline, complete with textbooks and examinations, doctoral theses and academic conferences. Mainstream ideas, and in the aftermath of the Versailles Settlement notably the ideas of the liberal wing of mainstream thinking, came to dominate curricula and to inform the wider public debate. Classical rationalisations of great-power rule of the world via 'the Concert of Europe' were abandoned, to be replaced by collective security thinking. The final demise of colonial empires (foreshadowed conceptually by the invention of the state three hundred years before), and the newer idea of self-determination, both became practical strategies. The ideas of the balance of power and its associated concepts, like the need for secret diplomacy and spheres of interest, were brought into disrepute.

From the Geneva headquarters of the League of Nations, serious attempts were made to put some of these ideas into practice. And in the universities of the 1920s and 1930s, many students of the new discipline were taught the merits of liberal ideas: of public voting by diplomats in international organisations; of the rule of law; of the promise of disarmament; and of foreign policies based on reconciliation.

In retrospect, this unique flowering of liberal thought, and (to a much lesser extent) of liberal practices in international politics, is quite amazing. Brief though it was, it constituted the first effort by intellectuals and statesmen alike to apply ideas of enlightened self-interest to international politics. Intellectually, it had many faults, described especially well by Inis Claude (1962; 1964). The most important flaws were its attempt to meet power with power (an exercise better conducted with the help of realist ideas); its undue reliance on law and organisations; and its failure to confront the need to transform, rather than to tinker with, the system. Underlying these problems was a basic misunderstanding of the classical debate. Not only was mainstream realism consciously rejected, but the much deeper insights of the truly radical thinkers, linking world politics to social change, morality, ethnicity, ideology and economic processes, were almost wholly ignored.

The demise of liberalism was signalled after less than two decades by the publication of E.H. Carr's *Twenty Years Crisis* in 1939. This work owed its devastating impact not just to its efficient critique of liberalism (thereafter to be known disparagingly as 'idealism' or 'utopianism'), but also to changing world events: the global economic depression, the failure of the League, the imperialist activities of Hitler, Tojo and Mussolini. With the outbreak of the Second World War, realism was wholly reasserted, and there began a twenty-year period of further distortion in the study of international relations. As the war ended, the United Nations Charter symbolised the new mood with its watered-down framework of reformist institutions, re-establishing the concept of great power rule and blurring the distinction so sharply drawn under the League between balance of power and collective security.

In the early postwar years, both academics and opinion leaders of the wider public conspired together to replace the discredited orthodoxy with a new one even more monolithic and even less respectful of the classical heritage. So powerful were the distaste for appeasement, the disillusionment with idealism, the cynicism about progressive international law, that for a generation mainstream scholars became somewhat less imaginative than political leaders. Even while anticolonialism and nonalignment doctrine spread across the Third World; while the General Assembly was debating human rights and disarmament; and while historic plans for an integrated and peaceable European Community were being worked out, teachers were presenting their students with textbooks of power politics and editing anthologies which resurrected Machiavelli and Bismarck.

At its Cold War extreme in the 1950s, mainstream activity in the discipline was so strongly gripped by the one-sided realist paradigm that it barely deserved to be termed a 'debate'. So confident were many authors of their understanding of the basic political structures of the world and the forces that moved them, that they permitted the discipline to become the handmaiden of superpower ideology. In the United States especially, the sober and prudent rules of international conduct as laid down by the general theory of classical realism came to be twisted and misused. Such basic notions as 'order', 'stability', 'balance' and 'vital interest' became self-serving justifications for intervention, for an East-West arms race and even for anticommunist dogma (Hoffmann, 1977). Mainstream thinkers of the realist persuasion began to write normatively in an effort to correct this tendency, offering their restatements of the classical doctrines less as straightforward texts than as conservative critiques of current practice (Morgenthau, 1948; Kennan, 1952; Bull, 1977).

Traditionalism, then, dominated the first half-century of academic international relations throughout both the liberal and realist phases. Seen from the 1980s, it was an unimpressive period, despite the publication of fine work by a handful of major scholars like Quincy Wright (1965) and the occasional appearance of important ideas such as functionalism (Mitrany, 1966). Throughout both its liberal and realist phases, little progress was made beyond ideas which had been developed in previous eras (Hinsley, 1963). Despite the trappings of professionalism, the discipline was staffed mostly by people trained in other fields – law, diplomacy, history, journalism – and the research methods employed were unchanged from those of the classical period. The most serious shortcoming, however, arose from the narrowing of the widely balanced classical debate. In most Western universities, the radical teachings of the fringe classicists on such topics as imperialism, dialectics, pacifism, justice, natural law and revolution were regarded as falling outside the 'commonsense' paradigm formed by the mainstream, with its static, state-centric, view of the international system.

THE BEHAVIOURAL REVOLUTION

By the 1950s some of these shortcomings came to be recognised, though not all. The resultant upheaval lasted into the 1970s, forming the second 'great debate' of the discipline. Unlike the long-standing realist–liberal debate, the new exchanges focussed on methodology rather than upon ideas as such. Known as the 'behavioural revolution', it was an attempt to replace both classical and traditional orientations by scientific method. A wave of energetic younger scholars, mainly in the United States but with adherents in various parts of Europe and the Soviet Union, saw reform as the product of new techniques. They sought to introduce systematic procedures for data collection and analysis; to link their scholarship with work done in 'hard-core' behavioural sciences like economics and psychology; to educate themselves in relevant aspects of epistemology and philosophy; and thus to replace ideographic statements with empirical generalisations.

The purpose was to create an objective science of world politics in which theories would be explicit and findings would be cumulative. Major assumptions of the past were attacked, especially the mainstream view that world politics was a unique field of action, necessarily different from politics within the state because states had governments to keep order, whereas the world at large did not. For behaviouralists, politics was politics, and decision making was done by people, whatever the level of analysis under consideration.

With the autonomy of the discipline thus under challenge, the door was opened to the introduction of 'interdisciplinary' approaches, borrowed from other fields of social science. For the first time in the history of the discipline, the international relations shelves of the libraries became stocked with books containing mathematical symbols and graphs. Students began to learn statistics, computer programming and simulation, while professional conferences offered sections on polimetrics or welcomed such exotic colleagues as systems theorists and content analysts.

Such methodological radicalism provoked outraged response from the many in the discipline who either could not, or would not, adjust to the new wave. The mutual criticisms spilled over into polemical exchanges, marring the academic literature of the 1950s and 1960s. Behaviouralist excesses offered cheap targets for the traditionalist reaction: abstruse jargon, incompetent use of mathematics, the trivialisation of important matters in the effort to find something that could be quantified. But the movement as a whole had a substantial worth, which slowly gained acceptance. Although it never conquered the discipline, it did manage to occupy some of its commanding heights. As it ran its course from the 1950s to the 1970s, it produced a substantial literature (for example, Jones and Singer, 1972; Rosenau, 1976; Sullivan, 1976; Morgan, 1981), and it left an imprint that seems likely to be indelible. That imprint included several of behaviouralism's original objectives, such as the widespread use of interdisciplinary approaches; the exploration of new units of analysis like system, decision or perception; the creation of entire new subfields like foreign policy analysis; and the accumulation of comparable and usable stocks of data.

More generally, its contribution to the ongoing international relations debate added far more than an unprecedented attention to quantitative research methods. The most significant impact came in the early years of the movement, when searching criticisms by leading behaviouralists exposed the faulty assumptions of the realist paradigm. It became clear that states could no longer be treated as the only actors in the international system, and certainly did not behave as unitary actors. Power was by no means the only motivating force in state behaviour, and in any case was hard to define and nearly impossible to measure effectively. The balance of power was shown to be partly mythical, and in any case was at least as likely to lead to instability as to the 'order' claimed for it by the realists. Textbooks were shown to contain shocking biases and ambiguities (Rosenau, 1977). And there was more, effectively drawing a picture of confusion and inadequacy in the central assumptions of the discipline.

This disconcerting turn in the international relations debate produced some lively and varied effects. By the late 1960s the dilemma had become profound, because the criticisms were undermining the previous paradigm *without* providing any promising alternative. The discipline seemed to be in the unique position, historically, of having no general theory at all. One scholar nicely captured the mood of the period in a short article: 'Where Have All the Theories Gone?' (Phillips, 1974).

Response varied more according to temperament than to any intellectual rationale. Many fled to the safe haven of area studies, full of facts and supposedly free of the tangles of theory. Philosophically inclined traditionalists moved right back to the classical period, seeking new enlightenment in Pufendorf and Vattel, Burke and Hume (for example, Donelan, 1978; Beitz, 1979; Linklater, 1982; Mayall, 1983). A few mainstream traditionalists, especially textbook authors, chose to dismiss the swathe of criticism, continuing to teach and write as if nothing had happened. Those interested in strategic questions sought to reinforce realism, rather than abandon it, by cementing their analysis in a mass of steadily more technical material about military capabilities. Their logical opponents in the debate, the peace researchers, went the other way, reasserting liberal values and foreshadowing the post-behavioural phase that was to follow.

But it was among the strict behaviouralists that the most interesting, and also the most confused, responses were to be found. At first, optimistic frontiersmen sought to start afresh in the entire theory-building enterprise. They explored the requirements of theory, the general nature of social science, conceptual frameworks and pre-theoretical schema. Briefly, it became an era of 'theory of theories'. But it soon became clear that metaphysical frameworks alone would yield little of solid worth, while many scholars were also fully aware of analogous difficulties in fields like psychology and sociology. Reluctantly, they set aside the question of general theory for the time being, and instead concentrated on specific, narrow questions to which answers might reasonably be expected. For them, the new task in the debate was to build 'islands of theory', backed by solid evidence but presumably standing in an ocean of ignorance.

POST-BEHAVIOURALISM: GENERAL FEATURES

During the 1970s, therefore, international relations became fragmented into specialisms. Although the discipline had more members than ever before it nevertheless seemed superficially to have weaker general theory. Some of the specialisms were old, like international law or institutions, while others were new like quantitative studies or forecasting techniques. Some were orthodox, as decision making had by now become; others radical, like sociobiology or conflict theory. Some seemed likely to be ephemeral, such as ecopolitics; others here to stay, like strategic analysis. As the decade progressed, more were added, most notably the politics of international economic relations.

Against this splintered background, the sharpness of the traditional-behavioural debate died away. There was a general acceptance that empiricism had its limits and that the vision of a truly positive social science of world politics could never be fulfilled. The mainstream became eclectic. Despite calls for relevance and the purposive abandonment of supposedly 'value-free' research, values were sometimes specified, sometimes not. The new pattern was carefully recorded in K.J. Holsti's fourth (1983) edition of a major text, exemplifying the updated mainstream judgment. There, classic topics like ethics stand beside a behavioural analysis of negotiation; traditionalist views of the state system are complemented by a cautious treatment of strategic theory; among the new subfields, conflict resolution is included but interdependence is scantily treated.

Specialisation and eclecticism were, however, minor features of the behavioural decade in comparison with the most important issue. What was to be the newly enthroned general theory of international relations? By the end of the 1970s, after centuries of classicism and a half-century of experiments successively with liberalism, realism and behaviouralism, the answer at last became clear. It had two parts. First, realism was not dead; it had merely gone underground, and continued to control thinking in the behaviourally tinged mainstream. Second, realism now had serious competition. For the first time since the establishment of international relations as a serious academic discipline a half-century earlier, a debate that recalled the classical era in both range and quality was beginning to re-emerge.

John Vasquez (1983) has charted the unconscious persistence of the realist paradigm among the behaviouralist researchers of the 1950–80 period. Most of them did not come to terms with their 'ocean of ignorance', and never fully recognised what was necessarily entailed by their own harsh criticisms of the traditionalist theories. Instead, they continued to employ the realist set of assumptions without being aware of doing so. This was especially true of the major effort and achievement of the period, namely quantitative research. 'Colour it Morgenthau', the inspired title of a 1973 conference paper, rightly became a catchphrase to describe the tendency (Vasquez, 1979).

As had long been insisted by the critics of behaviouralism, there were several reasons for this state of affairs, all inexorable. There was not only a psychological problem, of overcoming the mental obstacles to a paradigm shift – serious though these obstacles can be. There was also a problem of method, because behaviouralist procedures themselves obstructed the view of what was happening. Behaviouralism stressed empirical work: gathering facts. In itself, fact-gathering seems to be an objective exercise. But it actually is conservative in the ideological sense, because it records the status quo, building a record of things as they are and as they have been – ignoring questions of what might have been and what ought to be. Thus, under the guise of 'science', the behavioural movement unwittingly became an apology for power politics. Even the most sophisticated of empiricist advocates, such as Michael Nicholson, came to accept that 'the activity of social science is redolent with politics and morality' (1983, p. 235).

Furthermore, the behavioural commitment to collecting 'hard' data tended to reinforce the state-centric assumption of realism, because most such data (international events, trade statistics, armaments) are generated by officials and automatically overstate governmental influence on the course of history. The price of an MX missile is included; the passions of an Islamic revolutionary are not. Those scholars who tell themselves that their work in studying society is both objective (value-free) and inductive (theory-free) until *after* they have collected and fully assessed all the relevant facts, are deluding themselves. Their selection and interpretation of facts is necessarily guided throughout by both values and theories. Barefoot empiricism can yield only a jumble, or at best an explanation dictated by unconscious assumptions. And so the behavioural experiment became the strongest argument of the century for a return to the basic postulate of the classical era. Both to explain the world and to know how best to act in it, one must begin with a general world view.

POST-BEHAVIOURALISM: THE INTER-PARADIGM DEBATE

Discussion of fundamental questions did not die away completely during the long reign of traditionalism and its behaviouralist aftermath. But only a minority of scholars explored the assumptions of the discipline, questioned its worth, or asked troubling questions about its relationship to policy. Their work never threatened to alter the course of the mainstream. Only with the arrival of the post-behavioural phase did it begin to do so – but then with such effect that Maghroori and Ramberg (1983, ch. 1) felt justified in christening this phase the 'third debate' in international relations, comparable to the earlier liberal-realist and behaviouralist-traditionalist exchanges. The new debate consisted of confrontation between opposing perspectives of the most general kind, variously known as frameworks, perspectives or paradigms. These were all terms intended to convey a world view more basic than theory, including values as well as empirical findings, and often discussing matters regarded as irrelevant in the former mainstream. Early attempts to establish just how many paradigms there were produced a varying count (for example, Lijphart, 1974; Banks, 1978; Taylor, 1978; Pettman, 1979; Kent and Nielsson, 1980; Smith *et al*, 1981). But by the 1980s it seemed generally agreed that there were three. Rosenau has given them (in Maghroori and Ramberg, 1983, p. 3) the precise names of 'multi-centric', 'state-centric', and 'global-centric'. But the more widely understood terms 'pluralist', 'realist' and 'structuralist' seem likely to persist, and some authors use colloquial alternatives, such as 'cobweb', 'billiard-ball' and 'layer-cake'.

Within each paradigm, not only are different actors identified, but different forces are seen to be acting on them, with different effects. Debate between the paradigms therefore has to overcome direct contradictions. The most important differentiation between paradigms, and one that causes frequent confusion, is that each seeks to explain different outcomes, or dependent variables. Pluralism aims at the behaviour of *all* politically significant groups in world society, whereas realism confines itself to the behaviour of states, especially powerful states. Structuralism is designed to explain global class formation, in terms of income and wealth as well as political power.

Historical perspective will be needed to show why it was this period, rather than any other, that produced such a basic change in the discipline. But some factors are already apparent. One was the publication, initially in 1962, of Thomas Kuhn's *The Structure of Scientific Revolutions* (1970). For the debate, it did not matter whether Kuhn was right or wrong in his claim that the growth of knowledge proceeds by dialectical stages, with each plateau of 'normal science' succeeding its predecessor only after a turbulent confrontation between opposed ideas. What did matter was that his work encouraged radical re-thinking, focussed on deep 'problems' rather than on the routine 'puzzle-solving' that normally proceeds within the shared assumptions of a given paradigm.

Kuhn also pointed out that because there is no absolute truth and because human knowledge is forever expanding, any given paradigm must have limits in what it can reveal about the world. Paradigms become exhausted. Scholars find that 'anomalies', in the form of contradictions or questions with no answer, steadily become more disturbing as an old paradigm wears out. Straws in the wind of change for the traditional mainstream occurred far back, beginning with interwar perplexity over the problem of peaceful change. Later, Arnold Wolfers's recognition that states are not 'billiard-balls' (1959) was followed by David Singer's discovery that realism could not accommodate multiple levels of analysis (1961), and then by Martin Wight's worries about the incoherence of the paradigm (1966). Meanwhile, Karl Deutsch's extensive work showed that integration can be as effective as confrontation as a basis for security (see Lijphart, 1981).

Discussion of anomalies expanded rapidly as the post-behavioural phase progressed, although it was impossible to judge whether the real world was producing more of them, or whether it was merely that the changing awareness of the discipline enabled them to be seen more clearly. Few leading scholars other than John Burton (1982a) had the courage to tackle the greatest single anomaly, namely the doctrine that nuclear deterrence produces military security, although public concern had been highlighting that issue for decades. But attention was drawn to the increasing political mobilisation of people worldwide, with consequent shifts in values (Inkeles, 1975). The transformations resulting from rapid industrialisation were pointed out (Morse, 1976), and there was widespread analysis of material scarcity in the global 'commons' and the need for an appropriate trade-off between efficiency and equity in access to ocean resources. Together, such issues made the Eurocentric ideas of the mainstream tradition ever more anachronistic.

The most substantial discussion of anomalies, however, occurred in two of the oldest subfields of the discipline, political economy and international organisational studies, both revitalised by a wave of new issue-areas and a consequent surge of scholarship. The fashionable topics of the 1970s, interdependence (for example, Young, 1969); transnational organisations (for example, Keohane and Nye, 1971; 1977) and regime analysis (for example, Krasner, 1983) together produced mounting evidence that realism was impotent to explain what was happening. In the face of these new challenges to the prevailing paradigm, prominent mainstream scholars put pen to paper to defend the faith. The notion of global social justice was sharply attacked (for example, Tucker, 1977);

interdependence subjected to repeated critical scrutiny; state-centric assumptions reasserted (Sullivan, 1978; Waltz, 1979); the political significance of multinational corporations tied back into national interest theory (Gilpin, 1975; Krasner, 1978). But none of this defensiveness could hold back an increasing sympathy with the scathing judgment of Vasquez's exhaustive study of recent theory: 'the realist paradigm is an inadequate guide to inquiry' (Vasquez, 1983, p. 225).

Anomalies existed also in a more basic and ideological sense, and their exposure became the intellectual domain of the structuralists, or dependency theorists. The mainstream had long assumed that whatever the shortcomings of the inter-state system, it did at least have the capacity to promote progress by individual states, because they possessed sovereign freedom within a rudimentary framework of global law and order. In the 1970s this claim was challenged. Forced upon the Western discipline by the vigorous advocacy of scholars from Latin America, Africa and the European peace research movement, structuralism became the new paradigm most closely tied to the classical ideas of Hegel, Marx and Lenin.

Its exponents argued that most states were not free. Instead they were subjugated by the political, ideological and social consequences of economic forces. Imperialism generated by the vigour of free-enterprise capitalism in the West and by state capitalism in the socialist bloc imposed unequal exchange of every kind upon the Third World. Militarism and inequality, economic ruination caused by intolerable debt burdens, and the widespread violation of social justice and human rights were all attributed to the structure of the international system. The great powers fought out their conflicts of interest on the territories of the South, always using periphery peoples as low-cost labour and occasionally as cannon fodder. Understandably, these ideas caught the imagination of much of the educated public across the Third World, and contributed an acid tone to the North-South debate that spanned the decade.

In the West, structuralism made slow headway. It was significant in that it helped both to establish development studies as a new subfield and to fuel the growth of political economy within international studies. But it failed to establish a grip on the centre. Traditionalists dismissed it as mere polemics, while behaviouralists paid it the more respectful attention of subjecting it to formal tests in order to demonstrate its empirical flaws. Only for those who accepted the essential message of classicism – that all social science is, at base, ideological – did it become a major inspiration. Peace researchers, especially, adopted the theories (for example, Galtung, 1980a; 1980b) while a few mainstream scholars made a contribution (for example, Cox, 1981) and in the United States an active group led by Immanuel Wallerstein (1976, 1980) employed it as the foundation of a grandly historicist interpretation known as 'world system analysis' (see Thompson, 1983).

POST-BEHAVIOURALISM: MAINSTREAM CONFUSIONS

For mainstream scholars, the post-behavioural phase was not a comfortable one. The realist paradigm might be crumbling, but most academics shrank away from structuralism as an alternative. Arguments over anomalies caused more confusion that confidence. Proponents of the ideas of every past era continued to publicise their views, while new ones developed alongside them. More books were published, new journals were started, novel professional associations were founded in order to encourage defection from the established organisations.

It was clear that something fundamental was changing in the discipline, but what form should the new pattern take? Superficially, pluralism seemed to be the answer. It offered a general scheme, apparently not too different from tradition, within which a scholar could locate his or her particular interests. The effect, however, was not so much to clarify the general paradigm as to confound it. Because most scholars were reluctant to abandon their old paradigm, they simply qualified it and added points to it. Instead of a genuine paradigm shift, 'pluralism' came to mean an inconsistent list of things worth saying about international relations. The resultant world view became ever more complex as the economy of explanation offered by the pure version of realism was lost.

For participation in the ongoing debate, 'pluralism' as realism-plus-grafted-on-components did offer a tactical advantage. Criticism from the other paradigms could be deflected by the claim that it was directed at a straw man, because the pluralist-realist accepted both state-centrism *and* a role for multinationals; dependency theory (within limits) *and* mercantilism; ideology *and* national interest as motives of foreign policy.

Alternatively, a few scholars did see the contradictions, and took them seriously, but still could not abandon their former convictions. This group set about the task of securing a deeper reconciliation. Believing that 'the world is more complex than the typical globalist or realist conceptualisations would lead us to believe' (Maghroori and Ramberg, 1983, p. 231), they argued, contrary to Kuhn, that it was possible for the discipline to employ the best ideas of more than one paradigm, simultaneously. Among the most sophisticated efforts in this direction were Richard Ashley's incorporation of a Hegelian version of structuralism into power theory (1980), and the attempt by Mansbach and Vasquez (1981) to splice both foreign policy analysis and interdependence into realism.

POST-BEHAVIOURALISM: THE WORLD SOCIETY PARADIGM

Other scholars recognised, often with reluctance, that if pluralism were to serve the discipline constructively, then its contradictions with other paradigms would have to be faced and not evaded. How far would the necessary paradigm shift have to go? What assumptions would have to be changed? What new evidence would have to be gathered to subject the new pluralism to proper tests? What implications would there be for policy making? These questions became the province of the 'world society' paradigm, so christened by John Burton (1972b) and developed extensively in his other writings (especially 1965; 1968; 1979; 1982a). Further elaboration can be found in the writings of several contributors to this book, especially A.J.R. Groom (e.g. 1975) and C.R. Mitchell (1981a; 1981b).

Seen as a set of ideas in its own right, and not as an emendation of older approaches, the simple logic of pluralism immediately threw up a series of counter-intuitive assertions. If states were no longer to be treated as the single set of primary actors in the world society, then multiple sets would have to take their place. These would have to be political parties, business firms, ethnic communities, ideological groups, and many others – some fully politicised, others apparently less so. If the behaviour of all these groups was to be understood, then their values would have to be analysed. Value analysis would therefore cease to focus on international stability, national security, and other items associated only with states, and instead shift to human needs and other basic concerns. Some of these values would be confined to a given local group, others shared cross-nationally. Interactions between groups would have to be analysed comprehensively, covering all forms of conflict and of cooperation, so that power politics would become one category, but only one, within the new scheme.

Beyond these fairly straightforward implications of a pure theory of pluralism, there remained the toughest of all issue-areas: conflict. Throughout the history of the international system, conflict, in the form of the security dilemma, had been recognised as the core problem. From Machiavelli via Hobbes to Morgenthau and Kissinger, the realist doctrines had commanded authority because they alone, among the ideas of the great debates, both confronted the issue and had an answer for it. And from Grotius via Kant to Woodrow Wilson and David Mitrany, liberal ideas had correspondingly either failed to meet the issue head-on, or had offered inadequate reformist solutions.

To develop a pluralist logic of conflict and its efficient management therefore became the principal concern of the world society theorists. Their objective was to discover, in the literature of social science, ideas which would enable the international relations discipline, for the first time, to view conflict much as the physician regards pain. In medicine, to suppress pain with sedatives or painkillers is not enough; the main therapeutic effort must be directed at the underlying disorder. So, in the world society, the forcible conflict-suppressing devices so long employed – power balancing, peacekeeping, hostile intervention – would need to be replaced with other procedures which would not only control conflict symptoms, but also develop the capacity of the world society to become a self-regulating system capable of avoiding destructive conflicts.

The search for relevant insights dictated a close alliance between the world society thinkers and the work of the peace research movement, with its heavy concentration on conflict analysis, and also a wider excursion into the literature of the behavioural sciences to find ideas which could illuminate the problems of fear and insecurity at the inter-state level. The world society perspective, therefore, was forced to go beyond the standard talking points of the post-behavioural phase – interdependence, the extreme complexity of decision making, the activities of transnational actors – to consider also the linkages between domestic and international conflict, the successful record of conflict management in domestic contexts, and the academic literature on problems of deviant behaviour, perception, human needs and political socialisation.

Detailed exposition of world society ideas, insofar as they are understood in the early 1980s, is the task of other chapters in this book. The lesson to be drawn from a review of past thinking is that the new paradigm is firmly rooted in the intellectual history of the discipline. It resolves many of the anomalies contained in older perspectives (although, as Kuhn reminds us, it will certainly develop anomalies of its own as normal puzzle-solving work gets underway). In the spirit of the classical debate, it offers a vision of the world as a whole, combining the empirical and the normative. Unlike much of the optimistic forecasting literature, it does not seek to describe a preferred world that does not yet exist. Instead it draws upon elements that already do exist, both in real-world activities and in ideas about them, to compose a new portrait of the world society. As yet, the portrait is crudely drawn and unfinished. But it holds not only the promise of better understanding, but also the prospect of improved management of political problems.

2 The Post-Behavioural Debate: Indeterminism, Probabilism and the Interaction of Data and Theory

Robert C. North and
Matthew R. Willard

In 1969 Knorr and Rosenau published their widely read symposium on tradition and science in international relations – an attempt at clarifying some of the issues raised by the so-called behavioural revolution and its impact upon a field that has always been controversial. Their approach was even-handed and reasonable. 'If all the authors subscribe to the basic tenets of careful scholarship,' they asked in an introductory chapter, 'why do they argue so intensely about how to approach international phenomena rather than about the phenomena themselves? Will the debate about approaches ever end and move on to more substantive concerns?' (1969, p. 3).

Since there was no clear answer at the time, it seems worthwhile, now that well over a decade has passed, to inquire how the matter stands today. To what extent has the field taken seriously the editorial admonition to the effect that progress lies 'not in tradition *or* science, but in tradition *and* science; not in rejecting one approach and favouring another, but in rendering each the servant of the other'?

A fair-minded and useful assessment of a decade's productivity in the field – whether 'traditional' or 'scientific' – would require at least a volume and possibly two or three. This chapter will therefore attempt an oblique stab at the issue by addressing some problems which, although not widely recognised until recently, may have contributed to contention and uncertainty. In general, these problems fall into four categories: the relationship between perceptions and 'reality'; the tendency of both scholars and policy makers to confuse 'map' with 'territory'; the interactive nature of social systems; and the confusions arising from the emulation of nineteenth-century physicists. It is the central thesis of this chapter that data, rigorously and wisely used, are indispensable for the judicious management of these problems.

'HARD' AND 'SOFT' SCIENCE

Approaches to theory in global politics have tended to differ in terms of the degree of 'hardness' or 'softness' of conceptualisation, formulation and testing (Rapoport, 1970, pp. 17–18). Theory of the 'softer' kind has varied from loose conceptualisation – not much more than intuition, narrative and speculation – to the development of systematic, fairly rigorous but essentially indeterminate assumptions, propositions and axioms (Frankel, 1973, p. 15). Those who have pursued 'hard' theory have tended to employ rigorous testing and ruthless rejection of falsified propositions, as in classical physics.

A common response to the hard–soft issue is to focus on the selection of data and methodology: should the theoretician immerse himself in history, philosophy and law and then derive and 'test' his propositions through intuition and the exercise of judgement? Or should he pursue the tight logical organisation that the natural scientist demands? Should he gather quantifiable data and subject it to statistical analysis? Should he insist upon the iron-clad canons of verification that the physical scientist requires? A major purpose of this chapter is to direct the attention of both 'soft' and 'hard' schools elsewhere: with what assumptions about the universe and about humankind should our investigation start? With what 'realities' should our theories be compared? What are their essential characteristics? Which aspects must be assumed and which can be ascertained, verified and possibly measured? How do we treat the idea of causality?

Possibilities for rigorous theory about global politics necessarily begin with our view of human beings and how they interact with the physical environment as well as with each other. Proponents of 'soft' theory normally assume that human affairs, unlike the physical universe, are indeterminate and essentially non-predictable. Typically, they draw upon Plato, Aristotle, Hobbes, Rousseau and other classic sources, but start their historical analyses with the establishment of the European state system as marked by the Treaty of Westphalia in 1648.

Proponents of 'hard' theory also assume that human affairs are indeterminate – in the sense that iron-clad laws of behaviour do not apply – but unlike their 'soft' theory colleagues, they accept the idea that outcomes can be explained and predicted in terms of statistical probabilities. Many rely heavily on quantitative analyses and mathematical modeling. In establishing rules of falsification and criteria for theory assessment, hard-liners – often in spite of assumptions of basic indeterminacy in human affairs – commonly try to emulate the physical sciences.

Throughout the years of debate there have been areas of consensus as well as of controversy. Many agreements have been of the 'yes, but . . .' variety – pauses for breath before the responding hammer blows – but others have been quite genuine. Among contending writers there has usually been a widespread consensus that

data must be accumulated and systematically analysed, that every fact should be substantiated, that generalisations should not exceed the scope of the data, that alternative explanations should be considered, that discrepancies should be acknowledged and taken seriously, and that the observer should use his imagination and guard against his biases (Knorr and Rosenau, 1969, p. 4).

Who has been right – the traditionalists? The 'social scientists' (or behaviouralists)? Can such questions be answered satisfactorily? Should they even be asked? After a peaking of debate between traditionalists and social scientists in the late 1960s, some new 'post-behavioural' tendencies began to emerge (Choucri, 1980, p. 113). Many traditionalists increasingly incorporated into their thinking some of the fundamental concerns of the 'scientists' – especially those pertaining to the requirements of theory and the means for testing it (George, 1979a). On the other hand, numbers of 'scientists' began to express dissatisfaction with their progress, which all too frequently had fallen short of previous expectations. 'Oddly enough,' wrote Paige (1978, p. 336), 'it now seems that in the sometimes vicious but often beneficial polemic between the "traditionalists" and "behaviouralists" . . . both sides were "right" but for "wrong" reasons.'

The traditionalists were right, Paige concluded, not because human affairs cannot be studied by scientific methods and not because cherished values must necessarily be sacrificed in the process, but because 'man is a creative being who can envision worlds yet unknown and can strive purposely for their attainment'. The behaviouralists were right,

not because they insisted on broadening the study of politics beyond laws and formal institutions or because they insisted upon qualification and new methodologies, but because their search for more satisfying ways of explaining patterns of political behavior brought them face to face with man. In man, capable of both innovative and patterned behavior, the two schools met (1978, p. 336).

During the 1970s, serious criticisms of scientific assumptions, concepts and methods were launched by scholars who themselves had been deeply involved in cultivating them. In its eagerness to become scientific, wrote Almond and Genco (1977, p. 489), 'political science has . . . tended to treat political events and phenomena as natural events lending themselves to the same explanatory logic as physics and the other hard sciences.' There was an illusory search, for some powerful equation, some crucial experiment, some basic computer simulation, and the ultimate theory. But it became clear that political regularities do not follow statistical regularities; that historical change alters apparent regularities at frequent intervals; and that social learning (including learning the results of research) also alters behaviour (Almond and Genco, 1977, pp. 489, 494, 506). One response to these difficulties was to seek the explanation of variance in political behaviour in more basic economic, social and psycho-cultural forces. But this meant, Paige commented, that 'while political scientists had rediscovered the "wholeness" of society (after Aristotle and Confucius) they had "lost" politics' (1978, p. 337).

Many of the charges aimed at 'social scientists' could also be levelled at some of their critics as well. The traditionalist may proceed as though, having underscored the inappropriateness of physical concepts of causality for the explanation of human affairs, he is now free to explain human outcomes without regard for his own caveats: he writes about the 'cause' of a war as if there were only one primary cause; he uses loose generalisation to condemn generalisation; he denounces causal linkages as fallacious and underscores the unique characteristics of each situation and outcome – yet he takes national leaders to task for failing to heed 'the lessons of history'. Worst of all, he remains blind to his own inconsistencies.

At least some of the difficulty appears to emerge from misperceptions, or at least differing perceptions, of what scientific procedure is. Traditionalists and would-be social scientists alike have been trained since elementary school to use data (in one form or another) to test hypotheses and thus demonstrate – even prove – what is apocryphal, what is false, what is real, and what is true. Students, teachers, policy makers and the general public demand facts (as if scientists, experts, candidates for office and anyone in a white lab coat had 'facts' in their pockets like loose change) and suspect fraud, conspiracy or other skulduggery when responses fail to confirm their own fundamental convictions, causal experience or indoctrination.

Nobel Prize-winning physicist William Lipscomb provides us with a somewhat different perspective. 'Scientists do not work by adding one fact to another,' he asserted. 'Scientific method comes into play only after you make your intuitive jump. You use it to test your idea but not in the generation of ideas' (1981, p. 85).

PERCEPTIONS AND REALITY

In the field of global politics, the generation and testing of ideas is a difficult task because reality and 'facts' tend to be elusive. This elusiveness starts with some of the qualities of all living things that set them somewhat apart from the inanimate universe and is compounded by the relation of our central nervous system (and its perceptions) to reality. The relationship between the 'real world' and the way an individual perceives and interprets it may be one of the most critical considerations affecting the way people conduct themselves in global politics.

Since the mind cannot perform without structuring reality and thereby often oversimplifying or distorting it (George, 1980, p. 57), it follows that for a scholar, as for a decision maker, it is his or her *image* of the world, and not necessarily the actual world, that is accepted as real. This consideration can lead to serious problems – especially in international conflict. As in various other human activities, people in politics are not always objective in assessing their own motivations or charitable in assessing the motivations of others. The usual human tendency is to perceive the best in one's own motivations and to impugn the motives of one's competitors – and even one's colleagues and friends. Often, such reciprocal suspicions lead to a 'mirror-image' effect (Burton, 1972b, p. 75). In the 1970s, for instance, Chinese leaders perceived Soviet leaders as motivated by a desire to 'encircle' China, whereas Soviet leaders perceived the reverse.

In all human activities, people perceive only part of what they 'actually' perceive. Because of the way the central nervous system works, however, a person may experience the same sensation from different stimuli, or different sensations from the same stimulus. In any case, what a person has experienced or has been taught will tend to shape what he or she believes, perceives and expects (Kuhn, 1970, p. 193). The way we perceive reality is also influenced by what we are concerned with at any given time (Jervis, 1971, p. 125).

George has observed that these personal constructs and beliefs, acquired during the course of an individual's development, are essential to the perspectives and policies shaping any society or nation. These constructs and beliefs provide the individual with a relatively coherent way of organising and making sense of what would otherwise be a confusing and overwhelming array of signals and cues picked up from the environment by his senses. Our images and beliefs are indispensable, but they necessarily simplify and structure the external world (George, 1980, p. 57). What this implies is that each person establishes, maintains, adjusts, and sometimes feels impelled to defend his or her own image of reality.

To some extent, then, people tend to perceive and believe what they want to perceive and believe (a flying saucer), what they 'choose' to perceive and believe, and what they expect or are disposed to 'imagine'. Such tendencies toward selective perception, rationalisation and belief – the propensity of individuals to accept as true those things that are consistent with their personal frames of reference – is well established in individual psychology (de Rivera, 1968, pp. 20, 444; March and Olsen, 1976, pp. 64–5).

To the extent that any of our highly subjective images is false, warned Halle (1960, p. 316), 'no technicians, however efficient, can make the policy that is based on it sound'. In this context, the 'minds of men' observation acquires significance. Each of us constructs the reality in which he or she operates, and each takes his or her perception of it as authentic (de Rivera, 1968, p. 21). Thenceforth our perceptions, choices and actions tend to be shaped by it (Holsti, 1967, p. 25). Being predisposed to accept our beliefs as true, we commonly allow this acceptance to bias what we see, hear, taste, smell and feel. This is as true for the politician as it is for the scholar who studies him.

LANGUAGE: THE CONFUSION BETWEEN 'MAP' AND 'TERRITORY'

Many of our confusions about reality start with the languages we speak. Just as a map represents but is distinct from territory, so language represents but is distinct from things, relationships, states of being, and possible future outcomes. The usefulness of a map or of a language depends on the similarity of structure between the empirical world and the particular map or language. If the structure is not similar, then the traveller or speaker may be led astray, mistaking the map for the territory. In politics, a particular country is referred to as a democracy merely because it so identifies itself. A society taking pride in its free-enterprise economy may impose so many regulations, controls and special subsidies that very little truly free enterprise remains in it. A people which is 'nationalist' is seen as aggressive by some, and as loyal by others (Burton, 1972b, p. 69). Thus words (as well as numbers) can lie. 'Especially in the social sciences, we must watch out for the tyranny of words' (Samuelson, 1970, p. 8).

At the extreme, an uncritical reliance on language may lead to a fallacy. Having found a name, we mount an expedition to find – or invent – some 'reality' to match it (Kelly, 1953, pp. 43–4). We hunt the Jabberwock or dream up the widget. Thus, the patriot may declare with confidence that 'since our country has a people's government, it cannot possibly be imperialistic', or 'as a peace-loving nation, it is inconceivable that we should be guilty of aggression'. Noting such semantic witchcraft, Korzybski concluded (1933, p. 89) that all languages possess a 'certain metaphysics' whereby a structure is imposed on the world – perhaps wrongly. And because language perpetuates ideas over time as well as communicating them, the structure may become rigid. It is well to remind ourselves that 'while we can easily become slaves to words, they are meant to be used as tools of thought' (Burton, 1972b, p. 73).

The relevance of this becomes clear if we now consider some of the difficulties stemming from differences between living things and the inanimate universe. If the generation and testing of ideas is made difficult both by perceptions and by language, it is further exacerbated by disagreement over what theory is, what law is and whether or not the two words can be used interchangeably. Generally, the concept of law implies 'hard theory', although, paradoxically, it is not unusual to find soft theorists using it. Whereas a theory is sometimes referred to as an hypothesis (or a set of hypotheses) which has been partially tested and remains tenable, a law is commonly defined as the statement of a causal relationship which, to the best of our knowledge, always occurs. Some scholars use the word theory to cover the explanations which account for the operation of a law.

Causation is a troublesome concept in many disciplines, but in global politics it poses particularly difficult problems. The harder and more successful sciences are concerned with establishing causal relations and general laws, and disciplines aspiring to scientific status often seek to emulate them (Bateson, 1979, p. 230). In the physical sciences causal laws are often assumed. When such a law appears to be violated by facts, the scientist reformulates it. But even in the physical sciences, causal laws are 'essentially working assumptions or tools' rather than verifiable statements about reality (Frank, 1961, p. 65). The physicist normally approximates a reality he infers, measuring real-world deviations from it, and then extrapolating his results (Blalock, 1964, p. 17). Within an appropriate conceptual framework, such procedures may not be entirely out of reach in the field of global politics. The word law thus refers to regularities of process whereby, given certain initial conditions, a particular – *and no other* – outcome may be expected to occur. To explain why something occurred is to show why it *had* to occur, because nothing else could have occurred under these conditions (Dahl, 1965, p. 87). Such a 'lawful' theory, strictly defined, would presumably be, *ipso facto*, deterministic and unlikely to win widespread acceptance in the field of global politics.

In order to establish causal relations and general laws, then, it would appear to be incumbent upon the social scientist to concentrate on systematic patterns of human conduct (Frohock, 1967, p. 141). Almond and Genco have referred to attempts in this direction as a serious error, however.

In our fascination with powerful regularities and uniformities which have the properties of causal necessity or high probability we have overlooked the structural aspects of human and political reality. Not only is political reality a universe of choices, but the choices do not have equal values. Much of social and political change has to be explained neither by strong regularities, nor by weak regularities, but by accidental conjunctions, by events that had a low probability of occurring (1977, p. 512).

INTERACTIVE ASPECTS OF SOCIAL SYSTEMS

The study of global politics is further constrained by the consideration that social systems, like biological systems, are open, not closed. They are also equifinal and multifinal (Young, 1964, pp. 61–80; 242–3). Conventional physics, by contrast, deals only with systems that are closed, that is, isolated from their environments (nothing enters or leaves the system), and final, that is, wholly determined by their initial conditions. Living systems exchange materials and information both internally and with their own environments, so that any given final state can be reached from different initial conditions (equifinality) and via different routes: multifinality (von Bertalanffy, 1968, pp. 40, 132–6, 140, 148–9). Because so 'many different outcomes can arise out of basically similar events and conditions,' and vice versa, it is difficult to decide which 'causal' chain is correct (Singer, 1979, p. 25).

In the study of human affairs, especially politics, it is commonplace to accept the concept of cause as a force acting to produce a response (Blalock, 1964, p. 17). This is a basic error. One human being, no matter how powerful, cannot causally 'force' another to do anything. Through reward (or the promise thereof) or coercion (or the threat thereof), one actor may persuade another to comply. But the complier remains essentially independent, that is, he or she can choose to suffer torture or die rather than submit. It is misleading, then, to interpret individuals, groups, communities, states or other organisations as causing social outcomes in the way that rainfall 'causes' wheat to grow or an apple is caused to fall downwards from a tree.

Instead, social outcomes must be seen as stemming from *interaction* among actors as opposed to one actor directly causing another's behaviour (Cronbach, 1975, p. 116). When two or more human beings interact, 'the motivation and behaviour of each is likely to be responsive to the behaviour of the other' (Chein, 1972, p. 10). Indeed, all of us respond not only to events in the environment, but also to feedbacks emanating from our own (sometimes quite unconscious) testings of the situations in which we find ourselves (Miller, Galanter and Pribram, 1960, p. 16). In global politics, a confrontation among two or three countries, involving many millions of people, may appear to multiply the number of 'mirrors' many times. This is likely to make the determination of cause and the prediction of outcomes exceedingly difficult. 'Once we attend to interactions,' according to Cronbach (1975, p. 119), 'we enter into a hall of mirrors that extends to infinity.'

FROM CLASSICAL PHYSICS TO MODERN SOCIAL SCIENCE

In the social sciences, considerable dispute and frustration have been generated by attempts to emulate classical physics – a discipline that could be characterised as mechanistic, deterministic and fundamentally incompatible with whatever we think we know about the uncertainties of human affairs. But in this century, classical physics has moved towards substituting probability for determinism, in recognition that physical phenomena may result partly from principles implying a rational order, partly from random elements of contingency (Thompson, 1964, p. 23). If contemporary physicists have abandoned the building block concept as inappropriate to matter, then those concerned with volatile human institutions might also become much more probabilistic and approximate in their approach (Capra, 1977).

The basis of the problem lies deeper, however. Contrary to a widely-shared assumption, even natural phenomena do not obey exact laws (Compton, 1935, p. 7); even the 'so-called laws of physics are only hypotheses, points of departure . . .' (Rapoport, 1970, p. 16). Distinguishing determinacy from indeterminacy in physical and social systems, Popper referred to the more irregular, disorderly and unpredictable 'clouds' at the left end of a continuum and to the more orderly and predictable 'clocks' at the right end. 'Clouds' are of moisture, gas, gnats; also schools of fish and human societies ('clouds' of people). Each insect within a cloud moves randomly except that it turns back toward the centre whenever it begins straying too far from the swarm. 'Clocks' include the solar system along with such man-made objects as precision instruments and motor cars. 'If determinism is true, then the whole world is a perfectly running, flawless clock, including all clouds, all organisms, all animals and all men.' But if, on the other hand, indeterminism is true, 'then sheer *chance* plays a major role in our physical world. *But is chance really more satisfactory than determinism?*' (Popper, 1972, p. 208).

Physicists and philosophers have tried to build models of human choice based upon the unpredictability of quantum jumps, but Popper rejected these as too circumscribed. Some snap decisions may approach randomness, but 'are snap-decisions so very interesting?' Are they characteristic of human behaviour? Popper thought not. 'Thus we shall have to return to our old arrangement with clouds on the left and clocks on the right and animals and men somewhere in between.' But even after this has been done, we have only made room for the major issue. 'For obviously what we want is to understand how such nonphysical things as *purpose, deliberations, plans, decisions, theories, intentions* and *values*, can play a part in bringing about physical changes in the physical world' (Popper, 1972, p. 229). What we need is something intermediate in character 'between perfect chance and perfect determinism – something intermediate between perfect clouds and perfect clocks.'

A similarity between ancient thought and trends in contemporary theories of physics is an assumption of unity in the universe. 'The one is made up of all things,' wrote Heraclitus of Ephesus, 'and all things issue from the one.' So, too, according to Nobel prize-winning physicist Erwin Schrodinger (1956, p. 87) 'there *is* only one thing and . . . what seems to be a plurality is merely a series of different aspects of this one thing, produced by a deception (the Indian MAJA); the same illusion is produced in a gallery of mirrors, and in the same way Gaurisankar and Mt Everest turned out to be the same peak seen from different valleys.'

Philosophically, one need not necessarily accept the monistic, single-element assumption about the universe. Here the relevant

consideration is that what at the last turn of the century were referred
to as the 'building blocks of matter' are now seen to 'defy all forms of
objective location in time and space' (Heisenberg, 1930, p. 24). Not
only is everything at once a unity and also an array of components;
everything also appears to be here and there at the same time. 'If we
ask . . . whether the position of the electron remains the same,'
observed physicist J. Robert Oppenheimer (1954, pp. 42–3), 'we must
say "no": if we ask whether it is in motion, we must say "no".'

So it was that as physicists developed quantum theory in the 1920s,
the clocklike model of nature was challenged and to a large extent
replaced by the view that indeterminacy and chance are fundamental
to all natural processes. In modern physics, mass-matter is viewed as
a form of energy, a 'bundle' of energy. To some considerable degree
'all clocks are clouds,' rather than the converse (Popper, 1972, p.
215). In other words, '*only clouds exist*, though clouds of very
different degrees of cloudiness' (Almond and Genco, 1977, p. 490).
Given these perspectives in the world of contemporary physics there
does not seem to be much justification for making clocks out of
global politics.

Modern insights into the world of sub-atomic physics often seem to
transcend language and conventional reasoning in ways that bewilder
even social scientists, who are accustomed to indeterminism
(Heisenberg, 1958, p. 24). In trying to explain to himself 'why, after
one once knew precisely the position and velocity of a particle, its
future could not be determined exactly,' Heisenberg saw 'that this
indeterminacy was indeed the result of ignorance, not merely a
practical ignorance, but one of an inherent and unavoidable kind. Its
source was *the disturbance of an object by the act of observing it*'
(Meade, 1978, p. 217). A resolution of the paradoxes of atomic
physics could be accomplished, Heisenberg concluded (1930, p. 62),
'only by renunciation of old and cherished ideas', the most important
of these being 'the idea that natural phenomena obey exact laws'. If
the idea of iron laws of causality is under challenge in the 'hard'
sciences, then the social scientist has no choice other than to face up
to the problem of indeterminacy.

THE PROBLEM OF INDETERMINACY

In physics the turning point was a meeting in Brussels during the
autumn of 1927 (Meade, 1978, pp. 232–3). From a series of debates
centring on disagreements between Albert Einstein and Nils Bohr

(one of Heisenberg's former students) came the Copenhagen interpretation of quantum theory, which denied the capacity of the human mind for dealing with anything but ideas. This position challenged any notion of a one-to-one correspondence between theory and reality. According to this bold new perspective, 'the complete description of nature at the atomic level was given by probability functions that referred not to underlying microscopic space-time realities, but rather to macroscopic objects of sense experience' (Stapp, 1972, pp. 1098 ff; Einstein, 1936, pp. 349 ff.). Indeterminism, which until 1927 had been equated with obscurantism, now became the ruling fashion.

Even in the hard sciences, moreover, investigators had to be reminded not only of the difference between map and territory, but also of the confounding outcome of making maps in the first place. Physicists could no longer speak of the behaviour of the particle independently of the process of observation. Heisenberg asserted (1958, p. 24): 'even in science the object of research is no longer nature itself, but man's investigation of nature'. In the world of Nils Bohr, 'there are no atoms; only observations. The atom is a creation of the human mind, to bring some order into the chaotic pattern of observation. The paradoxes and conflicts of the atomic world originate in the workings of the human consciousness' (Meade, 1978, p. 233).

The Copenhagen interpretation provided a philosophical basis for Popper's reference to controls imposed by 'clouds (a combination of freedom and control) as "plastic" in contrast with the "cast-iron" controls of clock-like systems' (1972, pp. 215 ff). From there it was an easy step to see that 'what we are being offered is a model for understanding and explaining the world which includes people's interactions with themselves, with each other, and with the physical universe' (Almond and Genco, 1977, p. 503).

To date, however, much theory in the field of global politics has focused on relationships between constants. Traditional balance of power theory, to select only one example, often proceeded as if the capabilities of major powers in a system – A,B,C,D, and so forth – were fixed, country by country, although alliance patterns might change. Values, motivations, intents, expectations and purposes were often treated as a fixed attribute of a given country. Even obvious forms of change were often frozen, as in a photograph, as if relations between nations proceeded mechanistically. Physics, on the other hand, now reminds us that even matter, which seems fixed, can be viewed as packaged energy. Thus, if even nature is basically dynamic and probabilistic, then it seems less reasonable to treat human institutions as inert. Once the phenomena of global politics are perceived to be in unremitting motion, the possibility emerges (to the extent to which data are appropriated, collected, aggregated and applied) for tracing communication, population, energy, resource and technological flows in a never-ending pattern of 'who gets what, when and where' and 'with what consequences'.

Belated recognition by social scientists of the Copenhagen interpretation and its implications for the formulation and testing of their theories – together with the accumulation of research lessons – may explain in considerable measure the trend toward the post-behavioural revolution in the field of global politics (Choucri, 1980, p. 113).

Despite considerations of approximation, indeterminacy and probabilism, the physicist (unlike the social scientist) can often make point predictions – predictions to a point in time or in a particular sequence of events. This capability results mainly from the type of problem the physicist deals with, and the fact that cardinal, as opposed to ordinal (rank and order) values are available. To a large extent – though not entirely – the social scientist is limited to ordinal values and hence to directional (or trend) rather than point-value predictions (Meehl, 1967, pp. 103–14).

In view of the indeterminisms, approximations and probabilistics of contemporary physical sciences, moreover, the question arises whether deterministic assumptions and models can be of any use at all in the study of global politics. Or must all our approaches be strictly probabilistic and plastic? The possibility that 'all clocks may be clouds' does not in itself preclude the use of deterministic models. For purposes of theory formulation and testing, the deterministic position does have certain advantages, even in the social sciences. There are important uses for the inelastic tool – the yardstick, the assumption of rational decision, the deterministic model. In ways somewhat comparable to those of the physicist, the social scientist can approximate a reality he infers (however arbitrary the model), measure the real-world deviations from it, and then extrapolate his results. Such procedures can constitute a powerful adjunct to theory formulation and testing provided the 'iron-clad' model is not confused with the 'cloud-like' reality that the investigator seeks to explain.

For the evaluation of any theory, it should be formulated in such a way that it can be tested against reality; it is considered falsifiable if its explanations or predictions are susceptible to tests that are not easily survived. A theory is strong, 'hard' or rigorous if it is capable of predicting an improbable event, or if its explanation of an event holds up in circumstances wherein the probability of success for such an explanation is extremely low. Regrettably, some of our predictions in the field of global politics have not been pushed much beyond 'the-sun-will-rise-tomorrow' stage.

In addition to the difficulties involved in the testing of theory so far identified, we must take account of the problem of inadequate data. Data for the rigorous testing of hypotheses in the field of global politics are normally hard to get, incomplete, inconsistently selected and aggregated by gathering agencies, often all but incomparable between one country and another, and almost always full of errors in their raw state. There are relatively few guidelines for the selection or construction of indicators; there is little or no precedent for the selection of rates of change, and there are few criteria for determining when or if a model can legitimately be adjusted or modified. Even more basically, scholars disagree over where to look for 'causes' (does war begin in the minds of men, in institutions, in both, or somewhere else?) – and over the nature of causality in human affairs and, indeed, whether it exists.

According to what criteria, then, and how ruthlessly should a theory falsified by rigorous test be rejected? In formal systems of logic, an elaborately constructed argument can be overturned by a single contradiction. Should this criterion be enforced in the field of global politics? Within a broad philosophy-of-science approach, there are two contrasting perspectives. According to a 'hard' view, each theory must be subjected to increasingly severe tests, since it is only in this way that its weaknesses and limitations can be discovered. From a 'soft' perspective, a reasonable measure of agreement with observed facts may constitute the empirical criterion for a satisfactory test.

For the 'soft' position, Lakatos has maintained that 'we cannot prove our theories, and we cannot disprove them, either' (1970, p. 99). If an investigator has a theory, tests it, and secures the expected result, this does not prove that the theory is correct – only that the hypothesised relationship holds in this one case. Even if that same hypothesis is successfully tested in many different situations, it could still be possible that it holds for reasons other than those suggested by the underlying theory (Christensen and Butterworth, 1976, p. 262).

Suppose, now, that a theory is falsified. Is that the end of the matter? No. If a hypothesis does not survive an empirical test one is often at a loss to conclude whether the theory is wrong, the data were in error, the selection of indicators was faulty, or the analytic tool misapplied. If the hypothesis survives for one country but not for another the difference may be that a critical domestic variable was operating in one but not in the other. Under such circumstances it is difficult to avoid a certain amount of experimentation; reiterative, almost trial-and-error analysis; consideration of auxiliary *ad hoc* hypotheses; and adjustment and even readjustment of theory (North, Holsti and Choucri, 1976, p. 437). Even then, the possibility still exists that 'a theory that is "falsified" may indeed be a true theory' (Hilton, 1976, p. 167). As Lakatos concluded, the 'demarcation between the soft, unproved theories and the hard, proven empirical basis is non-existent: all propositions . . . are theoretical and, inevitably, fallible' (1970, p. 100).

If truth is elusive and nothing can be definitively proved, then what is the use of obtaining and analysing data? Why not stick to the formulation of theory? There are at least two major reasons. First, data – however inadequate – put the investigator in touch with reality. Without data, the theoretician deals with maps at the expense of territory. He runs the risk of spinning persuasive fantasy. Admittedly, even the best data, having been ripped from their territorial context, may amount to a fragmentation of reality that can be used only with great caution. Nevertheless, aside from intuitions, data provide the investigator's only access to reality. Second, and at least equally important, data arrangement and analysis open new horizons for the investigator – the possibility of identifying new connections (as well as new contradictions) – and may also assist in the generation of new ideas and intuitive leaps. The obtaining of data and its skilful management are thus an integral part of what Lipscomb (1981, p. 85) saw as the artistic creation – as distinct from the 'scientific' testing – of theory and the possible emergence of better theory.

THE COPENHAGEN REVOLUTION AND THE STUDY OF GLOBAL POLITICS

Deriving from the Copenhagen interpretation, these considerations amount to a major revolution for all the sciences, 'hard' and 'soft'. While solving none of the problems peculiar to the social sciences, the new perspective at least clarifies both the similarities and the differences between them and the purely physical sciences. In the field of global politics we need no longer feel a compulsion to emulate nineteenth-century physics, nor to discard prematurely the intuitions that appear to be unsupported, nor to abandon rigour. From this perspective there can be no 'falsification before the emergence of a better theory' (Lakatos, 1970, p. 19). But how is a better theory to be achieved? As a response to this troublesome question, Lakatos advocated what he referred to as 'sophisticated methodological falsification' and a series of theoretically and empirically 'progressive theories'. Sophisticated methodological falsification 'makes no attempt to isolate a theory and then try to validate it. Validation is a part of the process of theorising. It is empirical, but not infallible' (Christensen and Butterworth, 1976, p. 275). A series of theories is 'theoretically progressive' to the extent that each subsequent theory achieves more theoretical content than a previous one, and it is 'empirically progressive' to the extent that some proportion of the excess content is corroborated. Lakatos saw (1970, p. 119) a theory that possessed both as representing what he called a 'progressive problem shift'. A theory without both amounts to 'a degenerative problem shift'. These procedures constitute a 'research programme'.

Purely negative, destructive criticism – like refutation or demonstration of an inconsistency – does not eliminate a Lakatosian research programme. 'Criticism of a programme is a long and often frustrating process, and one must treat budding programmes leniently' (1970, p. 179). Indeed, the 'ability of a scientist to stick with his paradigm despite anomalies and discouraging results is important if any paradigm is to be fully exercised' (Hilton, 1976, p. 165). A causal or theoretical proposition is falsified only when, as an outcome of one or many research programmes, a better 'causal' or theoretical proposition is identified (Lakatos, 1970, p. 116).

This methodology amounts to an intensive feedback, adaptive and learning process whereby we move persistently back and forth between theory and data. Such a procedure tends to be slow and unspectacular. Moreover, the investigator requires considerable arrays of data, awareness of their limitations, and a capacity for managing and analysing them in rigorous and insightful ways. There is no guarantee – indeed there is small likelihood – of early or easy success, but the search for 'progressive problem shifts' would seem to offer the optimal possibility for long-term advancement of theory and testing.

The purpose of this chapter is not to obscure the unmistakable differences between the 'hard' sciences and the vastly more 'plastic' social sciences – especially global politics – or to minimise the gap that separates them on any 'cloud-to-clock' continuum. Nor is it our intent to plead for any particular conceptual, theoretical or methodological approach. It is our suspicion, however, that if traditionalists, would-be social scientists and eclectics alike (including both quantifiers and non-quantifiers) were to recognise the revolutionary implications of the Copenhagen interpretation for all sciences – and hence for global politics in all its aspects – and to meet head on both the new limitations and the unprecedented possibilities released by the new perspectives, many of the troublesome issues of the past would dissolve before our eyes and allow us to focus more effectively on the real problems that confront us.

3   The Subjectivity of Theories and Actions in World Society[1]

Dennis J.D. Sandole

A TALE OF TWO WORLDS

John Burton's views of the world, of human nature, and of conflict constitute a challenge to the corresponding views of 'political realism' or 'power politics'. Burton is not the first to challenge political realism, but his challenge is comprehensive. He perceives a 'world society' comprised of a multitude of actors, non-governmental as well as governmental, at all levels, interacting in ways which violate traditional state frontiers. Political realists, on the other hand, perceive a world primarily of governmental actors whose international relations violate traditional state boundaries only through war and threats of war.

Burton sees people in terms of basic needs (for example, identity, stimulation, and so on) which they will fulfil one way or another. If they cannot fulfil them in acceptable ways, they will do so in 'deviant' ways, including the use of violence. Political realists, on the other hand, tend to have a deterministic, negative view of people. No matter what masks they might wear, people are, at bottom, *evil*. And because they are evil, they are also untrustworthy, aggressive, and constantly attempting to gain, maintain or extend their dominance over others (and conversely, attempting to avoid being dominated by others).

Burton's approach to dealing with conflicts follows from his alternative view of human nature. If basic human needs can be fulfilled in a variety of ways, then, given the high costs of destructive conflict, it would be in the best *joint* interests of actors – persons, groups, organisations, societies – to pursue *cooperative* resolution of their conflicts. Realists would claim otherwise: for them what deters or terminates conflict is coercion – either the threatened or actual use of force. Consequently, realists tend to favour a 'hard' rather than a 'soft' line.[2]

Political realism has dominated political thought and action for centuries. Indeed, it has the status of what Kuhn (1970) calls a *paradigm* – a system of beliefs and values which for a time dominates the perceptions, thinking, and behaviour of some group or community. Burton, then, has taken on the 'establishment'.

There is a dominant view in philosophy which would argue that only one of these (or neither) presents a true picture of reality. For Descartes, with whom this view is identified, reality is a stable given. And to perceive it the way it 'really' is, all we have to do is to open our eyes and all will be revealed. If we do not then perceive reality correctly, it is because our sensory and information-processing systems have been contaminated by societal influences which must be exorcised. So pervasive is this view – and not just in philosophy – that Popper (1972) has dubbed it the 'commonsense theory of knowledge'.

But we now know – or think we know – that when we take a good look at what is 'out there', we may not agree on what it is we perceive, and *not* because we have been corrupted. If one person perceives a particular object and another perceives something else when looking in the same direction at the same time, then with regard to what the first has seen, the second may be said to be 'cognitively blind'. In other words, unless people have corresponding structures and contents in their belief and value systems, they will perceive different things. Accordingly, rather than say that either Burton or the political realists are right (and by implication, that the other is wrong), we can say that they live in different 'worlds'.

SEEING IS BELIEVING – OR IS IT?

We can almost hear the protest, 'But surely there is a real world out there which is either what the realists see or what Burton sees?' Let us examine this question with the help of the following theoretical statement: *to explain any human behaviour, we must take into account* (1) *the actor(s) involved,* (2) *the actor's environment,* and (3) *interaction between the actor and his/her environment.*

Analytically, the 'self' of the actor can be subdivided into two parts: mental and biological/physiological. The mental part is the repository of memories, the domain of beliefs and values, plus the expectations inherent in them. It is the stage upon which perceptions and ideas of self and environment are played out. The biological/physiological part, on the other hand, consists of the innate makeup of human beings – the senses, neurons, brain, muscles, and so on, plus the processes involved in the functioning and maintenance of the organism. The actor's environment can also be subdivided into two parts, the natural and the human-made. The natural world is comprised of the air we breathe, the weather we experience, the food we eat, the water we drink, the energy we consume – in effect, the sources of our physical maintenance. The human-made world, on the other hand, consists of all the systems, processes and things created by people.

Just as there is mounting evidence that *we* – in the sense of our biological/physiological selves – are largely what we eat, drink, breathe, and so on in our natural environments, so there is mounting evidence that we – in the sense of our mental selves – are largely what we have experienced and learned in our human-made environments. But while the evidence in the former case suggests that we are all members of the *same* physical world, the evidence in the latter case suggests, more and more, that we all live in *different* metaphysical worlds.

When a person becomes aware of something in his/her environment, what seems to have happened is this: physical energy from that 'something' has been transformed into 'information', that is, an electro-chemical representation of the external stimulus. This information then travelled through the nervous system to the brain where, against the background provided by beliefs and values, it was decoded into a 'definition of the situation'. This could take one or some combination of the following forms:

(1) a *bare sensation* – the person feels that something is 'out there' but cannot identify it.
(2) *recognition* and *identification* – an answer to the question, 'What is it?'
(3) *analysis* and *explanation* – an answer to the question, 'Why?' or
(4) *interpretation* – an answer to the question, 'What does it all mean?'

Those who follow Descartes believe that different people perceiving the 'same' thing might have different definitions in the sense of explanation or interpretation, but they should have the same definition in the sense of recognition. In other words, in a very basic sense, people should live in the 'same world'. But this is precisely what is being challenged by anthropology, by the work of Kuhn, and others. When two people with different beliefs and values look at the 'same' thing, they may not only have different analyses and interpretations, but also different identifications of it. It is in this sense of recognition and identification that people can live in different worlds.

And it is not only among members of radically different cultures and linguistic systems that the different-world phenomenon exists. 'Every man speaks a language somewhat of his own', Kenneth Boulding (1962, p. 295) tells us, 'and even messages that are in languages that we think are mutual to the sender and the receiver get filtered . . . through the private languages of each individual'. So, even within the same society there may be different groups or subcultures whose members perceive different worlds.

Even members of different professions 'have their own specialised means of communication and discourse'. This applies as much to scientists as to anyone else (Boulding, 1956, p. 171), and it is not merely members of different scientific communities but also different members of the same scientific community who may perceive different worlds (Kuhn, 1970).

If scientists – who can lay some claim to being among the most intellectually rigorous and 'objective' members of society – can be 'cognitively blind' to each other's perceptions, if they can experience different identifications of the 'same' thing, what does this say for the rest of us? Whether we are scientists, politicians, or laypersons, *inference* is involved at all stages of the perceptual process, and not just at the levels of explanation and interpretation. To perceive anything at all there must first be some corresponding theory, model, hypothesis or concept among our beliefs and values. Without these constructs, nothing can be identified; without them, we cannot have perceptions. So, there are no 'givens', no 'facts', except in terms of the meanings provided by these constructs. Consequently, Descartes' view, with its implied 'dogma of immaculate perception', is certainly problematic if not totally absurd.[3]

REALISM AND THE SELF-PERPETUATION OF CONFLICT

Realists hold their particular view of the world not only because their perceptions of it are mediated by shared beliefs and values, but also because their responses to it have influenced it to the extent that it conforms to (and therefore confirms) their expectations. In other words, the perceived world of realists is more and more of their own making, not just in terms of the lenses through which they view 'reality', but also the reality itself. Since realism has been a guide to political action at least since the fifth century BC (Purnell, 1978, pp. 23–4), it may seem unfair to charge present-day realists with responsibility for the way the world is. But though they may not have made the world the way it is, their actions nevertheless contribute to keeping that world in place.

The process by which this happens is insidious. It operates everywhere, yet it is not easily seen. It is succinctly embodied in a famous statement by W.I. Thomas: 'If men define situations as real, they are real in their consequences'.[4] The process we are talking about is the *self-fulfilling prophecy*.

Let us imagine two actors, A and B. Let us assume that A and B hold negative views of one another; moreover, that they have developed these views, not through personal experience of one another, but through learning from parents, peers, teachers, etc. Let us further assume that these negative views are not valid.

In any case, A and B *expect* each other to behave badly. Against this background, A does something which confirms B's expectations, behaviour which B defines as a threat to its security. B responds in a power-oriented way, which confirms A's expectations that B will behave in an untrustworthy, aggressive manner. A then responds defensively, but what is defensive for one is offensive for the other, and B experiences yet another confirmation of its expectation that A will behave in a negative manner.

As this 'bite-counterbite' process escalates, and the reciprocal expectations of A and B become more and more confirmed, so does the realist world within which they both operate. What was once untrue, or not so true, has, over time, become very true. Not only have A's and B's beliefs and values been strengthened by positive reinforcement, but the outcomes, even in 'objective' terms, conform more and more to their expectations.

Hence, Merton (1968, p. 478) tells us that 'many Americans of good will' experience their negative ethnic and racial beliefs 'not as prejudices, not as prejudgements, but as irresistible products of their own observation'. Mark Snyder (1982, p. 60) reports that assumptions about race, sex, physical appearance, and so on, 'are reinforced by the behaviour of both prejudiced people and the targets of their prejudice'. And at the international level, Morton Deutsch (1982) tells us that 'both superpowers are right to think that each wants to increase its power at the expense of the other'.

The upshot of all this is that the realists seem to have the edge on Burton. But this is more illusory than real. Through the self-fulfilling phenomenon, political realism encourages the very perceptions and behaviour which strengthen and sustain the environment which many find so hostile – the environment about which they feel so tense and insecure.

There is clearly in realism an element of counter-productivity: the very actions which actors take in pursuit of security have the opposite effect, of increasing *in*security. Arms races, and the insecurities they produce, are an obvious example. Looking at the potential link between arms races and war, it is clear that realism, as a self-perpetuating system, can encompass what Deutsch (1982) aptly calls 'malignant social processes'. Indeed, it is hard to imagine anything more malignant, more self-defeating than nuclear war, for it would probably lead to what Bryant Wedge and I have referred to as 'globicide' (1982). Yet there are indications that we may be moving in that direction. Are we stuck with this state of affairs or can we extricate ourselves from it?

WE HAVE MET THE ENEMY AND HE IS US

We have said that political realism has the status of what Kuhn (1970) calls a paradigm – a system of beliefs and values which for a time dominates the perceptions, thinking, and behaviour of some group or community. Once a set of images has come to have paradigmatic status for a particular community, its members have no need to debate and justify every assumption and move they make. Consequently, they work on select problems in terms of theories, techniques, and standards legitimised by the paradigm. Kuhn refers to this as 'normal science'.

Successful normal science generates feedback which leads to further refinement of the paradigm. This in turn leads to greater scope and precision in the paradigm's subsequent demarcation of legitimate research problems, theories, techniques, and standards. Successful normal science, then, facilitates the strengthening of the paradigm's hold over the perceptions and behaviour of its practitioners, just as the self-fulfilling prophecies of political realism strengthen its hold over the perceptions and behaviour of its adherents.

But there is an interesting paradox built into the normal science process – the stronger the paradigm becomes, the more potentially vulnerable it is. That is, the more refined the paradigm, the more likely it is that deviations from its expectations will be found. These anomalies may be either novelties of fact or theory, that is, novelties of identification or explanation-interpretation. When normal science starts to behave in this manner, it has begun to fail.

Some anomalies may eventually be assimilated by the paradigm. But when they are not, a period of crisis may ensue. Such periods are characterised by, among other things, a questioning of basic assumptions, and a proliferation of competing contenders for the paradigmatic throne. When one of these alternative systems replaces the traditional paradigm, a 'scientific revolution' will have occurred.

But there is another paradox in the normal science process. Although deviations from paradigmatic expectations should stand out sharply against the background of increasing paradigm refinement and articulation, it appears that the stronger the paradigm, the more difficult it is for practitioners to notice anything which might call it into question. There is an element of resistance here, and it is often unconscious.

Popper (1972, p. 63) provides us with a clue why this might be so. 'Subjective knowledge', such as our beliefs and values, 'consists of maturing innate dispositions.' In other words, our mental world has a biological basis. Since a major function of the biological/physiological world is its own survival – as indicated by the *homeostatic* processes (Cannon, 1939) – it would seem that the beliefs and values we learn over time would somehow reflect this need to survive. To put it another way, it would seem that we learn the 'lessons', the beliefs and values, most relevant to our survival.

The need of the organism to survive may be viewed in terms of a hierarchy. At the bottom lies the survival need in its most basic biological-physiological sense. Once this level of needs is satisfied, then with assistance from the natural and human-made environments, the organism develops and pursues the fulfilment of needs of greater complexity and sophistication. In terms of Maslow's 'hierarchy of needs' (1968), the organism moves from (1) physiological to (2) safety to (3) belongingness to (4) esteem and finally to (5) self-actualisation needs.

The notion of needs is an important element in Burton's work. Expressed initially as *social-biological values* (1972b, pp. 127–30), he views them as 'connected with survival, personality development, and self-maintenance within any social environment'. Some of the particular needs he has in mind are *identity, recognition, security, rationality*, and *control* (see Sites, 1973). Though these are universal, different cultural systems may employ different means for satisfying them. Needs represent the imperatives of the organism's self-maintaining properties; the organism survives through their fulfilment. And again, the beliefs and values which the organism develops and internalises are relevant to fulfilling these needs. Accordingly, the longer we exist in terms of certain beliefs and values, and the more they are confirmed and reinforced, the more relevant they become to need-fulfilment and therefore to survival; in effect, the more 'biological' they become.

As our beliefs and values become more biological, so they become increasingly resistant to change. Resistance is of two types, both of which operate at the unconscious level: *cognitive* resistance and *evaluative-affective* resistance. The *cognitive* dimension of images (Boulding, 1956) provides us with descriptions of our 'self' plus natural and human-made environments; these are our beliefs. The *evaluative* dimension provides us with rankings, priorities, a sense of what is important and preferable versus what is not. These are our values. And the *affective* dimension provides us with the biological-physiological energy with which to defend beliefs which our values define as important. This energy derives from our emotions.

Cognitive resistance is related to cognitive blindness. To recapitulate briefly, perception is a function of experience which has taught us to perceive what in fact we do perceive. What we perceive are not raw sense impressions, but rather sense data transformed into intelligibles by our beliefs and values. If something is 'out there' for which we do not have a corresponding image, then we will not detect it; we will be 'blind'. This blindness turns into cognitive resistance when, in the face of the continued presence of an anomaly, our images do not undergo the transformation necessary to detect it.

In practice, our prevailing beliefs and values have usually been successful in the sense of facilitating satisfaction of our needs. In terms of Maslow's hierarchy, safety needs are particularly relevant to our security and, therefore, to our survival. Included here are what I call the needs for predictability, regularity, and stability. The need for predictability is fulfilled each time the expectations inherent in our images, our beliefs and values, are confirmed; the need for regularity is fulfilled when the predictability need is fulfilled most of the time; and the need for stability is fulfilled when the regularity need is fulfilled most of the time. When our beliefs and values have worked for us in this sense, they will not be surrendered lightly. The biological/physiological realm cannot yield immediately to anomalies in our perceptual field. As Jervis (1976) has argued in his analysis of the perceptual process in international relations, not only will people assimilate incoming information to pre-existing beliefs, but their beliefs will be highly resistant to discrepant information.

But cognitive resistance can lead to disaster. A belief or value may previously and over time have proven its relevance to survival of the organism. But circumstances change and anomalies emerge as ← indicators of those changes. If anomalies are not detected and identified, traditional beliefs and values may prove detrimental to the survival of the organism. In other words, at some point in time it may be the anomaly, and not the tradition, that is relevant to our survival.

Anxiety can alert us to the possibility that our images may no longer be relevant to our survival. Through anxiety, we experience what Festinger (1962) calls *cognitive dissonance*, the phenomenon of breakdown between image and reality. When cognitive dissonance occurs because of a breakdown between expectations and behaviour, or between expectations and environment, we can attempt to reduce it by changing our expectations, our behaviour, and/or our environment. But these are not necessarily easy, straightforward actions. They may involve a great deal of time, effort, difficulty, and frustration. In the meantime, relief may be found in the form of the so-called *defence mechanisms*. These include (Hilgard, *et al.*, 1971, pp. 454–62) *rationalisation* (providing plausible explanations to conceal the nature of one's motives), *projection* (attributing one's own negative traits to others without recognising them in oneself), *reaction-formation* (giving strong expression to motives and behaviours which are directly opposite to one's true feelings), *dissociation* (severing connections between ideas and appropriate emotions), and *substitution* (replacing unapproved goals with approved ones). People characterised by these tend *not* to be aware of them.

The defence mechanisms are an example of the second of our two types of unconscious resistance: evaluative-affective resistance, or what Jervis (1980) calls 'motivated errors'. They are supposed to protect our self-esteem and protect us against excessive anxiety, especially in the face of continuing frustrations. This can be highly functional if the mechanisms operate for relatively short periods of time and are ultimately replaced by more realistic modes of adjustment. But to persist in using them is to flirt with the dysfunctional and perhaps even to court disaster. They involve self-deception, a denial or disguise of reality. As long as they operate, the people concerned will remain blind to the changes in their environment which may be crucial to their survival. By implication, the beliefs and values that would otherwise come under fire remain unchallenged and intact.

Now it is interesting that it is the same biological-physiological processes that are, at one and the same time, unleashing anxiety to alert us to the possibility that something may be wrong, but also attempting to protect us from that anxiety and therefore shield from challenge and threat certain beliefs and values. Given this anxiety-defence 'balance', one wonders what it would take to bring about a shift, a motivation to change rather than to preserve those beliefs and values.

HALTING AND REVERSING THE SLIDE

In order to halt and reverse 'malignant social processes', we would have to undermine the operation of *negative* self-fulfilling systems. And we would have to do this by counteracting the tendencies towards cognitive and evaluative-affective resistance. With regard to the self-fulfilling phenomenon, the obvious solution, as Merton (1968, p. 478) tells us, is to change 'the initial definition of the situation which has set the circle in motion' – to question and change the original assumption so that 'the consequent flow of events (would) give the lie to the assumption'. And what better way to achieve this objective than by, in Merton's words, 'mass propaganda and mass education'? Unfortunately, Merton himself (pp. 478–9) recognises that educational campaigns alone, even when accompanied by goodwill, 'cannot be counted on to eliminate prevailing ethnic hostilities'. Snyder (1982, p. 68) agrees: 'Apparently, goodwill and education are not sufficient to subvert the power of the stereotypes.'

This is particularly true in cases where beliefs and values were born out of trauma. Take, for instance, Japanese perceptions of defence issues, particularly those concerning nuclear weapons. Or take the support of Jewish communities worldwide for the State of Israel. Or take the intensity of Soviet feelings regarding their perceptions of vulnerability to attack. In this regard, the Soviet Union has experienced a traumatic event, the scale of which few nations, including the United States, have ever experienced: the surprise attack by Nazi Germany on 22 June 1941. This 'left an indelible mark on Soviet consciousness' which still influences their perceptions of, and behaviour toward the outside world (John Erickson, 1981, p. 16). American political leaders and their Soviet counterparts may live in the same world of political realism in general, but they clearly do not live in the same world with regard to June, 1941. It is this distance between the two – an emotional as well as cognitive distance – that accounts for what Ralph White (1982) has referred to as America's 'woeful lack of empathy with the Soviets'.

Beliefs and values which have come into existence through trauma, grief, and pain are particularly difficult to 'communicate with', let alone change. In addition to the cognitive blindness, cognitive resistance, and the evaluative-affective resistance which operate at the unconscious level, there may also be evaluative-affective resistance at the *conscious* level. And here we can see the phenomenon of the nearly 'knee-jerk' aggressive response to belief and value threats.

When an American nuclear-powered ship, laden with nuclear-tipped missiles, slips into a Japanese port; when the PLO accuses Israel of genocide; and when the American government accuses the Soviet Union of preparing to initiate a war against the West, then, among appropriate Japanese, Israelis, and Soviets, the phenomenon of 'seeing red' will be operative.

'Seeing red', or hostility, is an indication that the body, in a biological sense, has been violated. We are talking again about needs. In Maslow's scheme, if the safety needs (predictability, regularity, stability) are assaulted by persistent bombardment of anomalous stimuli, then beyond some crucial threshold, the body may be forced to respond with what I call the 'Lorenzian line of defence'. As Lorenz (1967) points out, intra-specific aggression is innate and is meant to enhance, rather than impede, species-survivability. Consequently, we would expect the organism under persistent and increasing threat to employ ultimately the last line of defence available to it – aggression.

Whether we talk about protecting the safety or any other needs, we are, in any case, talking about what Burton calls 'role defence needs'. These are concerned with 'the protection of needs once they have been acquired' (Burton, 1979, p. 73). By implication, role defence also concerns the protection of beliefs and values which are associated with these needs. It also means the protection of roles as such – 'the individual attempts to secure a role and to preserve a role by which he acquires and maintains his recognition, security and stimulation' (*ibid.*). Burton argues that no explanation of conflict at any level would be complete without taking role defence into account: 'It is a need for which biological evidence is available, for it explains the behaviour of dominant members of packs and the main fighting within species that takes place' (*ibid.*).

There is also anthropological evidence for role defence. Merton (1968, pp. 483–4) refers to the classic study by Malinowski of the Trobriand Islanders (1922). Amongst the Trobrianders, it is a moral virtue for men to be successful with women, but 'excessive' pursuit of sexual success applies only to the political elite, and not to 'lesser' males. The lesson which Merton draws from this is:

moral virtues remain virtues only so long as they are jealously confined to the proper in-group. . . . For clearly, only . . . by holding these virtues exclusively to themselves, can the men of power retain their distinction, their prestige, and their power.

Though Merton does not use the term, this is role defence in a nutshell. It seems to underly what is for him the major reason why educational campaigns alone would not counteract self-fulfilling processes. Role defence, the need to maintain social distance between oneself and others, between the dominant in-group and the minority out-groups, is for Merton (p. 482) 'rooted deep in the structure of our society and the social-psychology of its members'. Consequently, we will always find some way to maintain this distance, to defend our roles. In general, we seem to do this by disliking others, by defining them in negative terms, *no matter what they do*. For instance, we dislike them because they are not like us, but we can also dislike them when they are like us. This transmutation of in-group virtues into out-group vices is a classic example of 'damned if you don't and damned if you do'.

This implies that even if the Palestinians were to behave more like the Israelis (according to Israeli perceptions), the Israelis would persist in defining them negatively. And even if the Soviets behaved more like the Americans (as perceived by the Americans), the Americans would continue to dislike them. It is because of this phenomenon that Merton has decided that educational campaigns alone will not do the trick.

For Merton what would, in conjunction with education, do the trick is appropriate institutional developments and changes in the social, political, and economic environment. These 'deliberate institutional controls' could reduce considerably, if not stamp out altogether, environmental support for negative stereotypes and prejudices. In this way, a 'halt can be put to the workings of the self-fulfilling prophecy and the vicious circle in society' (Merton, 1968, pp. 489–90).

There is, however, a chicken-egg problem here. It would seem that to bring about appropriate changes in institutions, there must first be corresponding changes in beliefs and values. But the opposite case could also be made – that to bring about changes in beliefs and values, there must first be corresponding changes in institutions. This is an old problem. Does war lie in the minds of people? Or does it lie in their social, political, and economic environment? It lies in both realms, and the practical question is how to bring about psychological and institutional change simultaneously, especially during periods when intense role defence is operative. Indeed, during such periods, when beliefs and values are being consciously defended, and anger, aggressive behaviour, and conflict are prevalent, vicious circles can only be exacerbated. Realism as a self-perpetuating system can only be strengthened.

But hostility or 'seeing red' may have a positive as well as a negative side. To counteract the tendency towards resistance, cognitive dissonance could be actively increased. The resulting anxiety could eventually overwhelm the defence mechanisms and create new opportunities for the reorganisation of conceptual categories. This would in turn allow threatening anomalies to be detected and assimilated, in which case they would cease to be threats.

Accordingly, though intense role defence, or conscious defence of beliefs and values, may be moving the system closer to detonation and collapse, the accompanying sense of crisis may pave the way for a halt and a reversal. Some kind of shock may indeed be necessary to dislodge us from the long-term, progressively reinforced internal scripts which influence us to continue behaving in a self-destructive manner. The obvious question at this point is: are there any 'shock waves' running through political realism?

THE DECLINE AND FALL OF REALISM?

Crisis is experienced emotionally as massive dissonance and is interpreted as a breakdown between expectations and the way events are actually unfolding. It can be particularly painful. It is because of this intensity, this pain, that crisis can constitute the kind of shock that would be necessary to bring about a paradigmatic shift, a 'scientific revolution'. According to Kuhn (1970, ch. 8), the symptoms of crisis are expressions of explicit discontent, debates over basic assumptions, a willingness to try anything, and a proliferation of alternatives to the establishment paradigm. Is any of this happening with regard to political realism?

Our discussion thus far suggests that it is. Karl Deutsch (1981, p. 167) reinforces the suggestion: 'Governments are undergoing a deterioration in their cognitive capabilities at the same time that their ability to destroy themselves is increasing.' Apropos the deterioration of cognitive capabilities, the President's Commission on Foreign Language and International Studies, in its report, *Strength Through Wisdom* (1979), argues that the level of competence among Americans in foreign cultures and languages 'is nothing short of scandalous, and it is becoming worse'. Elise Boulding (1982, p. 59) states the problem succinctly:

There has been no growth of internationalism in the United States. Less than 1 percent of college-age Americans are enrolled in any course that focuses on international issues or areas; less than 2 percent of high school graduates have any foreign language competence; less than 5 percent of teachers have any exposure to international or foreign area studies.

And *Strength Through Wisdom* (p. 8) reports that 'those who graduate from an educational system so glaringly deficient in this vital area carry their ignorance with them into their adult lives'.

Apropos the increasing capability of governments to destroy themselves, there are the frequent manifestations of mass opinion – for instance, the hundreds of thousands who have been demonstrating in Europe, the United States, and elsewhere against nuclear weapons and nuclear war-fighting policies. Then there have been some interesting displays of elite opinion, even among the military, such as Lord Mountbatten. There is also 'Generals for Peace' (1982), a group of retired senior officers from NATO countries. There are also the political elites, such as the Palme Commission which is the East-West complement to the Brandt Commission on North-South relations (1980). In its report, *Common Security* (1982, p. 1), the Palme Commission argues that 'every year has uncovered new evidence that humanity may eventually confront the greatest danger of all – worldwide nuclear war'. George Kennan has put forward dramatic proposals for ending the nuclear arms race (1981) and he has joined other former top-level members of US administrations – McGeorge Bundy, Robert McNamara, and Gerard Smith – to urge, among other things, the beginning of a 'careful study of a policy that could help to sweep this threat (of nuclear war) clean off the board of international affairs' (Bundy, *et al.*, 1982, p. 767).

It is not just the *practice* but also the *study* of international relations which is in a state of disarray. For instance, McClelland (1972, p. 15) indicates that 'issues have been raised which call into question a number of long-established orientations to the field', thereby producing 'conceptual disturbance'. Rosenau (1973, p. 15) has said, 'What was yesterday's secure knowledge . . . has become today's pervasive doubt. . . . Confidence has given way to uncertainty.'

What does all this have to say about the dominant paradigm in international relations? John Vasquez (1983, p. 223) has found in his major study of the field that 'propositions based on realist assumptions do not do as well as those that reject realist assumptions'.

In both the practice and study of international relations, then, there are signs of discontent, debates over basic assumptions, and indications of a willingness to try something new. There have also been some attempts to develop alternatives to political realism. For instance, with regard to the way international relations is theorised about or studied, a number of alternatives, including Burton's 'cobweb' model of world society, have been proposed. And with regard to the way relations are practised, and not just at the international level, there are, among others, proposals from Burton as well as Kelman (1972) on problem-solving, from Morton Deutsch (1973, 1982) on cooperative processes, and from Pruitt (1981) on integrative agreements.

Accordingly, all the ingredients of crisis, in the Kuhnian sense, seem to be present in both the study and practice of international relations. Moreover, crisis seems to be occurring at other levels as well, for example, 'in the classroom, in the streets, in business, and in administration' (Burton, 1979, p. 31). Consequently, there is a greater chance that paradigmatic shifts – shifts in beliefs, values and corresponding behaviours – will take place at one or more of those levels. But crisis may not terminate in paradigmatic change. It may lead, instead, to an augmentation and refinement of the traditional paradigm and consequently, to the assimilation of the anomalies which gave rise to the crisis. In other words, crisis, even at all levels, might lead to confirmation, and not replacement of the establishment paradigm.

Burton (1979, p. 161), however, has argued that 'there is now evidence of a paradigm shift'. We certainly have the crises, the 'shocks', at all levels. And we have responses to these in the form of alternative ideas. At this point, we certainly have the bases for the 'educational campaigns' discussed in the previous section. But there is more. There have been some attempts to put these new ideas into practice, to institutionalise problem-solving alternatives to threats and violence at all levels. One of these is the University for Peace within the context of the United Nations.[5] Another is the National Peace Academy in the United States.[6] And there are still others, in the United States and elsewhere, where the objective is to train professional 'conflict managers'.[7]

It is one thing to talk about alternatives to violence, about cooperative problem-solving, and even to develop such alternatives. But it is something else – *and more suggestive of a paradigmatic shift* – to begin to create the infrastructures which would support and actively encourage problem-solving approaches to conflict resolution. So, perhaps Burton is right.

CONCLUSION

Political realism apparently began life as a positive response to threats to human security. But it seems to have become a pathological 'bad' – what we might call ideological or 'vulgarised' realism. In a sense, realism has failed, and with it what we have called the Lorenzian line of defence. At the international (nuclear) level, aggression not only fails to facilitate the survivability of the species but has become positively detrimental to it.[8] But the insidious nature of self-fulfilling processes means that pathological realism still prevails throughout much of the world. However, the world society perspective suggests not only that this state of affairs can be turned around, but also that the beginnings of such a reversal may actually be underway.

Only time will tell whether this view is right. In the meantime, it is interesting to note that some realists have begun to redefine realism back to its positive role. For instance, Herz (1981, p. 184), has said:

I progress now beyond my previous emphasis (and) align myself with (those) who recognize the outdatedness of many traditional interpretations of power and national interest.

He goes on: 'Realism yes, but a more sophisticated one . . . which distinguishes "real" facts and situations from the views actors and publics have formed about them'.

Perhaps when time has told, we will be able to declare: *Realism is dead! Realism is dead! Long live realism!*

NOTES

1 An earlier version of this paper was presented at the Annual Conference of the British International Studies Association (BISA), University of Southampton, England, 15–17 December 1982. The author gratefully acknowledges comments received at that time, plus comments made subsequently by Michael Banks. Special thanks are also due to Mary Lynn Boland for typing the various versions of the paper.

2 Though political realism has been expressed in a variety of ways (see Dougherty and Pfaltzgraff, 1981, ch. 3), it tends to be characterised by these fundamental dimensions.

3 See Boulding (1956, p. 14), Kaplan (1964, pp. 131–41, 268, 375, 385), Kuhn (1970, p. 126), and Popper (1972, p. 64).

4 Cited in Merton (1968, p. 475).

5 See *University for Peace: Basic Documents* (1981).

6 See *To Establish the United States Academy of Peace* (1981).

7 Wedge and Sandole (1982) discuss one of these – the MSc Programme in Conflict Management at George Mason University, Fairfax, Virginia.

8 Given that the self-preservation function of Lorenzian defence is achieved through the control of events in one's environment, then the failure of realism is also the failure of control. In Richard Ashley's analysis (1981), this is the failure of *technical* realism (plus the failure of *practical* realism in being overtaken and dominated by technical realism).

Part II
THE STRUCTURE OF THE WORLD SOCIETY

4 World Society as Cobweb: States, Actors and Systemic Processes

C.R. Mitchell

The insight that the structure of the global system is somewhat more complex than that suggested by the pattern of interactions between the governments of legally separate states hardly seems revolutionary in the increasingly complex and interdependent world of the 1980s. It is accepted in all undergraduate courses in international relations that some attention, at the very least, must be paid to transnational actors such as the EEC Commission or the nonaligned movement, to networks such as the protagonists in the Islamic revival, or to 'non-state actors', such as the Kurdish Democratic Party or the PLO. Yet the abandonment of the 'state-centric' approach is a recent innovation. Only a few years ago standard textbooks concentrated heavily on state actions and maintained a strict separation between domestic and international politics.

One of the most thorough-going assaults on the state-centric approach to the analysis of international relations was launched by John Burton in the late 1960s, when he proposed a 'world society' approach using a 'cobweb model' of global structure as a contrast to the then more familiar 'billiard ball model'. Burton set out his views in two books and a number of major papers (Burton, 1968, 1972b, 1974), while Banks (1978) has contrasted and compared not merely the state-centric and world society approaches, but those of the 'structuralist' school and an intermediate approach between state-centric and world society, talking about four competing paradigms. However, in spite of this wealth of direct material on the world society approach and the idea of the cobweb model, many of the ideas appear incomplete and in need of further explication. This essay, therefore, attempts to consolidate ideas on the world society approach and the structure of the global system and then to link them with the general analysis of systems structure and behaviour. To do this it will be necessary to review briefly the main outline of the approach itself.

THE COBWEB METAPHOR AND WORLD SOCIETY

The central, and initially very simple, idea at the heart of the world society abandonment of traditional state-centric approaches to studying 'international' relations is that by the middle of the twentieth century there were far more interactions taking place between non-governmental actors than those which could justifiably be regarded as involving 'the state'. This idea necessarily implied that territoriality was becoming a misleading guide to differentiating and categorising relations. Relationships cut across formal state boundaries and frequently made nonsense of government efforts to control them at those boundaries. States were becoming 'penetrated' to a hitherto unprecedented degree (Scott, 1965) and it had become necessary to pay more attention to the impact of 'linkage politics' (Rosenau, 1969).

The initial conception led Burton to posit that something new had developed in the world which scholars tried to explain and national leaders to manipulate. It was now quite proper to speak of a 'world society' with a describable structure and set of complexly interacting processes. The new structure was quite unlike the disjointed and compartmentalised one previously represented by the traditional 'billiard ball' metaphor. It was becoming more integrated and interdependent.

If the world had changed in this fashion, then the problem was how one could describe it in a helpful and economical fashion, given that the conventional model where 'each state is represented by a government and is seen as an entity – a sovereign, independent unit' was more misleading than helpful. Burton's answer to this problem was a fruitful new metaphor: one of a world made up of networks of transactions that could be conceptually organised as 'systems' which interconnected, overlapped and interacted. Among these would be conventional but now less important networks of inter-governmental relationships. However, according to Burton, the bulk of these networks of transactions would be non-governmental, even if affected by the activities of governments in the latter's attempts to regulate them.[1]

With such a structure existing 'out there' and waiting to be explored, the most appropriate metaphor would be that of a complex cobweb or set of cobwebs, with the strands representing relationships built up as a result of increased contact and communication on a *global* rather than merely *national* scale. 'In practice, there are so many direct communications, or systems, that a world map which represented them would look like a mass of cobwebs superimposed on one another, strands converging at some points more than others and being concentrated between some points more than between others. The boundaries of states would be hidden from view' (Burton, 1972b, p. 43).

To this simple but striking metaphor ('the cobweb model') Burton linked the idea that particular networks of transactions could profitably be regarded as forming *systems* of interaction. Thus, they could be differentiated from one another while remaining linked through sharing particular entities as elements in the system. This point emphasises that the 'model' of the world as cobweb is a three-dimensional one. It is possible to envisage the global set of cobwebs from side on, so to speak, and trace out the 'vertical' linkages. This delineates which cobwebs are connected to which other cobwebs, and which elements play a role in numerous networks, thus serving as key links in transmitting changes in one network to other levels.

From these simple beginnings, Burton launched into a complex analytical and prescriptive set of arguments about the contemporary nature of world society, the most appropriate strategies for governments seeking to achieve their goals at minimum cost in such a world, and the means by which a stable world order might be developed. However, it now seems useful to redirect attention to the basic conceptions because Burton and his fellow theorists, in their desire to apply the basic principles to practical problems of analysis and action, have neglected to spell out some of the nuances of the broad conceptions underlying the approach. They have ignored a number of apparently minor, but important distinctions that need to be drawn out from the original formulation.

If one adopts Burton's cobweb metaphor and world society approach as a basic framework to describe the global system, then there exists an obligation to be more specific about certain fundamentals. For example, what types of entity can form the nodes or 'points' in each separate cobweb of transactions; that is, what elements are in relationship with one another, or what units exchange something within each system? Furthermore, how can one locate such entities and their relational network in time and space? A second major problem is the exact nature of the 'relationship' between the entities; how can one describe and categorise the nature of what is exchanged between the elements, causing their attributes to change over time? What are the strands of the 'cobweb'? Moreover, where do they end or, more formally: what are the ways of limiting the membership of the set of entities under consideration, or delineating the limits of the network; where are the system boundaries? the process of communication and problem-solving, have an possible to devise some method of measuring the intensity of the various types of transactions between the entities in the network (or, indeed, of classifying the nature of the relationships between the elements). Finally, how, except on the grounds of some prior theory or trial-and-error can one tell which are important networks for illuminating any problem?

Such questions have been explored both by Burton himself and, indirectly, by other scholars who have adopted the bulk of Burton's ideas or a more limited transactional or linkage perspective. But some questions have been dealt with more comprehensively than others in the burgeoning literature on transnationalism and world society. The remainder of this article will discuss three problems. The first is relatively well explored, and concerns the question of the elements in transnational systems. The other two have been somewhat neglected. They deal with, first, the nature of the relationship between the elements in transnational systems – a key concept in world society as opposed to the less radical transnational approach; and, second, with ways of categorising the nature of the relationships between elements in such systems.

ELEMENTS IN THE SYSTEM

Probably the area in which the study of international relations generally has moved furthest away from the state-centric model has been in the development of a whole list of non-state actors that participate in and affect international politics. This trend reflects the realisation that, while national governments remain a potent influence within some parts of the global system, other elements have become equally, and in some cases more, influential.

Two of the most systematic treatments of this whole question appear firstly in a thoughtful article by David Singer (ch. 2 in Rosenau, 1969) and, secondly, in a more thorough-going attack on the whole state-centric approach by Mansbach et al. (1976). Singer argues that it is quite feasible to consider a large range of entities as potential elements in 'international' systems. These elements range from individuals, families (the Gemayel family in Lebanon, for example) or small groups, to governmental and non-governmental intra-national entities, national states (represented by their governments acting as a unit) and inter-national coalitions or organisations.

Singer argues that intra-national entities form by far the largest category of potential actors in transnational systems, a point supported empirically by Alger's investigations of the transnational linkages existing in a single United States city (see below, chapter 8). Non-governmental entities alone can include business organisations (the CBI); trade unions (the NFU), professional societies (ISA); ethnic, ideological and religious organisations (the Kurdish Democratic Party); political parties (SDLP); terrorist groups (Baader-Meinhof); and even separatist organisations (the Eritrean Liberation Front).

Almost as large a class are the governmental entities for, as Singer points out, this category includes not merely agencies of the central government (such as the obvious ones of ministries of trade, external affairs or defence), but organs of regional and local governments who can become international actors through both such mundane processes as 'twinning' and more overtly political activities like the GLC's recent efforts to have London declared a nuclear-free zone or Dundee District Council's links with the PLO. Singer's taxonomy is thorough and ingenious, and the only type of entity that does not fit very well into its categories is the genuinely a-national, 'multinational' corporation, which might have its headquarters situated territorially within one state, but operate on a wholly non-territorial basis.

In contrast to Singer's taxonomy, that developed by Mansbach *et al* abandons the distinction between family, small group and intra-national non-governmental 'actors'. But it provides a new category into which multinational corporations and other genuinely non-national entities can easily be fitted – that of 'inter-state non-governmental' actors, including such entities as the International Red Cross, the Comintern and IBM. They define six basic types of entity which can form part of what they refer to as a 'complex conglomerate system', characterised by the presence of any combination of the six actor types as elements: individuals, intra-state governmental, governmental non-central, nation-state, inter-state non-governmental and inter-state governmental.

Both the Singer and the Mansbach frameworks can be encompassed in the world society approach with little trouble and go some considerable way towards dealing with the question of what entities form the elements in Burton's transnational systems.

However, such taxonomies have their weaknesses. For example, do they exhaust the possible types of entity which might form elements in the systems making up world society? A brief reference to Burton's work reveals that the answer to this question is clearly negative, because the important elements in many transnational systems include *categories* or *collectivities*[2] of individuals not necessarily organised into some formal institution such as party, firm, union or other structure. Clearly, it is possible for Malays, Hindus, Chinese, anti-communists or nationalists to be regarded as 'elements' in some transnational systems (Burton, 1972b, pp. 36–45) just as the US Defence Department, Boeing Aircraft Corporation, American Metal Climax, the Rand Corporation and the Israeli Air Force are regarded as key elements in some other patterned interaction. Equally clearly, Burton regards it as fruitful to conceptualise at least some of his transnational systems to include (or even consist of) 'sets' of individuals whose common attribute, apart from their membership of the system, may be physical, behavioural, attitudinal or perceptual.

In some ways, however, arguments about what types of entity might form elements in the transnational systems making up world society are peripheral to that approach's main contribution to innovatory thinking. The crucial concept is less the entities engaged in a particular network of relationships and more the nature, and changing nature, of those relationships themselves. In all work on the world society approach, existing and altering relationships are the key focus of attention. The *structure* of the global system consists of the patterns of relationships that exist at any one time. *Processes* in that system consist of the manner in which these relationships change and evolve naturally, are deliberately altered, or are completely severed as when a boundary is imposed or reactivated and existing interaction prevented. In many senses, the *relationship* is the unit of analysis in the world society approach, and a clear delineation of the nature and classification of relationships is an important part of refining that approach.

THE RELATIONSHIP AS UNIT OF ANALYSIS

Unfortunately the world society treatment of this central issue demonstrates the difficulties of using a concept such as 'relationship' as an organising principle. These difficulties are, indeed, prefigured in Singer's efforts to deal with the problem. He argues that at least two meanings can be assigned to the concept of a 'relationship' between entities. The first he calls 'relationship as similarity of attributes' and the second 'relationship as interdependence'. The two are frequently interconnected empirically although it is not always the case that individuals, organisations or countries sharing attributes are necessarily 'interdependent' to any very great degree. In fact, quite the opposite might be the case. A country that has a relatively low GDP might be highly interdependent with others possessing a high GDP, and not interdependent at all with others sharing its economic poverty. The crucial question arising from Singer's point is what, precisely, is meant by 'interdependence' (Singer, 1969, pp. 36–7).

Burton's treatment of the concept is fuller than Singer's (and certainly fuller than that of Mansbach *et al*, who play down the question of the nature of a relationship and the types of relationship that can exist). However, he tends to use the term 'relationship' in two different ways, and he sometimes conflates them. The first is the idea of relationship as the exchange of something between elements in the system (trade flows, tourist movements, and so on). For example, it is quite clear that such 'transnational exchanges . . . including teaching abroad, study abroad, tourism, overseas religious missions, work in multinational corporations, participation in international non-governmental and international governmental organisations' involve movement, the flow of something, in this case people, between entities (Burton, 1972b, p. 47). The second usage, however, echoes Singer's ideas about relationship meaning a similarity of attributes, and involves entities which share attributes (ethnic group sense of identity, sympathies or common values).[3]

The whole world society approach has suffered somewhat from the dilemma of sliding from one meaning of 'relationship' to another, as indeed have all efforts to apply any form of systems analysis to international politics. One important task, therefore, is to sharpen the distinctions between the various definitions of the term, and then to suggest how it might best be used in making the details of the world society approach less ambiguous and, hence, more usable. A survey of the use of the term in the systems literature generally indicates that it has been used in at least six ways:

(1) 'Relationship' in the sense of coexistence in a spatial or temporal sense. Geographic proximity obviously has some claim to 'relate' objects to each other, as has temporal contiguity. However, this hardly seems important for analysing the structure of international politics, although Burton has mentioned this as a kind of 'systems' relationship as in the elements of a pictorial composition or the parts of some static whole such as a chair (Burton, 1968, p. 6).

(2) 'Relationship' in Singer's sense of similarity of attributes. In

this sense, we think of entities sharing something, such as a self-image as a group member, or some attitude, aim, sympathy or condition. This is connected with Burton's idea of members of *a set* being involved in a relationship by virtue of common possession, even though no exchange of anything tangible or intangible takes place and the entities may not be interdependent in any sense at all. It is possible for two people or groups to be hungry or even starving without any contact with, or even knowledge of, each other. Similarly, countries can share low GNP or high instability, communities be discriminated against or in revolt, yet be 'related' only in the sense that they are members of the same category.

(3) 'Relationship' in the sense of a logical or definitional interdependence. This type of relationship is one which exists when an entity's attribute logically depends on a necessary interdependence with another entity. One can be hungry on one's own, but not a 'cousin' or a 'husband'. Similarly, being a 'quarry' necessitates the existence of 'hunters', while being an ally or a bloc leader depends upon the existence of other allies or bloc followers. Such relationships enable an entity to be attributed the quality which defines it as a member of some special category.

(4) 'Relationship' in the sense of a mathematical or statistical interdependence which describes constant connections between variable factors. Thus, one talks about exponential relationships, or asymptotic relationship, or about the relationship between a circle's radius and its area. Again, this form of relationship will be important for studying international politics only if it can be revealed that empirical relationships between elements mirror those which exist in deductively produced mathematical systems.

(5) 'Relationship' in the sense of interdependencies that are causal rather than being logical, statistical or mathematical. The use of the term in this sense occurs when we talk, for example, of X's well-being as dependent upon Y's continued low standard of living, or A's sense of security being related to B's low level of armaments. Both these statements deal with bivariate causal 'relationships'.

(6) Finally, there are relationships for which the synonyms 'exchanges', 'transactions' or 'interactions' can justifiably be used. These involve the transfer of something between entities which can be indicated by observable flows or at least by the

effects, responses or changes brought about by such flows. The literature on systems analysis postulates that exchanges can be of three basic types: *material* flows (including personnel, such as experts); *energy* flows (including credit as well as electrical power); and *information* flows (including expertise) which is often the type most important for social and political systems (as well as being, unfortunately, the most elusive).[4]

However, our main point remains that even a brief reading of world society literature reinforces the conclusion that the most frequent meaning of the term 'relationship' in the approach is in this last 'relationship as exchange' sense, followed closely by its use in the 'relationship as shared attribute' sense. It can be argued that the two types of relationship are clearly, and probably causally, linked. Transactions and exchanges arise from the existence of shared attributes among entities (sense of identity, common values, or conscious sympathies). Equally, the growth of some pattern of exchange can lead to the development of shared attributes and – in Burton's terms – the *creation* of some 'set' of people sharing views, goals and aspirations, plus, perhaps, a desire to create some formal representative institutions.[5]

Because of this tendency to conflate two meanings of relationship in world society writings, we are led to a further question about its use as the main unit of analysis in that approach. This is whether it is possible to categorise different types of relationship (and hence transnational system) in any clear, useful and unambiguous manner, so that it is possible to distinguish different types of relationship and different kinds of transnational system. Such a step would be preliminary to drawing clear system boundaries and analysing the effects of one system upon another via linking elements.[6]

CLASSIFYING RELATIONSHIPS

At first sight the question of whether one can usefully categorise types of relationships appears nonsensical. A taxonomy of different usages of the term 'relationship' has already been suggested and it has been argued that the world society approach uses two of these categories (sometimes indiscriminately). Even if we merely concentrate upon the conception of 'relationship as exchange', we have suggested one approach based upon the nature of *what* is exchanged. Is a relationship not one involving flows of material (grain), energy (kilowatts), information (protest notes), or some combination of these?

Moreover, all scholars who write about transnational systems, not merely those who explicitly use the world society approach, assume that it is useful and possible to distinguish various types of relationship in order to talk about different systems. 'There is', writes Burton, 'in contemporary world society an increasing number of systems – some basically economic, scientific, cultural, ideological or religious' (Burton, 1968, p. 10). The implication is that it is possible to distinguish each different type of system on the basis of the 'nature' of the relationship involved. If this process of categorising types of relationship ('economic', 'cultural' and – presumably – 'political') is carried out so confidently by scholars writing about transnational systems, then it is a worthwhile exercise to attempt to clarify the basis upon which such categorisation takes place. If we are to be clear about what differentiates an 'economic' from a 'cultural' or an 'ideological' system, then some clear principles of classification must exist or else be created.

Two basic approaches to determining classification criteria for relationships, and hence for systems, have been used. The first is simply to revert to the question of *what* is exchanged and use that as the criterion for categorising (and, to a degree, measuring the intensity of) the relationships in question. It need hardly be pointed out that such classifications are merely more detailed versions of that which divides relationships into exchanges of material, energy or information. The *nature of what is exchanged* is the standard by which the type of relationship is determined. Such an approach does lead in a straightforward fashion to a useful ability to make statements about the (possibly changing) intensity of particular relationships, enabling scholars to analyse the comparative strength of various relationships, as well as about their fundamental nature. *How much*, as well as *what* is exchanged, becomes an interesting and useful question, even in respect of relationships that are based upon exchanges of information via messages, signs or signals. Much of the behavioural literature on the structure of international crises, for example, is based upon the principle that one can tell when those entities linked in some system are in a crisis by the increased intensity of their information exchange (see McClelland, 1961, on this).

Furthermore, the fact that one can use changing levels of exchange as a basis for making statements about the changing *intensity* of a relationship introduces the prospect of an alternative means of characterising, and hence classifying, relationships. If it is reasonable to characterise some relationships as 'intense' (and hence others as 'not intense') according to the level of exchange over a given period of time, then it should be possible to regard relationships as possessing other identifying qualities besides that of 'intensity'. Relationships can be regarded as multidimensional phenomena, able to be described by numerous attributes. A relationship might well be characterised as 'intense' or as 'cultural' or as 'exclusive', depending upon our ability to establish clear operational criteria for distinguishing intense relationships from non-intense, exclusive from non-exclusive, and so on.

This argument is hardly new. Efforts to characterise relationships, or at least to differentiate between them, are familiar in any work on international politics. Usually, these use some crude and often ambiguous 'main quality' approach, classifying networks of relationships as 'military', 'political', 'economic', 'social', 'ideological' without bothering to specify clearly what criteria are used to distinguish one type of relational network from another.

Such ways of characterising relationships obviously play a part in the world society approach, but in many ways the extension of the approach into prescriptive analysis (one of its great strengths) is based on the concept of relationships that possess the quality of being *legitimised*. This conception is a central feature. It also suggests that some networks of relationships are durable and can exist in their own right, while others are imposed and only kept in existence by the coercive and ultimately self-defeating efforts of those entities with some usable political power or economic resource.

Several points need to be noted about this concept of *legitimised relationships*. The first, frequently stressed by all who use a world society approach, is that legitimised relationships are not the same as 'legal' or 'legalised' relationships. The latter are frequently established by force and maintained through coercion or the threat of sanctions by the stronger against the weaker (many 'peace' treaties are of this nature). The whole point about legitimised relationships is that the entities involved in them accept them as being beneficial and, in some profound sense, 'right'. This conception can, paradoxically, include some relationships that are objectively or statistically unequal or one-sided, and others which involve the use of authority to cause elements to act in ways which, frequently, they would rather not. The point about this latter circumstance is that the action occurs, and the relationship is valued and retained, not because of any coercive element, but because the right of one element to demand conformity is recognised by the conforming units. A chairman is obeyed because he *is* chairman. His role is recognised as necessary and (even) beneficial. Hence, it is accepted, even when he demands conforming behaviour from members of his committee or cabinet. In slightly different terms, the crucial factor about a legitimised relationship is *its acceptance by those involved*. Legitimacy is not necessarily the same as symmetry or equality, although empirically there seems to be a close connection between the two concepts (especially in societies where egalitarianism is a major value).

The second point about relationships which possess legitimacy is that they tend to be self-sustaining, through their acceptability and because they fulfil some strong need for those involved. In contrast, non-legitimised relationships are those which are not acceptable to some of those involved and which thus contain elements of coercion or threat. The latter are maintained less because they are self-supporting than because the satisfied possess the means of imposing sanctions for ending the relationship on the dissatisfied, while the dissatisfied do not. Hence, according to Burton, a non-legitimised relationship contains strong elements of power without which the relationship would change or terminate because it fails to fulfil the needs of all those involved, and is unacceptable to some of them. The world society approach, therefore, makes a clear and important distinction between relationships among elements that are legitimised and those which are 'power' relationships involving overt or covert coercion.

Classifying relationships into those which are legitimised and those which are not returns us to the question of criteria. In seeking legitimacy, how one categorises a particular relationship involves no recognition of some quality *inherent in the relationship itself*. Characterising a relationship as 'legitimised' or 'non-legitimised' involves an assessment of the views, feelings or attitudes of the entities involved. This goes some way towards explaining how relationships can change radically over time without any apparent alteration in their fundamental structure as, for example, colonial and imperial relationships gradually altered. What is acceptable to entities at one point in time can, with changes in the views and values of one or other of them, become wholly non-legitimised at a later period. Legitimacy is in the eye of the beholder – or, perhaps more accurately, in the eyes of those involved.

A final point about classifying relationships into *legitimised* and *non-legitimised* categories is that one uses a totally different starting point from conventional analyses to ask questions about the fundamental nature of global society and what are its aberrations. For example, the world society approach begins by assuming that legitimised relationships should be regarded as a 'norm', in both a statistical and a prescriptive sense. In other words, in contemporary global society it is usual to find networks of relationships that are accepted by those involved and are thus both functional for the elements interacting, and self-supporting because of the mutually recognised benefits conferred by the transactions involved. The legitimised relationship is the norm, in the sense that the sheer number of such relationships far outweighs non-legitimised relationships involving power and coercion.

The contrast between this assumption and that customarily underlying power political, state-centric approaches hardly needs emphasising. In conventional analysis, it is assumed that coercive relationships are the norm. They are inevitable, given the structure of the inter-state system. Peace, accepted authority, legitimised exchanges and lack of coercion are the exceptions which are curiosities to be explained. In the world society approach, these latter phenomena are held to be normal, and the task becomes one of explaining the unusual circumstances that turn elements away from customary patterns of interaction and necessitate their behaving in some abnormal way. A whole new perspective emerges from such a simple reversal of assumptions.

Moreover, the world society approach also posits that legitimised relationships are the norm in a prescriptive sense; that is to say, the search for peace and a harmonious global society can best begin by rejecting the conception that stability and absence of violence can most surely be assured by the use of threats, coercion and deterrence. These are the very signs that existing relationships are non-legitimised and will inevitably lead to further conflict and violence so that their continued use will inevitably be counter-productive. What is needed is a search for ways of changing existing coercive relationships into those acceptable to elements involved. This would remove the need for threat systems to ensure continuation, or 'stability', to use the polite euphemism. In the best of all possible worlds, relationships would be entirely legitimised and durable because of this fact. (As can be seen, there is a strong infusion of anarchist assumptions in the world society approach.)

It is acknowledged by scholars who use this approach that such a complete Utopia is unlikely to be attainable. Even moving in the direction of fewer coercive and more legitimised interactions and exchanges presents major practical problems, not least in convincing

decision makers of the long run counterproductive nature of coercion
and the use of power to maintain relationships that are unacceptable
to others. However, world society analysis does at least offer an
alternative guide for action, a way out of the logical and empirical
impasse that the use of state-centric, power political ideas produces,
where the very factors that are supposed to produce security, stability
and absence of overt violence frequently give rise to the very
opposite.

LEGITIMACY: SOME CONCEPTUAL PROBLEMS

There are, naturally, a large number of difficulties and ambiguities
with the use of a 'legitimised relationship' as a core element in world
society analysis. There is only space to discuss two of these here and
to suggest ways in which such ambiguities might fruitfully be
clarified. The first problem is the tendency of world society writers to
assume that all relationships which involve the state and its agencies
are non-legitimised and involve coercion of somebody. Thus,
alliances are adversely contrasted with 'functional' transnational
networks which unite scientists, tourists and hosts, or sportsmen.
Government activities are held to be non-legitimised in the sense that
they interfere with exchanges that might otherwise exist. Government
attempts to regulate contacts between transnational ethnic groups,
like the Somali in Africa, or to prevent trade by establishing tariff
barriers, are given as examples of government activity which sets up
non-legitimised interactions as a substitute for those which would
otherwise exist.

The obverse of this argument is the implicit assumption that all
non-state systems are accepted by those involved, and hence are
networks of legitimised relationships. This is dubious. Is it really the
case that all transnational systems are legitimised because they (a) are
functional and fulfil needs for those involved; (b) are wholly accepted
because of mutual benefits conferred and thus (c) involve no coercion
of one element by another to ensure continuation? On *a priori*
grounds it hardly seems likely that, just as networks involving national
governments are by definition non-legitimised, all 'cobwebs' involving
other types of element are legitimised. With regard to multinational
corporations, many of the relationships and exchanges in which they
are involved are certainly not wholly accepted by related elements
(governments or growers) and undoubtedly involve strong aspects of
threat or coercion, even if, in most cases, this is not overt military

coercion. Nor should this be surprising. State agencies and institutions are not the only elements capable of using power and coercion. As Blau (1964) has pointed out, *any* entity can be in a powerful and coercive position through its control of desired goods and positions, both through its ability to do without what others can offer, and through its ability to find substitutes or alternative sources of supply. Such characteristics can apply as much to non-governmental entities as they can to national governments or their agencies. Hence, there appear to be no *a priori* grounds for regarding relationships involving governments as non-legitimised (although there are reasons for regarding this situation as likely), nor for regarding those involving non-governmental elements as necessarily legitimised. The matter is one for empirical investigation.[7]

The second major problem is the implicit tendency to treat the concept of legitimacy as though it were an either/or phenomenon, and the failure to allow for *degrees* of legitimacy. Burton, for example, frequently gives the impression that relationships either are clearly legitimised or they are not, although on other occasions implying that there may be degrees of legitimacy. If it is reasonable in principle and possible in practice to substitute the concept of a continuum of 'more or less' legitimacy, then some difficulties disappear, because discussion can then be couched in terms of *how legitimised* a particular relationship might be.

However, even banishing the problem of using a simplified dichotomy raises other, familiar difficulties about criteria. For example, in many situations it is obviously possible for some members of a particular element in a network of relationships to regard those relationships as highly, even wholly legitimised, while others in the same element regard them as unacceptable and hence non-legitimised. Are the relationships, then, partly legitimised, and how do we regard 'partly'? Contrast this case with the equally plausible situation in which all members of the elements involved are agreed that the relationship in question is tolerable, even if not being the best possible. Is this relationship also 'partly' legitimised and how should it be distinguished from that previously outlined?

At the extremes of the continuum, where members are decided about legitimacy or agree that the relationship is a disaster, there is no problem of categorisation. The real problem arises with relationships that lie in the middle of the continuum and which are legitimised to some (unspecified) degree, but not completely. Unfortunately, taking into consideration the world of greys and half convictions which we inhabit, as opposed to the black and white world of simple theory, such relationships are frequent. Indeed, empirical investigation may prove that *partly legitimised* relationships rather than *wholly legitimised* relations are the statistical norm, even if the latter might well be taken as the prescriptive norm.

CONCLUSION

In spite of these peripheral criticisms of the world society approach, and other minor *caveats* scattered through this essay, it is undoubtedly the case that the approach originally developed by John Burton is one that offers a completely fresh starting point for considering the nature of global society. In the sense of a term deliberately avoided thus far, the approach provides an alternative 'paradigm' for the analysis of international politics to that offered by conventional state-centric approaches.

We have already emphasised that adopting a world society approach implies not merely a down-grading of governments as the central focus of study, but is a major conceptual shift. An analyst need no longer take it as axiomatic that the starting point for explaining any global phenomena must be 'the state'. Such a realisation may appear simple, but its importance in developing a completely new approach to complex and multi-level phenomena that do not fit neatly into any state-centric model cannot be over-emphasised, particularly in the increasingly interdependent world in which we are all, decision makers, scholars and general public, becoming involved.

A second major advantage offered by the world society approach is that it leads explicitly to a set of prescriptions for efficient behaviour in that world, revealed by using the cobweb metaphor and transnational systems analysis. It suggests that peace and the avoidance of conflict might best be approached through the neglected, if difficult, process of strengthening legitimised relationships, and attempting to minimise or avoid the creation of fresh non-legitimised relationships. The latter will ultimately lead to conflict which, in the long run, will be more costly than any short-term benefits that might be derived. Thus, the whole emphasis in world society prescriptive analysis is less on ability to coerce others into maintaining undesired, unpopular and non-legitimised relationships and more on the ability to steer a conflict-avoiding course through improved decision making processes, efficient information processing, less inaccurate perception of the environment, and the monitoring and management of legitimised, 'functional' (especially transnational) systems, rather than their frustration or termination. The whole prescriptive package is based partly upon the conception of a system interacting with its environment and maintaining itself through internal adaptation and efficient information processing, rather than through brute efforts to make the environment adapt to it. It is also based partly upon the conception of clear, long-term calculation of interest and the avoidance of short-term and self-defeating policies of intransigent 'no change', even though these may suit the interests of those temporarily occupying decision making roles. While such a set of prescriptions may appear to be over-optimistic and even naive, the intellectual and practical barrenness of conventional state-centric, power political approaches is such that any alternative – even one less persuasive than the world society approach – needs to be taken seriously as a guide to action for success or even survival.

A last major advantage of the world society approach is its ability to include otherwise neglected interconnections between systems levels and between different types of relationship in an analysis. This is achieved through its emphasis on 'linking' elements, which form part of a large number of systems and which transmit the influences of changes in one set of relationships to others ostensibly isolated from the first. The downgrading of the state as the central analytical unit first clears the conceptual underbrush sufficiently to permit the analysis of a problem at levels other than that of inter-governmental activity.

All of these linkages need not necessarily be neglected by analysts using a state-centric approach – although, in some of the grosser 'analyses' lately fashionable, this does seem to have occurred, and the situation 'analysed' solely in super-power balance terms. But it is undoubtedly the case that they will be afforded an explanatory role secondary to the activities of governments. A world society approach does, at least, correct this ordering of priorities concerning major causal factors. At best, it can be argued (with some justice) that it provides an entirely new insight into the nature of the underlying structure of any complex situation with which state level decision makers might be struggling (often unsuccessfully) to cope. Neglect of such elements and relationships is likely to lead to policies which are, indeed, self-defeating and counter-productive. This alone is sufficient justification for regarding the approach as useful for understanding the increasingly complex transnational problems of the 1980s.

NOTES

1 'There is a system of states, and there are also transactions between businessmen, traders, research workers, television stations, drug peddlers, students and others. There are systems or linkages such as those created by amateur radio enthusiasts, by peoples with the same ideological or religious outlooks, by scientists exchanging papers and meeting together, by people behaving in their different ways' (Burton, 1972b, p. 36).

2 Mansbach *et al* take up a similar position, arguing that ethnic communities, such as the Greek or Turkish Cypriots, can be 'non-state actors' as well as such organisations as labour unions, industrial corporations or interest groups, for example, the CPSU or the Jewish Agency (Mansbach *et al*, 1976, p. 41).

3 It should again be emphasised that exchanges can arise between very dissimilar entities. To take extreme examples, a relationship undoubtedly exists between Lebanese Christians and the PLO, and one between the Provisional IRA and the Northern Ireland Office, but the entities involved in such relationships are hardly similar in attitudes or sympathies, while that which is exchanged is very different from a flow of trade or tourists. The world society approach would, one assumes, allow the existence of intra- or transnational systems linked by the exchange of threats, bullets and mutual hostility.

4 It is, of course, the case that exchanges involve all three types of flow. Information, for example, involves exchange of a material carrier (a diplomatic cable) or some form of energy (a radio message or some energy transfer down a 'hot line'). Similarly, material exchanges can also convey additional information. An arms deal involves the transfer of material (tanks, planes) but also information about the continued support of the transferer for the transferee.

5 It could equally be that – depending upon the nature of the exchange – the changed attributes of the elements in the system take the form of increased hostility, mutual antagonism and distrust. The world society approach does not preclude the existence of intra- or transnational patterns of harmful interaction or exchange, such as between the Christian community in South Lebanon and the Palestinians, nor ignore its malign effects.

6 If one takes the *nature of the relationship* involved as the criterion for determining the type of transnational system under analysis, then the same criterion can be used for fixing system boundaries (which elements are in, and which are out, of the system). System boundaries are indicated by a marked change in the nature of the relationship linking the elements under scrutiny. Thus, because the nature of the relationship between Egypt and Israel was very different from that between Egypt, Syria and Saudi Arabia in the period 1967–73, the two sets of relationships can be regarded as forming *analytically* separate systems.

7 This raises the question of how one can safely operationalise the legitimacy or non-legitimacy of a relationship. Burton suggests evidence of opposition, electoral support, stability of government or absence of overt coercion as good starting points, but this practical problem does seem intractable.

5 The Decision Maker and Social Order: The End of Ideology or the Pursuit of a Chimera?

Richard Little

Recurring strikes, rising crime rates and escalating urban violence are characteristic features of contemporary society. Few people are unaffected by these manifestations of disorder and decision makers are under constant pressure to intervene and resolve the conflict. The interventions, however, are invariably controversial. Police actions during the riots in inner-city areas in Britain during the summer of 1981, for example, were praised by some for controlling the violence and criticised by others for exacerbating community relations. Equally contentious, at that time, was the decision made by the British government to reject the demands made by members of the IRA who went on hunger strike in Northern Ireland – despite the deaths of ten men.

Public debate about official attempts to maintain social order is inevitable. It is generated by the divergent interests of those involved in the conflict. Strike breaking, for example, may be popular with those who are inconvenienced by the strike, but it will undoubtedly precipitate hostility among the individuals who have withdrawn their labour.

But the debate extends beyond those who are directly affected by the conflict. Social scientists, ostensibly objective and impartial observers, are also divided by their evaluations of how decision makers maintain social order. At one extreme, there are *pluralists* who associate order with the preservation of the democratic ground-rules which underpin the social system. Pluralists believe that, in general, decision makers in the West have been remarkably successful at maintaining a democratic order. At the other extreme, however, there are *radical* social scientists who associate order with the persistence of capitalism. They, too, accept that decision makers have demonstrated a surprising ability to defend the established order which they think operates at the expense of the majority of society. Although these two perspectives are competing, both lead to the common conclusion that decision makers in Western societies have managed to maintain a stable society.

John Burton, however, has made a very different assessment. For him, world society is characterised by 'massive violence, repression and exploitation' (1980, p. 1). In contrast to the pluralists and the radicals, he insists that decision makers have been persistently unsuccessful in maintaining social order. On the contrary, he believes that their policies have been self-defeating or counter-productive. In their attempts to promote harmony, they have generated conflict instead.

Burton acknowledges that in the past, decision makers were unable to promote harmonious societies. This was not because of man's inhumanity, but because of his ignorance. We did not possess the requisite knowledge to eliminate violence from our society. Understanding was tainted by ideology and decision makers pursued policies which reflected their ideological beliefs. As a consequence, efforts to maintain order almost invariably sowed the seeds for future conflict. Burton, however, is hopeful that developments in social science, particularly the work of sociobiologists such as Wilson (1978, 1981) will help to establish a non-ideological model of social order, providing the basis for the emergence of peaceful societies.

In this chapter I want to make two basic points. First, I want to show that Burton has developed an important and distinctive conception of social order which contrasts sharply with the more established models provided by the pluralists and the radicals. On the basis of his approach, Burton is able to assess the way that decision makers manage social conflict and to show why he believes their efforts are counter-productive. Second, I want to argue that Burton is, however, incorrect to assume that such a model can ever be non-ideological. Perspectives on social reality, I shall argue, are inherently ideological. The view of social order advanced by Burton must reflect his value system and it is not only erroneous but also counter-productive to assert that the resulting analysis can transcend ideology: there can be no end to ideology.

THE CONCEPTION OF SOCIAL ORDER: BURTON'S VIEW

When John Burton describes world society, he concentrates his attention on the evidence of social disorder: crime, unemployment, delinquency and violence are observed in all societies. While recognising that social disorder is worldwide, he denies that it is a necessary phenomenon. It is, he believes, within man's capacity to create peaceful and harmonious societies. Disorder is a product of ignorance. Burton also believes, however, that disorder persists because we leave decisions concerning our security, economic development, rights, welfare, even our relationships with each other, in the hands of people in positions of authority (1972b, p. 3). Such people, he believes, have quite mistaken views about the basis upon which order can be established. To create order they endeavour to promote and defend an integrated and coherent set of norms and values in society. The development of divergent norms and values are discouraged and constant attempts are made to reintegrate deviants into society. Deviance in terms of behaviour or belief is seen to pose a long-term threat to stability (1979, p. 52).

Burton contests this assessment and asserts that people adhere to a plethora of competing norms and values which any stable society must foster. A social order characterised by peaceful and cooperative human relations cannot be based on a single set of norms and values. Moreover, where decision makers insist on imposing their image of a homogeneous society, their actions often turn out to be a 'source of many unsolved social and political problems' (Burton, 1979, p. 45). In other words, by trying to squeeze everyone into a common mould, decision makers inevitably precipitate tensions for those people whose needs and interests are not served by the establishment conception of social order. Social stability is only effectively secured when individuals can satisfy their own needs and pursue their own interests; trying to 'reform' the deviants in society who are unwilling or unable to conform, can only promote disorder.

SOCIAL ORDER: THE RADICAL'S VIEW

Radical social scientists certainly accept Burton's view that exploitation and repression are characteristic features of capitalist societies. But they disagree profoundly with his overall analysis. The radicals centre their attention on a deep class division within society. They distinguish a narrow stratum where resources are concentrated, and separated from a much larger and more deprived stratum of people. The more extensive stratum is seen to be highly fragmented, with internal conflicts preventing the emergence of solidarity. Individuals are constantly divided against each other, unable to recognise the significant 'structural' division in society. The thin 'upper crust', on the other hand, is an essentially homogeneous group with compatible interests and a common view of the world.

Although decision makers do not advertise the fact, radical social scientists argue that they are fully aware that society is divided. They accept that their task is either to paper over the cracks and maintain the image of an integrated society, or, alternatively, where necessary, to use coercion to suppress the demands of dissidents. Such drastic methods, however, are rare because decision makers have become adept at manipulating the image of an integrated society and diffusing conflict. Order is maintained despite the deep and unbridgeable gulf in society. Indeed, there is often simply no awareness of the conflict of interest which exists between classes in Western society. As Marcuse puts it: 'In advanced capitalist countries, the radicalisation of the working classes is counteracted by a socially engineered arrest of consciousness, and by the development and satisfaction of needs which perpetuate the servitude of the exploited' (1969, p. 16).

In part, social engineering involves creating and propagating a particular image of society. The image depicts a society which tolerates a rich diversity of norms and values. But this image is an illusion, masking the fact that individuals, in practice, have no alternative but to conform. A group of women, for example, who marched from Wales to Aldermaston in the autumn of 1981, objecting to the values which underpin British defence policy, complained, in Marcusian style, of 'repressive tolerance' when they found on their arrival that they were provided with tea and toilet facilities. There is, argue the radicals, a neat division to be drawn between freedom of speech and freedom of action and by permitting the former, the authorities are often able to diffuse demands for the latter. As a consequence, individuals are effectively impotent.

From this radical perspective, Burton is only considering the surface features of reality. While he correctly observes that society operates on the basis of a set of 'consensual' norms and values, established by those in authority, he fails to see that officials recognise the objective conflicts which divide society. By manipulating societal images, they ensure that individuals remain unaware of the conflicts of interest between classes. The problem-solving techniques advocated by Burton are seen to facilitate the mechanisms for social engineering already employed with great success by officials.

SOCIAL ORDER: THE PLURALIST'S VIEW

Pluralists provide a third assessment of how decision makers view social order and stability. They draw a distinction between liberal and non-liberal societies: open and closed social systems. In liberal societies, argues the pluralist, decision makers see society as a complex web of competing groups: 'an intersecting series of social organisms, adhering, interpenetrating, overlapping – a single universe of groups which combine, break, federate, and form coalitions and constellations of power in a flux of restless alterations' (Latham, 1965, p. 35). These groups have their own values and beliefs and public policy emerges as the result of an incessant competition. As Dahl puts it, 'the making of governmental decisions is not a majestic march of great majorities united upon certain matters of basic policy. It is the steady appeasement of relatively small groups' (1956, p. 146). Policy makers believe, moreover, that it is this 'balance of power among groups that protect us from despotism' (Bowie and Simon, 1977, p. 134). It is, therefore, undesirable for differences among people to be suppressed. On the contrary, people must feel free to express their individual differences. One of the most intolerable features of totalitarian societies is seen to be the persistent attempts to create a consensus over values and norms, while the greatest virtue and strength of open societies is the toleration of continuously clashing values and beliefs. Decision makers, therefore, are seen to acknowledge that coherence is not a necessary attribute of a stable society and, indeed, to believe that attempts to create coherence could well precipitate conflict.

The pluralist considers Burton to be wrong in asserting that decision makers adhere to a homogeneous view of society. In fact, within the boundaries of the democratic system, any amount of diversity and lack of coherence can be tolerated. But toleration must have limits, otherwise incoherence can slide uncontrollably into chaos. Burton is seen to mistake concern about the limits or boundaries of the system for a desire to maintain homogeneity. According to the pluralist, authorities believe their major task is to ensure individuals can pursue divergent aims and express their values. Generally this task is seen to be trouble-free because groups are autonomous and their interests do not clash. Nevertheless, decision makers have a responsibility to intervene when friction between divergent norms and values can lead to violence. Local authorities, for example, are seen to prevent marches and demonstrations from taking place if it is believed that they will precipitate civil disturbance.

For pluralists, the limits of official tolerance are defined by the existing legal and political framework. Divergent norms and values can only co-exist if the framework is acknowledged: people must accept what are often called the 'ground rules' of democracy. Officials consider it to be imperative that groups do not achieve their objectives as a result of operating outside this framework. Such activity threatens the stability of the entire system. Officials, therefore, deal in a peremptory fashion with individuals who violate the ground rules. But this is not, as Burton suggests, because stability is considered to depend upon the acceptance of common norms or values, but rather because divergent norms and values can only flourish in a society where individuals operate within the ground rules.

THE INDIVIDUAL IN SOCIETY: BURTON'S VIEW

Whatever view is adopted about the nature of order, a problem remains for any social theorist about the relationship between society and the individual. Because humans live in close proximity, individual actions have social consequences. When an individual engages in an unfettered pursuit of self-interest, other members of society are inevitably affected. Social conflict occurs because of this interdependence among members of the social system. When thinking about how to resolve social conflict, therefore, decision makers must decide on the balance between the interests and desires of the individual and those of other members of society. In this section I shall extend the discussion of social order to examine the competing assessments of how decision makers relate individual and collective interests in society.

Burton insists that those in authority have a clear view about the relationship between the individual and society. They assume that a distinction must be drawn between the interests of individuals and the maintenance of social institutions and structures and that 'the interests of most citizens, over the long term, are best catered for by the preservation of social institutions and structures'. In consequence, 'individual values can be subordinated to social value'. Burton continues: 'officials believe that if they are to serve the long-term interests of individuals, then it is necessary, in the short-term, to place a curb on individual freedom and development' (1979, p. 55).

Restrictions of this sort are made easier because citizens are generally willing to see their freedom curtailed by the authorities. How then do policy makers interpret the actions of individuals who rebel and attack social structures and institutional values? Burton argues that such deviance is attributed by decision makers to a lack of socialisation; and the long-term interests of the deviants are seen to be best served by encouraging them to conform.

This assessment of the relationship between social and individual needs is challenged by Burton. The recent work of sociobiologists is said to demonstrate that a division between social and biological needs is artificial. On the contrary, many basic needs and drives of the individual have been designed, through evolution, to preserve the social group. Social behaviour is, in other words, genetically determined. Wilson (1978) argues, however, that this genetic conditioning has been supplemented by cultural conditioning – a process described as autocatalysis. As a consequence, many features of modern society which may reflect a biological origin (Wilson cites the example of war) have developed far beyond the dictates of sociobiological needs. Sociobiological needs can, in other words, be distorted by what he calls the hypertrophic influence of culture.

Burton builds upon this idea to suggest that institutional needs have a life of their own, and can thwart those genetically established needs which evolved to promote successful societies. Deviance, therefore, should not be explained by inadequate socialisation but by the failure of institutions to correspond to sociobiological needs. It follows that attempts to use the processes of socialisation to re-integrate deviants into society can be counter-productive. Burton argues that it is 'not possible to enforce social values that are inconsistent with individual values' and while coercion may produce 'immediate compliance', it is, in the long term 'a source of deviance and revolt' (1979, p. 56).

THE INDIVIDUAL IN SOCIETY: THE RADICAL'S VIEW

From the radical perspective, it is clear that decision makers seek to maintain social values and institutions. But their concern for established structures does not spring from any abiding interest in the general well-being of society. It reflects an awareness that existing institutions and prevailing social values provide the best available defence for the incumbent elite. Deviants, whether intentionally or not, pose a revolutionary threat because they can undermine the interests of those who possess power and authority. In the study of a wild cat strike, for example, Gouldner, a radical sociologist, noted that management 'tended to conceive of the strike as a *struggle for control* of the plant. . . . Behind each specific complaint . . . there is a hint of a fundamental challenge to management's status' (1955, p. 54).

How does the radical portray the way that decision makers deal with such 'threats'? The task is not considered to be easy because policy makers are perceived to be conscious of the objective rifts in society and the need to preserve the image of an integrated and cohesive community. Deviance jeopardises this image, and consequently requires careful handling. In extreme situations, a resort to force is possible. But decision makers are reluctant to adopt this tactic because it may have counter-productive consequences. In the case of the above mentioned wild cat strike, management distinguished between the power calculations of union leaders and the emotional response of the workers. They endeavoured, in the first instance, to deal with the workers, so as to avoid the power struggle with the leaders that the strike could so easily precipitate.

But radicals claim that this is not the only tactic used by decision makers to handle deviance. Their actions are frequently cloaked in the rhetoric of liberal ideology, at the heart of which is the sanctity of individual rights. Policy makers stress individual rights because, 'through emphasis on *the individual*, the possibilities for collective action are pulverised or reduced' (Mathiesen, 1980, p. 143). If one wishes to preserve the status quo, it makes sense to 'atomise' the members of the social system. Rather than stopping someone from organising a strike, it is preferable to ensure that the 'blackleg' who can break the strike is given full support. So, when the European Court of Human Rights ruled against British Railways in 1981 for dismissing three people who had failed to join a union, the court was, for the radicals, effectively undermining the power of organised labour.

From the radical's perspective, therefore, Burton has missed a crucial stage in the process pursued by policy makers to deal with deviance. The first step is to fragment society. Only if this tactic fails will policy makers justify their actions on the grounds of preserving social institutions. Radicals do, however, agree with Burton that human needs are not fulfilled in modern society. Marcuse, for example, has argued that 'the radical change which is to transform the existing society into a free society must reach into a dimension of the human existence hardly considered in Marxian thought – the "biological" dimension in which the vital, imperative needs and satisfactions assert themselves' (1969, pp. 16–17). However, whereas Burton argues that constraints on human needs will precipitate deviance, radicals emphasise the 'false consciousness' which blocks awareness of these needs. Society can, in effect, dehumanise the individual. Radicals are quite sure that policy makers rely heavily on this process.

For example, as unemployment reached three million in Britain in 1982, the Cabinet dismissed warnings of the possibility of widespread violence. According to press reports, ministers discounted the threat of violence not, as Burton's analysis might suggest, because they believed that the unemployed had been adequately socialised and would see that their current plight was designed to serve their long-term interests, but because past evidence indicated that the unemployed would become apathetic and dispirited rather than violent. To counteract this tendency radicals stress that individuals must be made aware of the degree to which their basic needs have been suppressed. Habermas (1971), for example, suggests self-reflection as a means of releasing the individual and creating a sense of autonomy and responsibility. More typically, radicals advocate politicising individuals, to bring them in touch with their real needs. But whatever technique is employed, it is designed in part to overcome the anodyne effects of the tactics employed by those in positions of authority.

THE INDIVIDUAL IN SOCIETY: THE PLURALIST'S VIEW

Pluralists offer a third assessment of how policy makers account for deviance, and endeavour to handle individuals who refuse to accept the rules and values of the social system. They argue that policy makers have a much more complex view of the issue than either Burton or the radicals appreciate.

Policy makers do not always resist demands for change or invariably try to prop up established social institutions. Nor do they believe that society's rules and institutions are immutable or inviolable. They accept that all institutions and norms in a liberal society (apart from the democratic ground rules) are susceptible to change. It is the function of the political system to find the balance between the rights of the individual and the demands of society. On any issue, from the right to abortion to the freedom not to use seat belts, the ultimate decision must reflect the balance of opinion as expressed through the medium of the political process. As the balance of opinion changes, so the norms and institutions in society will be modified. Policy makers accept that rules and institutions are in a constant state of flux. Nothing is fixed and unchanging.

Given this set of beliefs, how, in the pluralist view, do decision makers respond to deviance? First, they accept the distinction drawn by Merton (1961) between 'aberrants' and 'non-conformists'. The aberrant violates social rules without questioning their validity, whereas the non-conformist aims to bring about change in the social system. The policy maker does not condone either form. Deviance must be punished, if only to demonstrate that the behaviour is illegitimate. But it *is* accepted that the non-conformist may be drawing attention to a problem-area which has been overlooked by the political process. It is acknowledged, in other words, that no political system is perfect and deviance may be the only way available to get an issue onto the political agenda. The policy maker believes, therefore, that whatever the justification for deviance, the deviant must be held responsible for his action. Thereafter, it becomes the responsibility of the authorities to investigate the factors which precipitated the deviance.

The official response to the outbreaks of violence during 1981 in some of Britain's major cities can illustrate the pluralist assessment of how policy makers contend with deviance. The violence was condemned, and it was argued that deteriorating urban conditions did not excuse the violence. At the same time, there was an attempt to minimise the importance of the violence. It was attributed to 'hooliganism', and teachers and parents, the putative agents of socialisation, were partly blamed for the disorder. The authorities' initial response had to take this form; they reaffirmed that violence is neither necessary nor legitimate in an open society.

Once this point had been made, however, the government, acknowledging that the political system does not always work effectively, made highly visible attempts to investigate the causes of the violence and made public declarations of intentions to improve conditions in the riot areas. For the pluralist the investigations were more than mere window-dressing. They were designed to justify or legitimise a positive response by the government to the trouble in the inner-city areas, while not giving way to violence as such. The pluralist, therefore, considers that officials are more flexible and pragmatic than Burton supposes, and less Machiavellian than they are painted by the radicals. But whichever view is accepted, deviance does occur in any society. In the next section, I want to examine the competing evaluations of the 'control' mechanisms used by decision makers to prevent deviance from occurring. Burton, the radicals and the pluralists come to very different conclusions about their nature and effectiveness.

MECHANISMS OF SOCIAL CONTROL: BURTON'S VIEW

Decision makers, according to Burton, believe that rules are obeyed and order is maintained because of the coercive powers possessed by the state. He questions this belief. Deterrence, he argues, does not deter; statistics indicate that crime levels are unaffected by the coercive powers of the state. Moreover, empirical observation reveals that 'reasonable and rational citizens defy the law just because they are reasonable and rational in the pursuit of their goals' (1979, p. 88). When rules are obeyed, therefore, this is not, as officials believe, because the threat of coercion exists, but because of internal motivation. Burton supports this claim by pointing to recent studies which show a clear relationship between growing unemployment and rising crime levels. It is not the level of coercion which has changed, but the declining motivation to observe societal norms. Moreover, when coercion is exercised, Burton argues, it does not reinforce the desire among law-abiding members of the population to conform to established norms. All it does is to reinforce the deviant behaviour pattern of the law breakers. Thus, reliance on coercion is both irrelevant to the task of maintaining social order, and counter-productive.

MECHANISMS OF SOCIAL CONTROL: THE RADICAL'S VIEW

As far as radicals are concerned, officials are aware that their task is to keep serious societal conflicts in check. Moreover, they know that the use of coercion can be ineffective, or even counter-productive. Instead, officials rely on subtle mechanisms which make repression 'invisible' (Mathiesen, 1980, p. 292). Two parallel processes are involved. The first is the process of 'defining in' deviants who endeavour to precipitate change. By bringing individuals into the system and giving them the impression that they can reform it, conflicts can often be diffused. In the meantime, proposals for change can be diluted to the point where the new 'reforms' are meaningless and ineffective. Radical legislation can always be neutralised by 'trimming' and 'stripping down' (Mathiesen, 1980, p. 272).

The 'defining in' process, however also makes possible a parallel process of 'defining out'. Non-conformists become identified by the authorities as 'criminals' and this has the effect of making visible repression acceptable. As Lowi (1968) suggests, citizens obey authority 'largely because they do not feel they have any choice' (p. 52). On this basis radicals reject such pluralist views as those of Dahl, whose classic work on democracy (1970) argues that social stability rests upon peaceful adjustment rather than coercion. According to radicals, therefore, officials do not see coercion only as a deterrent. It is an instrument to be used, but only as a last resort against those deviants who refuse to be 'defined in' to the system.

MECHANISMS OF SOCIAL CONTROL: THE PLURALIST'S VIEW

Pluralists deny that decision makers base their actions on the assumption that social order can be maintained on the basis of coercion. On the contrary, they argue that decision makers adhere to the belief said by Hoffman (in Lloyd-Bostock, 1979, pp. 9–24) to prevail generally among social scientists. He argues that:

> The legacy of Sigmund Freud and Emile Durkheim is the agreement among social scientists that most people do not go through life viewing society's moral norms as external, coercively imposed pressures to which they must submit. Though the norms are initially external to the individual and often in conflict with his desires, the norms eventually become part of his internal motive system and guide his behaviour even in the absence of external authority.

The implication is that order is maintained, and rules adhered to, only if both are largely self-policed. Decision makers accept this because they know that the existing coercive powers of the state cannot accommodate a mass defection. If the public begins to ignore the established rules, then order cannot be maintained by coercion. Like bankers who would default if all their creditors were simultaneously to recall their money, officials administer more activity than they can actually police. They assume that they will never be called on to police all the activities simultaneously, just as bankers assume that they will never be asked to repay all their creditors at once. Because they know that their coercive powers do not extend far, officials are conscious of the need to maintain their legitimacy.

Pluralists believe that decision makers have a much more sophisticated view of the bases of social order than either the radicals or Burton appreciate. Rules are obeyed because they are seen to be fair and reasonable, and not because deviance is threatened with punishment. Of course, deviants must be punished, because the rules would no longer appear fair and reasonable if deviants were seen to prosper. But order must rest on a general acceptance of the rules because of the impossibility of policing the system in the event of mass defection. Pluralists insist, therefore, that in open societies, decision makers have to ensure that the rules they introduce are endowed with legitimacy and have a very broad base of support within the general public. Without this support, it quickly becomes impossible for the authorities to maintain order.

THE MANAGEMENT OF CONFLICT: BURTON'S VIEW

Whatever measures are taken by decision makers, however, no society can ever be completely free from conflict. Moreover, if it is accepted that conflict is an 'essential creative element in human relationships' (Burton, 1972b, p. 137) then a stable social system must be able to tolerate conflict and provide institutions for managing it. The real difficulty is that conflict can escalate and take undesirable forms. This section will explore the competing conceptions of how decision makers manage conflict.

According to Burton, officials assume that conflict occurs because of scarcity. So, if conflicts are permitted to run their course, then resources will be allocated on the basis of the level of power possessed by the competing parties. This makes no provision, however, for considerations of justice and equity. Burton believes that decision makers recognise that they have a responsibility to prevent the gross maldistribution of resources in society and he points to a variety of mechanisms, such as third-party arbitration and mediation, designed by decision makers to encourage parties both to change their minds about the way resources are allocated and to identify compromise solutions.

Burton is unconvinced that these mechanisms are satisfactory. He asserts that instead of resolving disputes, arbitration and mediation frequently lay the ground for future conflict, because they invariably deal with the overt issues which almost always involve a compromise over the distribution of finite resources. The conflict, therefore, is defined in zero-sum terms, so that any gain for one party must be made at the expense of another.

In contrast, Burton concludes that 'the resources that may be the main source of conflict and of unsolved problems may not be scarce' (1979, p. 103). Industrial disputes over wages and conditions, for example, are often settled by arbitration and mediation, only to recur at a later date. Burton believes that such conflicts often reflect a deeper source of discontent: the absence of worker participation in the decision making process. Participation will not mean that conflicts no longer recur, but it does mean that they will take a different form and will be amenable to more creative solutions.

THE MANAGEMENT OF CONFLICT: THE RADICAL'S VIEW

Like Burton, radicals argue that overt conflicts often fail to reveal the real sources of discontent in society. Unlike him, however, they see only one major source: the persistent, unresolvable conflict associated with capitalism. Despite growing affluence, people continue to feel that they are engaged in a struggle for existence. According to Marcuse, this is because 'former luxuries become basic needs' thereby creating an ever-expanding demand for goods in a capitalist system. This continuing struggle over scarce resources is inconsistent, Marcuse asserts, with the vaguely felt awareness that life could be fulfilled and contented. The result is 'diffused aggression' directed at 'any suitable target: white or black, native or foreign, Jew or Christian' (1969, p. 50).

But decision makers consider, say the radicals, that 'diffused aggression' is containable, if necessary by coercion. Such conflict will not undermine capitalism and can, therefore, be tolerated. Indeed, by deflecting attention from the real source of conflict, occasional outbursts of violence can even serve as a safety valve. The crucial factor is to ensure that the violence is contained. Radicals, therefore, contest Burton's assessment that officials are struggling ineffectually with conflict and violence in modern society, and argue instead that officials have developed a powerful repertoire of responses to contain the contradictions in society. In the long term these responses must fail; but in the short term, they appear to be remarkably successful.

THE MANAGEMENT OF CONFLICT: THE PLURALIST'S VIEW

For pluralists, the *raison d'être* of a democratic political system is to generate conditions whereby groups can themselves resolve their own conflicts. Officials are there, primarily, to defend the 'ground rules' of the system. Only two kinds of conflict should, therefore, precipitate official involvement. The first concerns conflicts where adjudication on the application of norms is necessary. The second involves cases where individuals operate outside the 'ground rules'.

Many conflicts arise because of disputes about the way rules should be applied. Legal institutions play an increasingly important role in such disputes – a desirable development which is given official recognition and support. This tendency is examined in detail by Chambliss and Seidman, who have examined different means of dispute settlement. They show that as society moves from the simple to the complex, and from the less stratified to the more stratified, dramatic changes occur in the methods used to manage conflicts. Where complexity and stratification are both low, disputes tend to be settled by compromise, often amicably, because the parties anticipate a continuing relationship. 'Businessmen do not bring law suits against customers whose trade they want to keep' (1975, p. 29). But as societies become more stratified and complex, disputants tend to be strangers to one another and lack the time, inclination and incentive to undertake the protracted business of reconciliation. Instead, relationships are necessarily governed by rules, as in a car accident, and disputes are settled in courts on a zero-sum basis.

The second kind of conflict which, according to the pluralists, requires official involvement concerns situations where individuals or groups, such as the IRA, violate the existing ground rules in order to precipitate change. In such cases, argues the pluralist, officials rightly recognise that there is no room for negotiation. The British government, therefore, was quite correct in 1981 to resist the demands of the IRA hunger strikers when they wished to be granted political status. By deviating from the ground rules, the IRA prisoners had acquired a criminal status and if the government had wavered it would have brought its own legitimacy and authority into question. Any negotiated settlement would have constituted, for the pluralist, counter-productive appeasement. There might have been short-term gains but at the expense, in the long-term, of all the benefits derived from a democratic system.

CONCLUSION: PROBLEMS WITH POSITIVISM

How can we account for these very different assessments of the role played by decision makers in the maintenance of social order? This question touches on one of the most fundamental debates in the social sciences. On the one hand, there is what Bernstein (1976) has called the 'mainstream' response. According to the mainstream view, social scientists must distinguish empirical and normative questions. On matters of fact, the mainstream assert, consensus can be achieved, whereas on matters of value, there will always be debate. So, while social scientists should be able to agree on how decision makers *do* maintain order, they will never agree on how decision makers *ought* to maintain order. Ideological considerations come to the fore as soon as a question takes a normative form. If competing assessments remain unresolved, this can only represent a failure to separate normative and empirical issues because, once separated, empirical questions can be definitely answered, provided the necessary evidence is available.

By making the fact-value distinction, mainstream social scientists are endeavouring to call upon the positivist methodology apparently employed with such success by natural scientists. But there are two problems. First, natural science has had success only because it describes the natural world in terms of abstract, theoretical concepts. Once social scientists try to follow this example, they find that the terms they use are infused with values. For example, when natural scientists cite the second law of thermodynamics and assert that the level of order in the universe is steadily diminishing, there is general agreement about what is meant by order and the conception excludes value considerations. However, when a social scientist states that there is mounting disorder in the social system, the analysis does not build upon a consensus. Agreement cannot be achieved because the concept of order is not only abstract but also value-laden. As Tucker (1977, p. 95) and many others have observed, what constitutes order for one person represents disorder for another. All abstract concepts in the social sciences have such value connotations (Little, 1981).

John Burton has endeavoured to overcome this difficulty by transcending the fact-value distinction. He suggests that once human needs are adequately understood, social scientists will be able to discuss values objectively and thus, like their natural science counterparts, transcend ideology. Order, for example, can be defined in terms of the fulfilment of human needs. In this event, only an inadequate understanding of these needs prevents the emergence of a consensus about the foundations for building harmonious or ordered societies.

This idea of values, however, reflects a positivist conception of knowledge. It presupposes that there are undisputed facts which can be used to provide the building blocks for an unchallengeable view of the world. Many philosophers of science contest this conception of knowledge and in doing so, pose a second problem for the mainstream approach in the social sciences. It has been argued, for example, that all theories are *underdetermined* by the facts. As Mary Hesse has put it:

Theories are logically constrained by facts, but are underdetermined by them: that is, while to be acceptable, theories should be more or less plausibly coherent with facts, they can be neither conclusively refuted nor uniquely derived from statements of fact alone, and hence no theory in a given domain is uniquely acceptable (1980, p. 187).

In other words, it is not possible to have recourse simply to facts as a means of resolving disputes about theory.

THE PERSISTENCE OF IDEOLOGY

Extending this argument to the social sciences, it follows that disputes about values can never be resolved by resorting to 'undisputed' facts. The hopes of early positivists in the social sciences who conceived that it would be possible, using empirical methods, to establish an undisputed body of social knowledge, are fast fading. Many now accept that social science can only proceed on the basis of competing models and that although an empirical method may refine these models, it cannot adjudicate between them. Rein's analysis of this problem (1976, p. 256) concludes that:

Reality can be constructed in different ways, that these constructions may be incompatible and that there is no final way to determine which is truer and no procedure for choosing among these constructions of reality because they are ideologies – that is, frameworks of interpretations where knowledge, values, and ways of organizing the world are inextricably interwoven.

On the basis of the same argument, Ward (1979, p. viii) argues, for example, that there are at least three 'world views' of the economy. The parts of each world view are 'mutually compatible and mutually reinforcing' and as a whole, each passes the test of being 'stateable in ways that contradict no known facts'. Although this view is anathema to the mainstream in social science, it represents an important component in the debate about the nature of social science.

If the anti-positivist view is accepted, it follows that the judgement about which theory to accept cannot simply be dictated by empirical considerations: the choice will largely be affected by our value systems. As a consequence, Hesse argues that before research is ever carried out, it is necessary to establish a 'prior commitment to values and goals'. A social theory should then be built on this foundation. Advocates of a social theory must, of course, seek for and respect the facts, but they must go on and 'appeal explicitly to value judgements and may properly use persuasive rhetoric' (1980, p. 203).

Radicals and pluralists can both point to a large body of literature which identifies and defends their ideology and the values which underpin their models. By dubbing this literature 'ideological' and 'non-scientific', Burton is refusing to fight a battle which must be fought if his ideas are to be influential. If it is accepted that there are a variety of world views which are 'workable' and 'defensible', Burton does himself a disservice by arguing that these world views are inconsistent with the 'laws of nature'. He has developed a complex body of theory which provides the basis for a new 'world view'. To be successful, however, he must argue the merits of the kind of world he wishes to see established. And to do this, he must take seriously the competing conceptions of how the world is and can be organised.

There is a choice about the kind of world we want to live in. As a consequence, the social scientist can never be a mere spectator. The possibility of reshaping the world which is being analysed must affect the nature of the analysis. Analogies with the natural sciences, therefore, are inappropriate because any analysis of the social world will be infused with the values of the analyst. In a world of competing values, the merits of any particular model, therefore, are not self-evident. No model is free from ideology. Since John Burton wishes to change the world, he has no alternative but to make the argument for change in ideological terms. It is counter-productive to dress one's values in natural science garb. A non-ideological model of social order is a chimera which it is a mistake to claim or pursue.

6 The Logic of Conflict: Its Origin, Development and Resolution

Anthony de Reuck

It is notorious that conflicts appear to lie along a spectrum according to how difficult they are to resolve, extending from those that might in imagination be composed with a modicum of good will, to those for which it seems impossible to conceive a reasonable solution. Any account of conflict resolution might be expected to explore the factors that give rise to these characteristics and to discuss the possibility that there exists a class of irresolvable disputes that can end only in victory or stalemate.

It is of course an established tactic for adversaries to announce that a particular issue is non-negotiable. This stiffens resolve in their allies and disheartens their enemies. People in conflict often sincerely believe that theirs is an ineluctable dispute that can only be concluded by death or victory. But to infer from this that some conflicts must be pursued to the bitter end is to be deceived by the ambiguity of the imperative 'must'. Here there is neither logical nor sociological necessity: the imperative is an act of choice, a decision on the part of the actors concerned. The response must instead be to question the rationality, but not the expediency, of this choice wherever it is made.

A totally irresolvable conflict would presumably imply a literally inevitable future in which adaptation was absolutely impossible. Some changes certainly seem inexorable and adaptation sometimes seems inconceivable, but that is a different thing altogether from denying in principle the possibility of alternative outcomes or of learning to solve the problems of legitimate accommodation.

This essay is an attempt at some clarification of the nature of conflict and of the possibility of resolving it, at the mundane levels of etiology, diagnosis, prescription and prognosis.

FORMULATING THE PROBLEM

A conflict situation is usually said to arise between parties (however defined and organised) who perceive that they possess mutually incompatible objectives. The more valuable the objectives the more intense the conflict. The more numerous the objectives, the greater its scope. The more parties there are in conflict, the larger its domain. These are the main dimensions of conflict.

The relations between the conflicting parties and their behaviour toward one another is a function of these dimensions and of the nature of the issues. Conflict behaviour accordingly takes many forms – bargaining, litigating, striking, fighting, for example – which are all attempts to decide the outcome in favour of one party or another. One may speak of various levels of conflict behaviour.

If the incompatibility at issue were misperceived – if it were illusory or readily circumvented – then the conflict would still exist but might be regarded as *unrealistic*. The goal of at least one of the parties might conceivably be to engage in conflict for its own sake; some communal violence might fall into this category, including the Nazi Jewish Holocaust. *Realistic* conflict is the pursuit of genuinely incompatible and extrinsic objectives (Coser, 1954).

The incompatibility may arise because the parties are like players competing for the same prize (such as government office or territory or raw materials) or disagreeing about the rules of the game (the Rhodesian constitution was an example). The former are conflicts of *interest* and the latter conflicts of *value*, though the distinction is rarely clear-cut.

In a simple view, realistic conflict can only be concluded when one side gains its objectives at the expense of the other. If the parties are evenly matched or become exhausted by the dispute so that neither side can win outright, they may agree to compromise – each gets a fraction of the loaf he wanted, which is proverbially better than having no bread. So universally is this thought to be the inescapable logic of conflict, that enemies develop a characteristic mentality whereby a gain or loss to one is experienced as a loss or gain by the other. Indeed it is this feature of conflict which distinguishes it from competition or games. Competitors in a market or in a sport cooperate to engage in ritual conflict. At the level of win or lose their interests are opposed; at a higher level they share the superordinate goal of competing for its own sake. But enemies are debarred from cooperating by their zero-sum conception of their relationship.

Rational conflict resolution implies reaching an accommodation – a new situation of compatibility – at minimum cost to the parties individually. Optimisation of the cost-benefit balance thus becomes a central feature of the process. The total gains or losses must be measured not only in terms of objectives attained, modified or abandoned (and evaluated against other opportunities postponed or foregone while those objectives were pursued), but also in terms of the costs incurred in bringing about the new compatibility. Let these latter be called the *costs of decision*. The distribution of the costs of decision between the parties and the question of compensation for costs already incurred become additional issues in the conflict.

So defined, the costs of decision comprise the costs of conflict behaviour whether the conflict is conducted reasonably and pacifically or by coercion and violence. They include the costs of bargaining or of going to law, or of going to war. These processes are listed in ascending order of cost (of decision) and descending order of rationality (of outcome). Rationality and costs are inversely related.

A distinction can be made between the *settlement* and *resolution* of a conflict (Burton, 1969, pp. 177–227). 'Settlement' is imposed by a third party such as an international court or a greater power. It could be a compromise which the parties feel they have to accept because neither party has the resources to oppose it. 'Resolution' on the other hand implies a solution acceptable to all concerned, which does not sacrifice any basic interest, and which no party will later wish to repudiate. At best, settlement reduces the level or intensity of conflict behaviour but it leaves the conflict situation substantially untouched. Resolution removes the very ground of dispute by eliminating or transforming the conflict situation.

In many instances a settlement is preferable to violent conflict, especially when the costs of decision have risen disproportionately above the values at issue. Time may make other issues more prominent, or may throw up alternative means to achieve the original ends. In this way the settlement may be transformed into a genuine resolution. Nevertheless, in the short term a settlement entails the costs of failure to decide. These may be the costs of injustice or of the continual drain of chronic low-level conflict (for example, the cost to all Ulstermen of communal violence; the costs to the entire population, black and white, of apartheid in South Africa). Conflicts are thus terminated in three ways: they can be determined, or settled, or resolved. That is to say, conflicts can be pursued to a conclusion and so won or lost; the outcome can be decided by external forces; or they can be transformed into problems for rational solution and resolved either at minimum cost or even possibly with gain to all parties.

The task of conflict analysis, then, is to relate the origin and development of a conflict to its termination, and to estimate costs.

THE FUNCTIONS OF CONFLICT

Conflict is always about change. Conflict is about change in social structure and institutions, in the distribution of resources, in human relations at many levels. It may be about who is to win or who is to play in the game, about the prizes they play for, or about the rules of the game. It may be about 'the name of the game' itself. Those who promote one form of change enter into conflict with those whose interest is to promote another, and both are resisted by those opposed to all change. At the same time each contestant seeks to pass the burden of adaptation to change onto the others. There are, therefore, always likely to be two sets of issues in any conflict: what changes shall occur and at whose expense. Thus conflict is about learning and adapting to change.

We see in conflict, therefore, both a cause and a consequence of change. It has innumerable and diverse causes and effects in society, and is not a unitary phenomenon. It is a symptom which accompanies the birth of much that is new in society and frequently attends the demise of whatever is outworn. It also sometimes signals the presence of ills in the body politic. It has therefore both destructive and constructive aspects. It can be both a warning and a promise: it heralds progress and growth as well as death and decay.

We are thus led to view conflict as a decision process which selects between alternative futures. There can be no question, therefore, of the suppression of conflict – alternative futures are forever before us – but violence can often be replaced by other decision processes which are either less costly and more rational, or more persuasive and less power-laden.

The *outcome* of the process of decision is for those most affected to choose. It is with the *process* itself that scholars are concerned. No one should prescribe the future for others; that they must be free to select for themselves. The scholar's concern is to explore the conditions for freedom and rationality in the decision process and for legitimacy for all in the outcome.

One may conclude from the preceding analysis that any general theory of conflict is likely to be a by-product of a theory of social and cultural change, and also of a theory of learning an adaptation to change, including the *adoption of new values*. Conflict resolution is about rational decisions; it is about converting conflicts into problems involving a search for alternative futures and accommodations.

THE ORIGINS OF CONFLICT

Conflict is about the legitimate distribution of future costs and benefits among men. It often arises because somebody benefits at someone else's expense. Or because this is suspected or anticipated and resented. The notion of 'legitimacy' is vitally significant. It depends upon existing relationships, upon people's 'identities' and with whom they identify – in a word, upon their definition of the situation. 'Legitimacy' is a value placed upon a relationship, and like all values it is subjective. Values may seem to be objective factors but they are not. They are assessments, and they may change.

It is convenient therefore to define a *conflict situation* in general as one in which the activity of one party actually or foreseeably comes to impose unacceptable costs, material or psychic, upon another.[1] These unacceptable costs may be called the *costs at issue* for the aggrieved. The objective pursued by the original actor may be called the *value at issue* for him.[2] The word 'party' implies an individual, a group or an institution such as a government involved in a dispute. The conflict might be described as *covert* until the aggrieved party becomes aware of the situation, when it becomes *overt*. Emerging awareness of costs and their origins can be important factors, of course, in the escalation of conflict.

It is also relevant for conflict resolution to note that the question of 'awareness' introduces a strongly inferential element, calling in complex instances for causal analysis of the situation and in all probability for an interpretation of other peoples' motives. It introduces the element of perception of responsibility, both in the sense of causation and in the sense of motivation. Those who are unemployed may not be sure who or what is responsible, but they are conscious of the economic and social costs to them. A variety of theories will be urged upon them: the employers, the unions, the money supply, a world shortage of energy, government overspending or the capitalist system are all alleged culprits. Before a conflict begins, let alone resolved, there is plenty of room for analysis, for disagreement, and error – in identifying the parties or even in defining the issues.

The conflict situation is described as *manifest* or *latent* (Merton, 1968, ch. 3) according to whether the originating actor does or does not recognise and intend the costly consequences of his actions for the aggrieved party. The first party whose conflict behaviour becomes conscious and deliberate is often labelled the aggressor, whether or not he is the aggrieved party, as indeed he most frequently is.

The aggrieved party may protest. The author of the trouble may argue that his activity is legitimate and the costs should be tolerated, or he may make a reciprocal arrangement that compensates the other party for his losses. Reciprocity underlies most valid arguments for legitimacy.

But if the author of someone else's costs fails to legitimise his actions or to compensate his victim, then the situation develops into open conflict. Conflict proper begins when those aggrieved attempt to impose counter-costs on the originator. He in his turn is now likely to retaliate by imposing additional costs, thus embarking upon an escalation spiral which may well get out of hand. The sum of the costs to either side of both administering and receiving blows are the *costs of decision*. Collectively, they are the price that the parties jointly pay in order to reach a final accommodation.

In terms of rationality, the costs of decision to either side should not equal or exceed the values at issue; nor, of course, should they exceed what the parties can afford. But escalation all too often supervenes. War as a violent technique for settling international disputes is notoriously apt to incur costs of decision out of all proportion to the benefits sought. The 'irrationality' of much conflict-accounting is a factor to be considered again later.

As the struggle proceeds, the cost of battle itself becomes assimilated to the original issues: we fight on, so that our honoured dead shall not have died in vain. The only way to recover costs in an expensive dispute is for the parties to invest more in an all-out effort to reap the harvest of victory. In conflict, sunk costs are rarely discounted and, as Frank Edmead (1971, pp. 12–15) has shown, cutting costs presents especial difficulty, which may delay disengagement from a hopeless cause.

It is worth emphasis at this point that justice is never an absolute, it is always socially determined. It is what one is accustomed to consider as one's right. What in any given social context is legitimate in human relations, what constitutes distributive justice, what people value most and would fight to gain or to keep are decided by comparison with others. A sense of relative deprivation, relative that is to other reference groups, underlies any experience of injustice anywhere (Runciman, 1966). To experience injustice, however, it is not necessary that the situation of those aggrieved should deteriorate: it may be that the lot of their reference group has improved. It is *relative movement* of this sort that constitutes social change; and since every social change can lead to a change in values or to perceived injustice, so change leads to conflict. And conflict leads to change, in ever expanding waves of adjustment.

THE DEVELOPMENT OF CONFLICT

The dynamics of conflict (Schattschneider, 1960) depend upon the range of parties that involve themselves in the process. Every new participant adds or subtracts from the balance of forces, from the resources committed to the struggle and to the definition of the issues at stake.

It follows that a most important aim of strategy is concerned with controlling the spread of conflict. As new parties intervene in the dispute – always of course for their own ends, perhaps rationalised as the interests of those already involved – not only will they alter the balance of power but also the definition of the situation and the issues at stake.

In clearly defined conflicts of small scope, the relative strengths of the contestants are likely to be known in advance and the stronger side will prevail without an overt trial of strength because people are apt not to contest issues if they are sure they will lose. The hierarchical social pyramid may well be 'peaceful' in terms of vertical change because the outcomes of asymmetrical conflicts are fore-ordained. On the other hand, the weaker side may have greater potential strength provided it can be mobilised; and the stronger may hesitate to exert power if there is doubt whether the adversary can be isolated. Thus the values of the onlookers or of the system outside become part of the calculus of conflict. The balance is not decided nor the outcome ensured until the last reserves are committed and everyone concerned is involved.

It is now apparent that parties are not predetermined entities. They tend to be coalitions, more or less temporary alliances for a limited purpose, though some members may be corporate bodies with a quasipermanent existence and collective goals. And as a conflict situation evolves, parties tend to take on a dynamic quality as some members may find their objectives attained while others find the costs at issue increased. So parties tend to undergo fission and fusion and reformation: those who determine the outcome at the end are unlikely to represent all those who were in at the beginning.

It is the natural strategy of the weaker side in conflict to seek outside help. The Patriotic Front in Zimbabwe-Rhodesia sought the aid not only of the 'Front Line' African States but of the international community through the United Nations. The side formerly stronger becomes the weaker and will accordingly also look for allies. The white regime turned to South Africa and the multinational corporations. Thus the conflict spreads to new parties, each of whom introduces new issues and may try to redefine the whole situation. The original parties are liable to lose control of the conflict, as the Cypriots discovered when first Greece and then Turkey took a hand in their quarrel.

The maintenance of authority, on the other hand, depends upon effective control of those 'rules of the game' and hence of the right to legitimise new players. The capacity to communicate the taken-for-granted definition of the situation is the principal attribute of high status. This was the attribute denied to Ian Smith after UDI in Rhodesia by the even higher status of the British Government which defined his regime as illegitimate as well as illegal for the rest of the world.

Now, as Schattschneider (1960) pointed out: he who defines the issues, determines the parties; and he who determines the parties, decides the outcome in conflict. This is the prerogative of status. It is perhaps the principal attribute of social power, as Stinchcombe (1968, pp. 158–63) describes it – the capacity to define the situation so as to be able, by virtue of the norms and doctrines by which it is justified, to call legitimately upon other centres of power as reserves in case of need, so as to prevail in conflict with others.

It is evident that the issues decide the parties as much as the parties decide the issues. Unification and division are as much part of the strategy of conflict as its results. The more fully the conflict is developed the more complete is the consolidation of the parties likely to be on either side, and the more complete the polarisation into opposing camps. The development of one conflict is quite likely to inhibit the development of another. A radical shift of alignment is possible only at the cost of a change in the priorities and relationships of all the contestants. Thus conflicts compete for priority, for attention and allegiance.

In any social system there are innumerable potential issues and social alignments but only a few significant conflicts. Reduction in the number of conflicts to manageable proportions is essential to domestic politics: society survives because it establishes priorities among a multitude of possible patterns of cleavage. The very multiplicity of cleavages in modern society tends to temper the severity of particular antagonisms (Ross, 1920, pp. 164 ff). Polarisation of communities – as in Ulster or Belgium or Cyprus or Montreal – along single lines of cleavage over all issues and values can in the end disrupt social structures completely. The definition of priorities is the supreme instrument of power. By the same token, displacement of conflict, the redirection of attention and redefinition of the situation must be prime instruments of strategic behaviour.

Dominance among the conflicts presumably relates to three factors: first, to the intensity and salience of the issues; second, to the status and legitimacy of the parties; third, to the clustering of interests and coincidence of cleavages within a community.

Old issues which freeze obsolete social alignments and fossilise cleavages in society prevent new issues from arising to prominence. The new conflict of economic interests between the United States and the European Community is at present almost totally submerged in the old conflict of political values between them both and the Soviet Union.

In any well integrated system change is contagious and liable to ramify to the utmost limits of interdependence. Only in non-systemic segmented structures can change pass unheeded in neighbouring parts. Neither Medieval Europe nor Imperial China reflected upheavals at the other end of the continent, and the fortunate American Indians knew nothing of the fall of the Roman Empire. But in the modern world any change is far-reaching. The decay of the Ottoman Empire led directly to the Great War in Europe of 1914; the resultant collapse of the Russian, German and Austro-Hungarian Empires created Stalin and Hitler and the Second World War; the consequent dissolution of the British and French Empires led to a generation of terrible strife in the Middle East and South East Asia.

The purely legal distinction between domestic and international change (or conflict) appears increasingly artificial as the systemic interdependence of world society expresses itself; all parts of the system are automatically involved. Systems superior to those in dispute involve themselves as patrons of conflicting clients in the interest of self-preservation. So contagion rises to that level (if any) at which some supersystem stands in a symmetrical relationship with both sides in the conflict (Barkun, 1970).

CONSTANT-SUM OUTCOMES

Conflict is usually thought of and commonly defined in terms of incompatibility of interests, which creates from the outset a presumption that in the end 'someone will have to give way' – that not all parties can be satisfied. The conventional wisdom is that so long as the sources of satisfaction in this world are limited while the desires and ambitions of men are boundless, the outcome of any real conflict of interest must be such that any gain by one side must result in equivalent loss for the other. The accounting framework is in the logic of a constant-sum game. Where interests are not strictly incompatible, it might be argued, the parties can reach a satisfactory accommodation by bargaining without allowing the situation ever to attain the dysfunctional proportions of a really costly conflict. Only when the interests opposed are vital, irreconcilable and held to be legitimate on each side, will the possibility of escalation to violence exist.

This exposition of political logic appears to be homologous with the logic of economics, defined as the study of the rational allocation of scarce resources in the satisfaction of unlimited demands. Within this frame of reference Blau (1964) has spelt out some aspects of the political realism of Morgenthau (1967): for a state to be independent and secure it must have access to strategic materials, to have alternative sources of supply, to have the coercive means of taking resources if they are withheld, or to have an ideology that enables it to do without them. It is to be observed that most states do without them. Nevertheless it is in this framework that we have been accustomed to thinking about the sovereign state in world society.

Within this framework, international lawyers and mediators are asked to determine what division or settlement is 'just', that is to say, in accord with past decisions and practices. If someone must win and someone must lose, the problem reduces to that of deciding who shall win and who shall lose and by how much the victor shall gain. It could be less costly to forecast the outcome without going to war. Oddly enough, this course seems unreasonable perhaps because the outcome of war is so often a lottery. Despite gross disparities in power, the outcome is always uncertain – in Vietnam, for example – and the material costs of destruction are expected to be offset by certain psychic rewards.

VARIABLE-SUM OUTCOMES

But economics can also be defined as the logic of optimising decisions. Even within its own terms, the economic model of international rationality would be defective if it took no account of the principle of comparative advantage. Even for the most powerful state, economically or politically, mutual benefit must still flow from exchange relations with weaker partners who specialise in those goods and services they are best fitted to produce. It is clear that integrative influences in the relations between states normally predominate over the disintegrative and defensive postures of the power model. Certainly 'objective' conditions exist – structures, institutions, conditions of privilege – that give rise to 'objective' clashes of interest. But under modern conditions in the international field realistic discounted cost-benefit analysis – including allowance for the ultimate cost of preserving privilege, for example – is unlikely to favour conflictual over cooperative policies. Perhaps the other principal source of nonrationality in the behaviour of states is the fact that man is mortal and life is short. Costs that can plausibly be postponed until the next generation are all too often discounted completely. The case is even worse when the comparatively short life of governments is considered. Policies whose costs are likely to be experienced by the next administration may be cynically espoused, while those in which the benefits are similarly deferred are liable to total neglect. It seems likely that the most costly mistakes in conflict arise from errors in accountancy over the appropriate rates of political discount.

The nub of the argument is quite different, however. It is that in politics generally and in international politics especially, we are rarely dealing with scarcity at all. In international conflict of any importance we are hardly ever faced with a zero-sum situation. This springs from the fact that the political function is essentially the provision of public, collective or indivisible goods which by definition may be shared by all without loss to any. It is precisely because there exists a class of goods from whose enjoyment none can readily be excluded whether or not they have contributed to their provision that the political process steps in to provide them on a collective basis lest they be not provided at all (Olson, 1965).

It is not surprising, therefore, that the goods supplied by public authorities tend to assume a defensive character. They include, for example, internal and external security, economic regulation, social security, health and welfare services, environmental planning and conservation policies. They amount to insurance premiums needed to counter the risk of negative goods or 'bads'; they contribute less to satisfaction (unless security itself is a satisfaction) than to the negation of dissatisfaction.

The second branch of political goods takes the form of safety regulations against external diseconomies that create public 'bads'. They restrict, for instance, the private appropriation of certain key goods which would otherwise permit divisive pockets of unjust privilege: for example, preferential access to public office, to the courts of law, to the schools or hospitals or to the media of communication.

In international politics we are predominantly concerned with security, with independence and with other values that increase in distributive volume, the more each actor has of them. They are essentially collective goods. Security is not divisible and certainly not in unequal shares. One country's perceived security or independence leads to policies that increase its neighbour's sense of security and independence. Conversely when one country experiences insecurity and adopts defensive postures, its neighbours also feel insecure: the total insecurity is increased. These are not situations that can be analysed within a constant-sum framework.

The only class of goods of political relevance that is inevitably of a zero-sum character is the class of positional goods. That is to say, offices, roles or statuses in the system. There is only one Secretary of the Soviet Communist Party, only one President of the United States, only one Secretary-General of the United Nations, only so many seats on the Security Council. Conflicts to fill these offices and roles are doubtless win-or-lose in outcome but they are not the stuff of international conflagration.

Relations between the Soviet Union and the United States are sometimes interpreted in positional terms. Whereas formerly the Russians sought military parity with the Americans as the condition for stable deterrence, they are now, in some Western interpretations, on the verge of nuclear superiority. Soviet perceptions of NATO arms programmes reverse these interpretations. Jostling for world nuclear supremacy would be competition for a positional good, conducted according to zero-sum rules, if coming out on top were the sole or even the supreme value of the Soviet or the United States governments. But there are no conceivable circumstances in which the issue of nuclear supremacy on its own could be regarded as the sole value for either. The economic status, cultural prestige and political legitimacy, as well as the sheer survival of both regimes in the international system are issues of comparable significance to each.

Values are never singular: they come in hierarchies on a preference schedule, with those below expendable as costs for the attainment of those above. The price paid for values sought is the sacrifice of other values foregone. Values are never static: they wax and wane according to whether they are in scarce or plentiful supply, and they must be weighed against one another. The cost of the Vietnam war in lives, in neglect of the 'Great Society' and in waning US legitimacy, became excessive in the end. The United States government cut its losses and withdrew. Cost accounting in conflict is delicate and only those who pay can know when to stop. But an irresolvable conflict is possible only between adamantine parties with only one absolute value apiece. They would not be human.

THE PROBLEM OF RESOLUTION

The classical 'economic' solution to the problem of allocating external costs involves, first, a meticulous assessment of their origins, of their legitimacy and of their magnitudes. Second, the author of the costs, party A or A plus those who benefit from A's actions, must be induced to bear those costs – if necessary by law. Thus A and his allies compensate B. Or alternative means may be found for A to attain his ends, so that only negligible or acceptable costs fall on B. In certain circumstances, the costs could be shared by the whole community – for example if a great many people would be worse off if A's activity ceased. An extension of this approach might be to create a partnership between A and B to distribute the benefits as well as the costs among all of those most nearly affected.

What then is entailed by the problem of conflict resolution? It clearly does not imply universally opposing or diverting all activities which produce competitive or external costs for others – nearly all political change is likely to do so for someone. It does mean collective readjustment to such effects, accommodation and reallocation of the costs and benefits of change among the international community, in which account is taken of the disbenefits arising from failure to adjust. It also means realistic acknowledgement that when the costs of the struggle mount up beyond any potential gains, the time may have come to cut losses and close the account.

It must be evident that all such evaluations are intensely subjective. As we have seen, the costs and values at issue invariably come to incorporate the costs of decision. None of these is a constant: they all change with time. Evaluations are continually revised, generally upward, as investment in the conflict proceeds. This occurs because commitment to the conflict often tends to increase over time. As investment mounts – in resources that may range from time devoted to the dispute, to men trained and committed, to war material expended or to lives lost in battle – the only way to recover these costs is to win. Commitment to winning, therefore, tends to grow. And as investment increases, so perceptions of the value of the outcome increase – and with it the willingness to expend further resources. So a spiral process of incremental argumentation drives up commitment, investment and assessment of the values at issue. This is quite contrary to economic rationality which insists that past costs are sunk costs, that for present calculation only future losses or gains are germane.

The progressive rise in commitment and the strengthened resolution not to yield on the issues, appear to be aspects of the need to reduce cognitive dissonance. Increased investment must be matched by increased expectations of the gains to be won. Whether the game is worth the candle is not a *fact*; it is an issue for discussion and for intensive reassessment.

There is evidently no optimum solution that minimises the sum to all parties of the costs of decision and the costs at issue. Those who bear costs and those who reap the gains are all too often different sets of people, even within one party. In so far as they are subjective values and experienced by opposing parties, they are indeed incommensurable in principle. But not in practice. The everyday world of peaceful trading, competing, cooperating mankind rests upon a foundation of communicated and compared values: in a word, upon mutual understanding.

The obstacle to conflict resolution lies not so much in the limitations of a utilitarian calculus of rights and wrongs, or of gains and losses, but rather in the extreme difficulty of communication between enemies. Because to enemies, a loss to one is a gain to the other. The office of conciliator must be to enable the opponents to meet, not only to analyse their conflict but also to communicate with just sufficient comprehension for a mutually beneficial collaboration to ensue.

To resolve a dispute satisfactorily, it has to be converted at least implicitly in the minds of the parties to it, from a conflict that divides them into a problem they share and over which they must (to however limited a degree) cooperate if it is to be solved. This is a process of 'discovery' that cannot be taught, even by a conciliator: it can only be reached by the parties themselves.

The conciliatory role, therefore, is not to offer solutions but to facilitate learning and to stimulate the passages from conflictual to collaborative modes of interaction. This is the subject of Margot Light's chapter in this volume.

Here is the essence of the problem-solving procedure which we at one time called 'controlled communication' (Burton, 1969, 1972a). Accredited representatives of the parties in dispute are brought together to analyse their conflict with the aid of a small panel of disinterested consultants, professionally qualified in the social sciences, in conditions of complete confidentiality. The consultants seek to foster reconciliation but otherwise they are concerned only with rigorous analysis and never with advocating particular outcomes. Through cooperating with the panel of consultants over analysis, the parties learn to communicate with one another and eventually to collaborate together in joint problem solving (de Reuck, 1974).

The analysis, conducted by the parties themselves, in due course provides a common language and a common frame of reference. Within this shared code and frame of reference the parties may find it possible to redefine their relationship as a joint predicament jointly to be resolved (de Reuck, 1983).

CONCLUSION

A sketch has been offered of some of the points to be pursued in conflict analysis. In the process it may have emerged why all concerned may benefit from an appreciation that their conflict is not 'given', it is not an entity, ineluctable and refractory out there in the world. It is a fleeting process, a shifting pattern of issues and parties, of evaluations and perceptions. It is a predicament best solved by cooperation.

Resolution of conflict is through acceptable social change including acceptable changes in perception and evaluation of the situation. It requires an analysis as delicate as surgery or psychoanalysis. But the analysis cannot claim 'objectivity': it has to be that of the protagonists themselves if the change that they choose is to be truly acceptable to them – on all sides. This is the aim of the problem-solving technique.

NOTES

1 Rarely but conceivably, the motive for that activity may have been to impose costs on another for the sake of doing so. That is a case of considerable interest but we shall not concern ourselves here with such psychopathology.
2 By contrast, a cooperative situation is one in which the activity of one party confers benefits upon another – fortuitously if that is unintentional.

7 Psychological Processes in World Society

A.N. Oppenheim

The field of international relations as a whole, and that of international conflict in particular, bristles with psychological problems. How do the personalities of important leaders influence their foreign policy behaviour? Do their attitudes cause some of them to become more conflict-prone, or more obstinate in conflict resolution? Why do arms races escalate? How does deterrence work? How can we explain, and prevent, crisis behaviour? Do diplomats have certain attitudes in common? What are the conditions that produce terrorism? Do the mass media influence foreign affairs? How does the rhetoric of conflict affect perceptions and misperceptions? Are wars an expression of aggression? Do people draw the wrong lessons from history?

It is not difficult to see why there are few ready answers to such questions. In the past, few psychologists have concerned themselves with group conflicts or with international relations – such problems are regarded by most psychologists as far too broad and amorphous, too much in the macro-domain. Having suffered, in the past, from over-ambitious theories which tried to encompass all forms of behaviour, the modern psychologist tends to keep his nose firmly down. He may concern himself with *intra*-individual conflicts, or possibly with marital conflicts or conflicts between parents and children, but he will regard the problems of war or revolution as well beyond his horizon. Moreover, psychologists generally think of themselves as scientific and quantitative in their approach, using laboratory methods under controlled conditions or conducting large-scale social surveys; in their terms, the issues raised by international relations are vague, intangible and unresearchable.

The excitement of the early 1960s and the emergence of peace research as a field of study in its own right brought about some changes in this situation (Dedring, 1976). On the one hand, scholars in international relations became more interested in behavioural approaches and quantitative methods, and so began to ask 'better' questions; on the other hand, a few social psychologists, impressed by the dangers of nuclear warfare and stimulated by the hope of making a contribution to the solution of problems in the 'real world', were tempted to lend their skills and theoretical outlook to this important new field. At that time, some useful advances were made in the area of game theory; considerable simulation programmes were undertaken jointly with strategists or IR scholars; crisis gaming was developed, and various content-analytic methods led to an improved understanding of historical events. At that time, too, we saw the first efforts to develop the problem solving workshop as a method of conflict resolution (Pruitt, 1969; Hermann, 1972).

Sad to say, these early enterprises have but rarely led to firmly based and continuous interdisciplinary team work. Few psychologists have the necessary dual background, in IR as well as in their own field; they tend to remain wedded to whatever can be accomplished by means of their own particular approach, be this clinical case studies, group dynamics, public attitude surveys, or prisoners' dilemma games, on a take-it-or-leave-it basis while remaining deaf to such IR concerns as the nature of power, the various perceptions of the national interest, bureaucratic politics within the government machine, or the problems of deterring aggression. If this is where angels fear to tread, then in some cases others have rushed in, with mistaken applications of psychological theories, quantification seemingly for quantification's sake, or wild and errant speculation. This has no doubt led some psychologists to feel, rather self-righteously, that they should stick to doing what they know best, and that the conceptual distance between psychology and international relations is at present too great to be bridged.

THE MICRO-MACRO LEVEL PROBLEMS

But is this gap truly so wide? At first sight, the levels-of-analysis problem, from micro to macro, seems to emphasise the differences between the two disciplines. How can psychological researchers, used to working with school children, patients, small problem solving groups, or laboratory subjects, be expected to extend their concerns to world affairs and conflicts between nations without undergoing a paradigmatic shift or, at the very least, developing new methods and theoretical constructs? Part of the answer to our reluctant psychologist might be that, even at the highest levels of government, 'people are still people'. It may not be possible to study a whole nation, or an entire state bureaucracy, but at the nodal points in the decision making network there will be individuals or small groups or committees whose behaviour *can* be studied with our relatively limited means. Such people are not very different from 'ordinary' people, even though they have to deal with some 'extra-ordinary' problems: they have attitudes and prejudices, stereotypes, fears and memories, they must process information and assess risks, they form subjective images of their allies and opponents, and often they lack the knowledge, training and experience for the task they have to perform. Moreover, each of these decision makers is an actor in a complex, multi-faceted organisational scheme, and so our studies can extend beyond individual differences to the *organisational* determinants of foreign policy behaviour.

For example, why are nations sometimes caught by surprise, and how do they react to this (Whaley, 1973)? What happens to a crisis team under conditions of overload, and how can this be averted? How much power should a negotiator have? What are the most important differences between bilateral and multi-lateral diplomacy? How can military peace-keeping operations lead to conflict resolution and peace? In short, psychologists should not be expected to want to 'psychologise' everything, or to want to 'psychoanalyse' politicians and high officials, and neither need they feel too intimidated by the complexities of political, economic, military and ideological components of international life. They can make fruitful contributions by studying the behaviour of individuals and small groups in key positions (their dynamics round the table), and by showing, through organisational analysis, how decisions are affected by bureaucratic and structural determinants of the administrative machine.

One further suggestion may be helpful here: the adoption of the 'subjectivist' position. Thus, it is not necessary to make an exhaustive study of what might constitute 'the national interest' in a given situation; one only needs to know how the national interest is *perceived* by the groups and the individuals under study. Likewise we do not need to assemble all possible risks and options that might enter into a given negotiation, but only those of which the negotiators are aware. These subjectively determined images or percepts of a complex environment are a better guide to the understanding of behaviour than the so-called 'rational' or 'objective' approach.

PSYCHOLOGICAL ASPECTS OF CRISIS BEHAVIOUR

What, we may ask, has been accomplished so far, and what are some of the things that remain to be done?

Perhaps the biggest and most clearly established gains have been in our knowledge and understanding of *crisis behaviour*, its effects and its prevention. Not only psychologists, but several other disciplines have done valuable work in this area, so that we have evidence coming together from a number of strands: experimental, historical, observational, simulative and others.

Perhaps the most helpful theoretical framework for our understanding of crisis behaviour is that of reaction to stress, both by individuals and by organisations. In general psychological terms, we know that response to stress is usually in terms of an inverted U-curve, increasing stress leading – at first – to higher or faster performance but tending, beyond a certain point, to progressive decline and disintegration of performance, and ultimately to panic. Thus, the initial stages of a crisis can be experienced as stimulating, but if the crisis goes on, or becomes more severe, then some of the negative or maladaptive aspects of crisis behaviour will manifest themselves. It should be clear from this that different individuals and different organisations respond to a certain level of pressure in different ways: what is experienced as vigorous stimulation by one, may lead to near-disintegration in another. Even the same respondents may react differently on different days. Thus, the same 'objective' degree of stress may create different degrees of crisis behaviour in different settings.

The crises in which we are particularly interested here are those that may lead to war. Typically we have in mind small groups of top decision makers, each group heading its own state and placed centrally within some kind of command and information-processing structure. A crisis situation will affect both ordinary citizens and the leadership structure, but eventually fewer and fewer people will be able to affect its course, until in extreme cases its main effects are felt by a small, isolated group of top decision makers.

THINKING AND PERCEIVING DURING A CRISIS

What do people actually do, at the beginning of a crisis situation? For a start, they often work each other up into a crisis. They bring into play all the culturally approved attitudes and rhetoric of conflict:

they will threaten, posture and close ranks. In other words, their thinking and behaviour will become *polarised*: they see things in black-and-white terms, each side will project all kinds of negative qualities on their opponents while reserving only positive percepts for their own side, and they can henceforth only see 'one way out' rather than a range of possible alternatives. Communication with the opposite side is likely to break down, and they can no longer put themselves in their opponents' shoes; the latter therefore become dehumanised, treacherous and unpredictable. Subtle, long-range thinking becomes impossible; only practical, short-term issues are considered. The need for unity may become so great that a line of action may be chosen not because it is 'best' but because it is the only one that commands general agreement. For the same reason, people may 'sink their differences' in the face of a common opponent. In the short run, a certain amount of pleasurable elation, excitement and role expansion may take place.

The top decision makers are not, of course, immune from these processes – though one would hope that they can 'keep their cool' rather better in such a situation. On the other hand, decision makers are subject to many pressures and organisational constraints which do not affect the man in the street. Almost the first thing they will discover is that, in a crisis, the amount of communication increases manifold: more reports and telegrams are coming in, while more orders or requests for information have to go out. As a result, there is a considerable risk that the channels of communication will become clogged: not only will the existing communication personnel and machinery find it difficult to cope, but those who have to read, digest, consult and decide may find themselves overwhelmed. Strenuous counter-measures will be taken: more people will be put on certain jobs, bureaucratic red tape will be cut, more incoming messages will go straight to the top, telegrams and telephones will be used instead of letters, and the lights will burn till late at night. A wag once defined a crisis as a situation in which people run, not walk, along the corridors! A crisis means a lot of extra work, and requires more time – a commodity that is likely to be particularly scarce (Holsti, 1971).

Studies of crisis behaviour may highlight factors in international affairs of which we are not normally aware. One of these is the formation of 'mirror-images' or 'mirror-percepts': opposing parties may develop very similar hostile ideas about each other. Each may see the other as bent on world domination, as uncivilised and subhuman, as ruled by demagogues, as impervious to reason and common sense. Generally, this is part of the polarisation that takes place during the run-up to a conflict, and these hostile images serve, aided by the rhetoric of conflict, to 'justify' the use of force (Fisher, 1969). The building of such images is also very necessary in order to create internal unity and to stifle doubts and disagreements. The manipulation of the mass media becomes an essential element in this process, in order to create a 'united' nation.

Decision makers generally have a great fear of disunity – indeed, their forceful suppression of 'treasonable' activities can be understood in the light of such fears – and they often become the victims of perceptual narrowing. They quite deliberately cut themselves off from dissenting voices in their own country or among their allies, they sharpen the perceived contrasts between themselves and their opponents ('black-and-white thinking'), and they cannot bring themselves to think about the problems of future co-existence with their current enemies. At the very moment when they most need to engage in subtle consideration and awareness of each other's thought processes they will break off all communications and withdraw their ambassadors.

If the available facilities do not succeed in coping with the extra load, then a state of overload will come to exist. This is likely to cause the decision makers a great deal of trouble. At the very time when they need to be calm and rested, unhurried and well-informed, they will find themselves virtually cut off from events and from many of their advisors and informants, snatching a hasty sandwich or forty winks on the office couch, taking part in all-night crisis meetings and making decisions which may already come too late to influence the situation. They will experience the impact of the basic components of any crisis: high stakes, extreme urgency, great uncertainty, and the threat of internal disunity (Brecher, 1978; Snyder and Diesing, 1977).

DECISION MAKING IN A CRISIS

What happens to the quality of decision making under these conditions (Kahneman, Slovic and Tversky, 1982)? A good deal is known about this, both from simulation work and from content analyses of major real-life crises. The decision makers will start to experience stress phenomena. Their thinking will become polarised and oversimplified, with emotional overtones. Short-term objectives will be given precedence over long-term goals – though the latter might be in contradiction to the former. Perception will become more subjective: they will be unable to see how the conflict appears from their opponents' point of view, or from the point of view of interested outsiders. (These phenomena are sometimes described as 'tunnel vision'.) They will be less able to scan a wide range of possible options or to generate new ones, and they will find it difficult to anticipate counter-moves or to think more than one or two moves ahead. Hunger, tiredness and irritation will begin to affect their powers of concentration. Fear and anxiety (generated by uncertainty as much as by anything else) will cause more rigidity of thought, compulsive demands for unity, and the feeling that delays might be fatal ('any decision is better than no decision'). Reports about their opponents or proposals from them will be misinterpreted to a greater degree and influenced by fear-dominated projections. As a result, decision makers will tend to over-react, they will make exorbitant responses rather than offer 'yessable propositions' (Fisher, 1969), and thus the crisis will rapidly escalate and get out of control. It is a common experience of participants in a disastrous crisis that afterwards they cannot understand how it all came about (Janis, 1973; Janis and Mann, 1977). The well-known studies of the outbreak of World War I are a case in point (Pruitt, 1969; Snyder and Diesing, 1977). For a dissenting finding, see Maoz (1981).

When we start to think about preventive measures, it is useful to distinguish at least to some extent between *personal* and *organisational* factors in crisis decision making. If we were to observe a bureaucracy in a state of crisis we would note the communication overloads and efforts to overcome these, and the short-circuiting of lower echelons, of consultation, and of the information stores; as a result, decision makers become progressively more isolated and ill-informed, so that they are forced to extrapolate from an earlier (and possibly irrelevant) past. Inputs from sources which are not immediately concerned with the crisis will be ignored. The decision makers also become cognitively overloaded, with the consequences to their perceiving and thinking that we have noted.

Thus, there are really two kinds of overloads in a crisis: on the communication channels, and on the top echelon, and these affect each other. Likewise, time pressures affect both the organisation (consultation, information retrieval, use of faster and more informal communication techniques) and the decision makers (less time for discussion, loss of sleep, less tolerance of dissent, fear of delay, shortened time perspective, fewer options considered). Anxiety, fear and over-reaction under stress are partly caused by high risks, but also by uncertainty (lack of information) due to clogged communication channels or about the intention of others. Shock, surprise and tunnel vision may partly be due to the organisation's lack of anticipation and forward planning (Whaley, 1973). Palliative or preventive measures need, therefore, to take into account both the structure of the organisation and the personnel at the top. Ministries of Foreign Affairs differ widely in their capacity for handling excess communication loads; once the dangers of crisis behaviour are realised, it becomes obvious that a certain amount of 'slack' is needed to cope with crisis loads, yet in budgetary terms this is hard to justify. Few of them choose their staff on the basis of their capacity to remain subtle and flexible in a stressful situation, and even fewer offer training courses or engage in simulations to improve crisis coping styles. Planning departments, if they exist, are more likely to be dead ends than the source of long-range warnings and contingency preparations. The Cuban Missiles Crisis showed the advantages of having alternating crisis teams, to minimise the dangers of rigidity, polarisation, lack of sleep, and tunnel vision, but few governments have such teams available. Most still work on the assumption that in a crisis 'we all work just that little bit harder' – and therein lies the danger (Steinbruner, 1974; Allison, 1971).

CRISIS PREVENTION

It was noted earlier that wars and conflicts can have some positive or pleasurable effects, and the same can apply to crises. A crisis can 'clear the air', may create a feeling of team-work, could enable participants to find out 'who your real friends are', and may root out some deadwood in the organisation. A group which has weathered a number of crises successfully may feel that it has become very effective at 'crisis management' but this is a rather ambiguous term, for who is to say what constitutes 'success' or good management? From the 'national interest' point of view, a 'successful' crisis is one that yields an advantage yet ends short of war, and is handled with cool sophistication while deliberately causing crisis behaviour in the camp of an opponent, with perhaps some foolish decisions and loss of advantage – but to instigate a crisis deliberately is very risky, since the opponent's crisis behaviour may lead to dangerous over-reaction and will, at best, be unpredictable.

However, from the 'system point of view' good crisis management (of an inadvertent crisis) means giving your opponent a way out while maintaining 'face', thus hopefully leading to de-escalation and avoiding war. Perhaps the difference can be seen most clearly when we look at time as a variable: the deliberately instigated crisis will use shortened time as a means of exerting pressure (for example, by means of an ultimatum), while in an inadvertent crisis both parties will probably be willing to 'defuse' the situation by 'creating more time' to find solutions, for example, at the suggestion of a third party who will 'hold the ring'. Apart from time pressure, organisational rigidity (for instance, an inflexible military timetable which cannot be halted or reversed) can be another source of unexpected danger. The first efforts of any potential mediating party will therefore have to be directed towards extending time limits, and towards the creating of greater flexibility of thinking, perceiving and labelling (Mitchell, 1981a).

Thus we see that one effective way of reducing the likelihood of violent major conflicts is by creating more awareness of the dangers of crisis situations, and by developing the skills of crisis avoidance. It is possible to build decision making systems which are less vulnerable to crises (having more slack, more spare communication capacity, fewer rigid processes), and to man them with decision makers who are better selected (more stress resistant, with more flexible coping styles, and able to think several moves ahead, under tension) and better trained (for instance, by means of simulations). Most diplomats and politicians are insufficiently aware of the developing literature and knowledge on these topics because they have no background in the social sciences (Deutsch, 1973). As a result, they tend to favour older approaches to conflict prevention: they seek safety in various kinds of alliance structures; in some form of collective security such as the United Nations; in the ideal of international law and world government; or in balance-of-power policies such as still animate today's deterrence strategists. However, these approaches are often based on very primitive and unverified assumptions (for example, the so-called Domino Theory); they may create very unstable situations, not lasting safeguards; or they tend to 'freeze' the status quo (for example, Nato and the Warsaw Pact) so that they are ill-equipped to deal with change. What we need is a synthesis between old and new, in which many of these classical approaches are submitted to detailed analysis and modification and are then merged with newer findings, in an attempt at better understanding.

RECENT DEVELOPMENTS: COGNITIVE MAPPING AND GROUP IDENTITY

The findings of crisis research are by now well-established and have become widely known, although rarely applied. The whole area is a good example of collaborative and inter-stimulating work between social psychologists and others. Are there signs of *new* developments in social and political psychological research and theory which will have relevance to international affairs?

An interesting developing area concerns the study of the 'operational codes' of prominent foreign-policy actors (Axelrod, 1976). In the past, the field of leadership studies and the analysis of the personalities of particular international leaders seemed to have but limited relevance to political events; there were too many gaps between our psychological understanding of a leader's character and the behaviour of a nation in the political arena. This gap is now being bridged. There is a movement away from 'psychologising' and towards a more detailed understanding of the beliefs and percepts (the 'cognitive maps') which individual decision makers bring to a particular situation.

Imaginative use is being made in this research of the findings of cognitive social psychology: how leaders and elites see their world, how they attribute causes and effects, what they think are the 'lessons of history', what basic values they bring implicitly into their world views, and what 'social representations' (Forgas, 1981) they have of themselves and of their allies and opponents. These components can be built up into a picture of an individual's 'operational code' which helps us to make predictions and estimates of his future behaviour. We have here, once more, an example of taking the 'subjectivist' position. Obviously, operational codes are but one component in a complex process; we must never forget the impact of bureaucratic and organisational factors, of the stresses of crisis, and of the problems of information and communication processing. We must also wonder what will happen if and when this line of research becomes effective: when decision making elites are given a more accurate and sophisticated understanding and prediction of their own and their opponents' likely responses to a given situation, how will this affect the outcomes of an interaction sequence?

Adjacent to these studies are the implications of new work on the formation of group identity. In addition to his private self-percept, an individual develops numerous further group identities based, for example, on gender, on age, on status and on culture and nationality.

Such group identities can act both as unifying forces and as divisive ones: they create the 'us' and 'them' percepts to which powerful emotions and action potentials sometimes become attached. They may, at times, polarise the social perceptions of large groups of individuals and – as we have seen earlier – such group identities and labels become the focal points of prejudices and hostile images, of dehumanisation of the 'other' and glorification of the 'in-group'. In short, certain kinds of group identities can become conflict facilitators. We can see this most particularly in the fields of communal conflict, revolutionary movements, and terrorism, where quite often the aim is to break down some earlier group identity and establish a new one, with added implications of legitimacy: yesterday's terrorists are today's revolutionaries and, perhaps, tomorrow's recognised government. Such struggles for group identity can also be seen vividly in emergent or developing nations ('nation building') when they seek to submerge internal divisions and claim their own place at the table of high politics. The research now being done, for example, on the identity problems of black youth in Britain or of Palestinians or French Canadians, will have considerable relevance to our understanding of international affairs.

Such identities do not usually emerge spontaneously. They are the results of deliberate 'conscience-raising' activities such as leadership speeches, mass media manipulation, popular claims on history and 'destiny', and political education. Research in political socialisation in many countries is beginning to show that 'civics' lessons are not merely about presidents and constitutions but also about attitudes and values: about democracy and equality, about race and religion, about the role of women, about justice and the UN and about the place of one's own nation in the world (Torney, Oppenheim and Farnen, 1975). We know, of course, that politicisation does not only take place in civics lessons; our political values and orientation are also influenced by the mass media, by our parents and siblings, our religious organisations, our friends and by our own experience. But if we consider the quality of relations within the international system of the future, then clearly such educational programmes, both for adults and for children, can contribute towards greater or lesser conflict potential.

DETERRENCE

It is regrettable that there is little new work to report from another important psychological area: the study of deterrence. We are told that only the existence of nuclear deterrents prevents the super-powers from engaging in major, and world-destructive, war. The deterrent assumption is also widely used in measures of social control (the threat of imprisonment is supposed to deter the criminal), and generally in any persuasive situation where threats are available. Yet, after the predominantly strategic studies carried out in the 1960s, our understanding has hardly advanced. We simply do not know enough of what goes on in the 'deterree's' mind at the moment when deterrence breaks down. We all realise that the threat of legal punishment is not the most important factor that stops each of us from murdering someone with whom we quarrel; moreover, most murders are between family members or acquaintances, yet even these social bonds are an insufficient deterrent at the moments of extreme jealousy, anger, drunkenness, fear or other pent-up emotion when murder is committed. By analogy, simulation work has frequently shown how previously 'rational' decision makers, driven by a desperate situation, will commit 'irrational' and self-destructive acts. When events pursue their normal course, we cannot say if the deterrence is 'working', and when it breaks down, we know not why.

When we are dealing with ordinary social controls we can suggest that deterrence has two components: (a) the magnitude of the expected costs, or punishment; and (b) the likelihood or probability that these costs will be incurred. In a situation of full knowledge and high rationality (not a very common condition) the deterree is supposed to calculate the risks: he will avoid situations in which very high costs will be inflicted with great certainty; he may indulge in acts that carry but small penalties, rarely incurred; and he may, or may not, accept the risks in the middle zone, where the magnitude of the punishment or costs is quite high, and the probability is about even, or more than even. Whether or not he then 'takes his chances' will depend on the perceived gains or reliefs he may obtain if he 'gets away with it', and on the extent to which the deterrer can make him think that the odds are really less in his favour than he believes.

Obviously, in deterrence between states there are many other factors involved, and in the case of the *nuclear* deterrent we have the added problem that – while the magnitude of the cost can hardly be in doubt – we have no reliable way of estimating its probability since, mercifully, it has hardly ever been applied. Such probability will depend not only on technological factors, but also on the political will and determination (or on a 'doomsday machine') of the opponent and, most of all, on the extreme stresses of crisis decision

making. Despite the offensive-defensive swings of military technological advantage, deterrence is in the final analysis a psychological
problem, and one about which we need a great deal more knowledge,
to enable us to travel from mutually assured destruction to mutually
assured co-existence.

PROBLEM-SOLVING WORKSHOPS

One method that may help us move in that direction is the problem-
solving workshop, a technique that has been developed particularly
by John Burton (1968) as well as by Doob (1970) and by Kelman
(1972); see also Hill (1982). The problem-solving workshop, in its
form of 'controlled communication', seeks to apply in a real-life
conflict situation some of the principles we have learnt in the study of
conflict behaviour. It seeks to re-establish severed communications;
it counteracts narrowed and polarised perceptions of the conflict and
of the parties (indeed, deciding jointly who *are* the parties to a
particular conflict can prove most illuminating); it shows up the
dangers of tunnel vision and of mutual mirror-images; it deflates
conflict rhetoric while helping the parties to discover underlying and
hitherto inadmissible motives; and it seeks to establish a non-
censorious atmosphere of trust which enables the parties themselves
to generate alternatives to further fighting. In short, it engages the
parties in mutual problem-solving, in order to turn a win-lose (zero
sum) situation into one where both can gain (win-win, or positive
sum). To most participants this approach is novel, in that it gets away
from legalistic, territorial, logical, historical and military issues and
focuses, instead, on the deeper level of human needs, fears and
insecurities, hostile images, misperceptions and misunderstandings.
While probing the unique aspects of each conflict, the panel of
experts can help the participants by bringing knowledge and experience of other conflicts to bear, showing them the predictable
regularities in the typical conflict process.

Problem-solving workshops serve to re-establish a kind of mutual
awareness, and frequently go deeper. The parties come to realise that
often they have the same hostile perceptions of one another, and that
this paradoxical kind of mirror-thinking is part of the normal process
of conflict behaviour, born out of fear of internal disunity, projected
by distrust, and maintained by the suppression of alternative images.
From this, they begin to accept the subjectivity of their own
perceptions and this may lead to major perceptual shifts: they begin

to see that their opponents are not bloodthirsty animals, that they have difficulties of their own, that much of their hostility is caused by fear rather than by aggression, and that there are many misunderstandings to be cleared up. They begin to respect and to understand each other's problems, and can produce problem-solving ideas which go to the psychological heart of the matter. Indeed, after having shared such a prolonged series of 'mind altering' experiences and having, perhaps, arrived at a set of resolution proposals, participants typically find the 're-entry' phase the most difficult of all: the problem of convincing their own leadership and polity, who cling to their outdated perceptions.

So far, this procedure has only had limited and intermittent application; it has not yet been subjected to rigorous academic scrutiny, nor can it as yet point to a long list of 'successes'. Indeed, a 'success' under workshop conditions may, as we have seen, yet fail to convince the top decision makers since they have not been through the problem-solving experience themselves. More such workshops will hopefully lead to a more precise and testable set of theoretical guidelines and to increased willingness among practitioners to take part. Where conflicts lie along the major fissures in the international system, a continuously ongoing set of workshops may well be necessary.

THE RHETORIC OF CONFLICT

In passing, we have mentioned the 'rhetoric of conflict' but this is really worthy of study in its own right. We quote the Bible: 'an eye for an eye, a tooth for a tooth'. We sing 'Britons never, never, never shall be slaves'. We say that we 'have no alternative but to . . .' (haven't we?); or that 'because so much (innocent) blood has been shed, we must . . .' (must we?). And so we fight 'for our heritage'; we fight for a 'principle' (both are better, presumably, than fighting for a piece of land, for markets or for oil-wells); we 'serve notice' on others that we 'will not tolerate' certain things because they are 'the thin end of a wedge' and that our opponents, being 'intransigent', only have 'themselves to blame' if we 'teach them a lesson they will never forget' (but they may learn quite a different lesson!). Needless to say, there is a similar rhetoric of peace, in which the images tend to be somewhat rustic (swords into plowshares, lions lying down with lambs). The use of rhetoric is a form of persuasion beyond logical discourse, reasoned argument, or the maximisation of utilities (processes which are rare enough at the best of times); it seems, rather, to create an unthinking response, a gut reaction that will unite the audience and mobilise its action potential. It pre-empts and over-simplifies argument, it implicitly congratulates 'us' and dehumanises 'them' and it facilitates conflict because it enables us to 'act' and relieves us of the necessity to think, and to weigh alternatives – especially when we also know that, of course, 'God is on our side'.

Such a gut reaction would hardly be likely if this rhetoric could not appeal to a long process of political socialisation (both formal and informal), to religious teachings, the effects of the mass media, and the effects of various aspects of nation-building (such as one-sided history and geography teaching; the proclamations about sovereignty and national flags; the ceremony surrounding a Head of State; national language; national airlines and national songs). The function of conflict rhetoric is to appeal to these attitudes, stereotypes and feelings in order to create predictable reactions, and to stifle doubts and reasoned discourse. Such attitudes may have lain dormant for many years, but they emerge ready-made when triggered off by suitable rhetoric.

War and conflict should therefore never come as a surprise. We must never forget that in most nation-states war-making is an honourable profession on which more is often spent than on health or education, to which whole industries are devoted, and usually more than one government department. Our systems of religion, education and political socialisation prepare the young to think that war is not 'unthinkable' but can be glorious and exciting or, at worst, a necessary evil. In short, while we may go on thinking and saying that war and conflict are 'bad', both the state and the individual citizen are deeply prepared for it – in a way that is, moreover, grossly outdated and bears little relation to the possibilities of *nuclear* war.

COMMUNICATION BARRIERS BETWEEN RESEARCHERS AND PRACTITIONERS

Similar problems of language, rhetoric and outmoded thinking confront us when we ask why not more of these findings have been used and applied by the practitioners. If we assume that much of this knowledge is generated by academics (which is by no means always the case) then it has to pass through the following barriers: it has to be thoroughly researched and replicated by its originators and by others; it has to be integrated in a broader theoretical framework; it has to be scrutinised and technically evaluated by the wider academic community; then it has to find its way into training courses and textbooks; and finally, such courses and texts must be seen as 'relevant' by those who select and train our future practitioners. But frequently such knowledge is *not* seen as relevant, or not seen as 'knowledge' or, indeed, not seen at all! For example, in most countries neither the top diplomats nor their political masters will have obtained university degrees in international relations; they probably will have taken law degrees, or qualified in arts or in classics. Consequently their thinking habits, their ears and their language are not attuned to what IR has to say, partly because of the 'way it says it', using its own jargon and terminology.

To add to these communication difficulties, in some countries the field of IR has begun to use quantitative and hypothetico-deductive methods which, while adding precision and falsifiability to research findings, has made its books and learned journals even more impenetrable to practitioners untrained in the social sciences. Psychologists erect still further barriers to be crossed: of techniques, of statistical presentation, of theoretical concepts unshared, and of more fearsome jargon. Beyond all these barriers, and still further distrusted and misunderstood, are the conflict researchers with their different assumptions about 'successful' conflict resolution and their unpatriotically supra-national position. No wonder that, bar an occasional foray into academe, the busy practitioner just gives up.

We must also bear in mind that practitioners have their own hard-earned knowledge, and that they can teach academic researchers a thing or two. They do not see themselves as the products of irrelevant training, practising and applying the outdated doctrines of nineteenth-century power politics. On the contrary, most ministries of foreign affairs are supremely self-confident, they believe themselves to be successful, and to be almost the sole repositories of knowledge about the optimal conduct of international relations.

Perhaps what is needed, to take a leaf from our own book, is the development of a series of controlled communication meetings between academics and practitioners, for surely by overcoming these barriers and pooling our resources both sides will have much to gain.

Part III
APPLICATIONS OF THE WORLD SOCIETY
PERSPECTIVE

8   Effective Participation in World Society: Some Implications of the Columbus Study

Chadwick F. Alger

John Burton's disarmingly simple world society paradigm has two fundamental components. The first is an emphasis on realism. He insists that the world should be described and explained as it actually is – in all of its complexity. Because 'the interaction of states is only one of the many systems of interaction in world society' (Burton, 1974, p. 6), he asserts that 'a concept of systems interacting is more realistic than a concept of states interacting. A system has no geographical boundaries. The system comprises points between which there is interaction'. The simplistic billiard ball image of interacting states is replaced by the much more complicated image of world society as a set of overlapping cobwebs. The detailed implications of this 'cobweb' view of the world have been set out by Dr Mitchell in a previous chapter.

Why such a sharp break with traditional analysis? It is required in the light of the second fundamental component of Burton's global society paradigm, a forthright value position. Burton is concerned about the values implicit in approaches that make the nation-state the centrepiece of analysis, fearing that they will 'promote the status of state authorities and inhibit processes of political and social change' (Burton, 1974, p. 27). While other scholars certainly share Burton's concern for individual human beings, they do not assert it directly as a foundation for their inquiry.[1]

These central premises of Burton's work, an emphasis on genuine realism combined with the primacy of values, are important not only to our understanding of the present world society, but also to the opening up of new possibilities for the future. From his systems perspective, Burton foresees increasing interdependence and smaller and smaller political units:

If a systems image is more akin to the referent world than the billiard ball model, then we should anticipate the emergence of more and more, smaller and smaller, political units within a widening economic and cultural interdependence as political services develop and participation demands become effective. The increasing interdependence, promoted by communications and technology in industry, will further accelerate the growth of functional institutions (Burton, 1974, p. 27).

It is important to note that Burton uses the key term 'functionalism' in a very special way:

We are seeking relationships that need no coercive support – that is, essentially functional relationships that have their source in the organization of a scarcity of resources in the satisfaction of infinite demands. Such functional relationships are by definition associated with *participatory decision-making* processes: functional exchange relationships are *reciprocal* and involve the free decision-making of relevant parties (Burton, 1974, p. 25, emphasis added).

Writing in 1974, Burton asserted that 'functionalism will emerge in a world society as a means of dealing with interdependence', although he does not specify the time that this will require. It is the purpose of this chapter, building on Burton's world society paradigm, to suggest strategies that will help to fulfil Burton's vision of the future, and thereby help to overcome the very real counter-tendencies towards centralisation and exploitation.

CENTRALISATION AND DECENTRALISATION IN WORLD SOCIETY

To many this may seem to be an inauspicious time for Burton to suggest that world society will evolve toward smaller and smaller units linked together in a participatory and equitable interdependence that serves human needs. Actually there are strong tendencies toward centralisation, accompanied by militarisation. The yearly arms budgets of nation-states have risen to $550 billion, some thirty governments are selling $25–35 billion in arms to other countries each year, and in fifty-four countries armed forces control the machinery of government (Sivard, 1981, pp. 6, 7). Major powers have acquired new means for projecting their influence throughout the world – through military, political, economic and communications systems that employ missiles, planes, submarines, spy satellites and an array of communication facilities.

Centralisation tendencies can also be perceived in the growth of international organisations in many domains of human activity.

First, national governments have joined together to form new organisations that operate across national boundaries. These IGOs (international governmental organisations), now numbering 337, are concerned with cooperation in matters such as health, transportation, communication, development, ecology, governance for the commons (atmosphere, oceans, and space), and controlling and employing large-scale violence. Second, TNCs (transnational corporations) girdle the globe, moving technology, capital, profits, resources, labour, parts, finished products, and managers around the globe through complicated networks. Third are INGOs (international non-governmental (non-profit) organisations), now 4265 in number, covering all the important domains of human activity (agriculture, medicine, recreation, arts, religion, philanthropy, science, education, professions, and so on). Forty-five are federations of a number of international associations, such as the International Council of Scientific Unions and the World Council of Churches.[2]

From one perspective these three kinds of organisations are greatly increasing the number of people directly engaged in transnational functional relations. On the other hand, it can be argued that these organisational changes, overall, are tending to concentrate power in the world. Those that already have positions of influence, and access to resources that go with these positions, are those most able to acquire the new technology employed in transnational relations. This has tended to make powerful national governments relatively more powerful, huge TNCs even larger, and influential INGOs even more influential. Typically, the headquarters of the major organisations of all types are concentrated in the industrialised world.

The pervasive influence of nation-state ideology also tends to concentrate power. This ideology asserts that the world is composed of nation-states and that the agents of these nation-states do and should control the external relations of these states, because foreign policy is an esoteric subject that must be handled by the elite few that can divine the 'national interest'. Because IGOs are basically unions of national foreign policy elites, this means that the emerging network of IGOs is in the control of an elite that is even more distant from most people of the world than the foreign-policy machinery of national governments. In the same way, most people are not directly involved in the international activities of non-governmental organisations in their societies and have little influence over or knowledge about their international extensions – INGOs. Nation-state ideology also has a pervasive influence over research and teaching, thereby making the possibility of wider participation in international processes 'unthinkable'.[3] In this context the wide gulf between research and teaching about international relations, and research and teaching about participatory democracy, is highly significant.

The distinction in the market economies between public and private enterprise has also strengthened centralisation. Corporations wield tremendous global power, with widespread impact on rates of inflation, conditions of employment, availability of resources, and consumer wants. But even those people very active in domestic politics make little effort to exert influence over TNCs because they are considered to be in the private sphere, outside of politics.[4] As these corporations have increased their influence over the international involvements of societies, few people seem inclined to demand public control, partly because of lack of public competence in international affairs. Thus, both nation-state ideology and capitalist ideology inhibit popular control over TNCs.

On the other hand, there are also important forces promoting decentralisation of the world. The breakup of colonial empires and the continuing struggle of new nation-states for economic self-determination is one example. At the same time, many people in local communities and regions within Third World countries are demanding more local autonomy in defining their approach to development. This tendency is in response to the perceived failure of many centralised national development plans over the past two decades.[5]

Throughout the world ethnic and national groups within nation-states are demanding greater autonomy, and sometimes independence. Groups within old countries ask why self-determination in the twentieth century applies only to overseas empires and not to conquered peoples in contiguous territory. Groups within new countries are asking why self-determination has been limited to territorial units set up by colonial regimes and not extended to people forced into these Western style states by colonial masters.[6]

In the industrialised countries there are also strong decentralising tendencies brought on by growth in the size and functions of modern governments. Particularly in larger countries, many people perceive these governments as decreasingly responsive to their needs and are demanding that governmental services be decentralised. In the capitalist countries this includes demands for decentralisation of services usually provided by private enterprise, exemplified by a demand for simpler energy technology, under more local control, in place of giant power companies. Many people, particularly the young, are expressing their desire for decentralisation through communal and family life-styles that are as self-reliant as possible.[7]

WHY IS A PARTICIPATORY WORLD SOCIETY UNTHINKABLE?

Given the fact that there are both centralisation and militarisation tendencies in the world, and counter tendencies toward decentralisation, how might decentralisation be supported and encouraged? Answers to this question require deeper understanding of why a world society of a multitude of localities with symmetrical relations appears to be unthinkable to most people. For the sake of concreteness, the response to these questions will draw on eight years of research on the connections between a metropolitan area of one million people (Columbus, Ohio) and world society, sharing this information with local people and working with them in local organisations.[8] These findings have been discussed with people in many US cities, revealing a similar experience to that in Columbus. While the local context varies in other parts of the world, discussions with people in many countries reveal that for people everywhere a participatory world society is unthinkable.

Most people in Columbus perceive their community to be distant from world affairs. One man was asked in what ways he thought Columbus was linked to the world. He replied: 'Linked to the world? I don't think it is linked anywhere.' But like all cities it *is* linked, through international trade and investment, scientific networks, religion, ethnic ties, migration, tourism, the arts, sports, and so on. Many people are vitally affected by these networks because they affect prices, availability of consumer goods, availability of employment, and so on. Why can they not perceive them? Three factors seem to be important. First, people are systematically educated in ways that prevent perception of the links between their local community and the world. Young people are first educated about things in their local community and then about their local region or state (province). But information about the world connections of these territorial entities is omitted. This creates the impression that links to the larger world are distant – out beyond the nation. Despite the fact that people are increasingly affected by powerful world organisations, their image of the way the world works does not help them to perceive and cope with these intrusions on their life.

Second, norms for citizenship also contribute to perceptual gaps between people and the world society in which their life is embedded. Traditions of the nation-state system dictate that so-called foreign affairs are handled by a small elite who have special competence to discern the 'national interest'. This contributes to widespread apathy, and to ignorance about world affairs.

Third, these patterns of education and socialisation for citizenship build social structures that wall people off from the world. This means that nation-state traditions for handling foreign affairs are replicated in voluntary organisations – that is, they tend to be handled in a national office. For example, the 'foreign ministers' of labour unions, churches and a variety of nongovernmental organisations are as distant from local people as the foreign ministers of national governments. Because much adult education in matters of public policy takes place through participation in voluntary organisations, the tendency for international issues to be handled by the national office further isolates local people from the world.

As a result of these three factors, a cycle of apathy with respect to world affairs is created in local communities. It can be summarised as follows: people have no knowledge, therefore they do not participate; since they do not participate, they have no need to know; because they have no need to know, they are not interested in international education; therefore, they have no knowledge.

This cycle is reflected in the slight attention given to world affairs in local schools and colleges, the press and local politics. For the most part the international dimension of life is not perceived, is not a subject of learning, and is not at issue in local politics. As a result, local voluntary organisations with professional staff tend not to have specialised competence in international affairs, whether they be labour unions, churches, political parties or chambers of commerce. This means that local people who do acquire competence, and who wish employment in international affairs, must migrate to national headquarters. Valuable international talent moves away. The cycle of apathy is reinforced by this brain drain, producing a periphery mentality with respect to world relations in most local communities.

Of course, in cities like Columbus there are many educated people in upper socio-economic strata who are interested in world affairs. They attempt to fulfil this interest through internationally oriented voluntary organisations with programmes in adult education, international relief and development assistance, and international exchange. Educational organisations, such as world affairs councils, sponsor speeches and discussions on foreign policy issues. But the speakers, the materials and the issue agendas tend to come from the national government and the national headquarters of voluntary organisations. Thus they reinforce the traditional nation-state view of the world. Relief and development aid programmes are based on an altruistic impulse. But rarely do they offer opportunity for direct contact with recipients, or for direct participation in policy-making. For the most part, local activity consists of fundraising for programmes developed nationally. Exchange programmes, motivated by the belief that cross-cultural communication will in some way contribute to world understanding and peace, do offer direct links to people in other countries. But exactly how such links can overcome the tension and fear generated by growing nuclear arsenals is not very clear to participants.

Overall, these international activities do not provide avenues for participation in significant decision making. Agendas are set nationally, not locally. Although some who participate in exchange and development aid programmes may feel that they are part of strategies for peace and social justice, they only deal with symptoms produced by larger systems. Few participants even perceive these larger world systems, whose major dimensions are determined by powerful governments and corporations. For the most part, the activity of local organisations unwittingly supports these structures. Nevertheless, there is a tendency for local participants to believe that their efforts could greatly improve the world if only they could acquire the attention and participation of the mass of apathetic people around them. Because of this lack of interest, the participants tend to feel that they are a beleaguered minority in an alien sea. They deplore the fact that 'you can't do much around here because people are too parochial'. This attitude itself contributes to the periphery mentality in their community.

But, of course, all metropolitan areas, and many small cities and towns, do have their cosmopolitan operators. These are the people in banks which invest abroad, in corporations which trade and own branches and factories around the world, and in research organisations which participate in global knowledge networks. But such global activities tend not to be perceived by local people, even though they may walk daily past the office buildings in which they take place. For the most part the cosmopolitans that inhabit these nodes of world networks have more in common with colleagues in distant places than with their own community. They normally feel more responsibility for maintenance of world systems than for conditions at home. In particular, they feel little responsibility for sharing knowledge of world systems with local people. Why should they, when they perceive these local people to be in the periphery and to be uninterested in such things? The cosmopolitans tend to mock 'provincialism', especially of newspapers. Of course, by their own behaviour, along with that of the 'provincials' themselves, the gulf between them and local people becomes a self-fulfilling prophecy.

Ironically, some of the cosmopolitans attend distant meetings devoted to world problems that are also the concern of people in local governments and non-governmental organisations – problems such as hunger, energy, population, unemployment, inflation and human rights. But these local people live in a world isolated from the cosmopolitans. They may be vaguely aware that they are working on problems that transcend their country, but they see the links only as far as their state (province) and national government. They have been socialised to assume that things 'beyond the nation-state' will be taken care of by elites with special competence.

RESOURCES FOR CREATING A PARTICIPATORY WORLD SOCIETY

This brief diagnosis of the characteristics of local nodes in world systems indicates that there are strong traditions in teaching, research and citizenship that are restraining evolutionary development of the participatory world society envisaged by Burton. On the other hand, resources have been uncovered that could be employed in deliberate strategies to move in this direction. These can be viewed in three contexts: mass apathy, the agendas of internationally oriented voluntary organisations, and cosmopolitan actors.

First, mass apathy is supported largely by a false image of detachment from the world. Local people need concrete information about the links of local organisations and individuals to the world as it is reflected in a diversity of aspects of community life. This will require new kinds of maps and charts that will become as important as political maps in shaping people's view of the world. Through them they will come to understand how they are involved in global networks in manufacturing, investment, labour migration, inflation, religion, agriculture, pollution, and so on. These displays of local links to world systems will compensate for the distortions of maps which falsely suggest that people in centres of countries are distant from borders. They will demonstrate that the borders are as near as airport customs offices, satellite communications terminals, and even the living room of the transnational corporation executive down the street. Such maps and charts will also overcome the false impressions given by national statistics, those subtle conveyors of the nation-state view of the world. These statistics will be disaggregated to demonstrate local involvement in world networks, enabling people to perceive that their community is related to the world in special ways that are traditionally obscured. As a result, local people will be able to identify issues with respect to their external relations that are relevant to their needs. This will free them from national elite definitions of needs, based on aggregate national statistics and clothed in the mysticism of 'national interest'.

But new information will not alone enhance possibilities for local participation. It requires support in local organisations, the means through which people collaborate with other people in their community with common interests – unions, churches, farmers' organisations, chambers of commerce, and a diversity of special interest groups for environment, human rights, social justice, and so on. These organisations will have to disseminate relevant information, identify issues important to local people, encourage broad participatory decision making, and help to implement decisions via state (province) and national bodies and international organisations. This implies, of course, that these local organisations will begin to develop staffs with expertise on world issues. To make the point in nation-state terminology, the 'foreign offices' of voluntary organisations will no longer be confined to the national office. Instead there will be competence in 'external relations' in all local organisations that have permanent staff. These professional opportunities will slow the brain drain of talent away from local communities and will also diminish the periphery mentality that causes and is a consequence of this loss of local competence.

Second, once the mainstream organisations have shed the blinkers walling them off from the world 'beyond the nation-state', the context in which they operate will dramatically change. No longer will they perceive themselves as a beleaguered minority in an alien sea. Many people will be participating in activity related to a variety of world issues. Indeed, there will be much local conflict over world issues, and some unexpected coalitions. For example, local labour leaders might become active in support of UN efforts to develop rules governing the operation of transnational corporations. Small-business leaders might support them, but local people in transnational corporations would oppose them. Such direct participation in world affairs will tend to focus on specific needs, interests and issues. Organisations with a more general international interest would also be needed, to enable the community to perceive the totality of its involvement in the world and the long-term consequences. As more and more people in local communities self-consciously participate in the creation of the future world, it will be important for them to have visions of alternative possibilities.

Third, as people in other sectors of community life become more active and competent in world affairs, the former cosmopolitan operators will become more visible. On the one hand, they may be pleased that their expertise is more sought after in the local community. On the other hand, as local people become more competent in world affairs they will also seek more detailed information about the world activities of local cosmopolitans. This will lead to criticism and efforts to change their policies, on overseas employment, marketing, pollution, and other matters. They may also wish to evaluate and change the overseas technical assistance policies of local universities and research institutes. Supported by a growing number of experts in world affairs in a diversity of local organisations, more people will effectively be able to challenge the knowledge monopoly of the cosmopolitan operators.

As local people learn about the world networks through which the cosmopolitans control world systems they will find it necessary to develop their own networks in response. Transnational links will replace barriers between people working on supposedly local issues and their counterparts in other parts of the world. Issues such as environment, human rights, and hunger will be tackled through collaborative strategies, permitting powerful national governments and corporations to be challenged and international non-governmental organisations made more responsive to grass-roots needs. For example, an environmental group wishing to stop pollution by a local factory of a transnational corporation could use its world environmental network to prevent the corporation from exporting the pollution to a site in another part of the world. This would prevent the corporation from fighting local pollution controls by developing an alliance with local labour based on a threat to move the plant overseas, which would export jobs along with the pollution.

The evolutionary developments which have been described would grow out of existing decentralisation tendencies in the world. The critical difference between much current activity and what is being suggested is that this author is urging more local units, such as regions and cities, to overcome the constraints that nation-state ideology imposes on their perceptions. This would in turn lead to organised efforts, with wide participation, to formulate policies for their relations with the world. It should not be difficult to convince those active in decentralisation movements that local control of 'external relations' is a prerequisite. The overwhelming power of some national governments and transnational corporations is largely derived from their competence in controlling world systems.

CONCLUSION: COPING WITH WORLD PROBLEMS IN A DECENTRALISED WORLD SOCIETY

Evolution towards a decentralised world society could release new potential for coping with four of the seemingly intractable world problems confronted within the constraints of a nation-state system: aspirations for human rights, for a new international economic order, for a new international information order, and for a reduction in violence and warfare. Issues on these topics are being debated continually in a multitude of United Nations and regional international bodies. The outcomes will vitally affect all people in the world for years in the future. But most people in the world know little of the debates and have had no opportunity to express their views. The United States can be used as an example for illustrating how the nation-state paradigm has walled off the people from these issues and debates, preventing them from seeing how their participation in world society could help to ease these problems.

First, despite the fact that the United States has a relatively good domestic record in ensuring human rights to its citizens, it has a very poor record in working with people from other parts of the world to ensure rights on a world basis – reflected in the relatively few human rights conventions it has ratified. Instead, the United States tends to use human rights as a means of embarrassing the Soviet Union in order to gain advantage in power politics.

Furthermore, human rights are frequently made subsidiary to US– Soviet conflict when the government backs repressive regimes. Why cannot those who support human rights in the United States move their government towards support of multilateral efforts to protect human rights? Partly it is because they lack the active support of domestically oriented human rights groups, who tend to place a national boundary around their efforts. These groups even use a different term, 'civil rights', which subtly supports the assumption that domestic rights are qualitatively different from rights of people elsewhere. Deeper understanding of how local people are directly involved in 'distant' human rights infringements (largely through their own national government and locally active corporations) would show how the nation-state paradigm prevents supporters of the same human rights from collaborating across boundaries against powerful interests whose power depends on maintenance of these boundaries.

Second, efforts of Third World countries to acquire economic self-determination have largely been resisted by the industrialised countries. In response, Third World leaders have been campaigning for 'global negotiations' that would lead to changes in the world economic structure, known as a New International Economic Order. The United States government, with support primarily from Britain and West Germany, has thus far prevented negotiations that the rest of the world is willing to accept. Obstruction of this process of peaceful change by the United States, in light of the growing gap between the rich and poor of the world, is sowing seeds of discontent and possible violence in the future. Nevertheless, few US citizens are even aware of the problem, and those that are aware seem unable to organise a movement for a change of policy. Yet many local people in the United States are struggling against the same centres of economic power as are Third World leaders. But they perceive unemployment, declining purchasing power, and the plight of the urban poor as strictly local, or at most national, problems. Perception of the degree to which these problems are affected by world systems would illuminate possibilities for networks that could bring new interests to bear in the formulation of US policy on global negotiations. Actually, many people in the United States have common interests with so-called Third World people. But the interests cannot be acted on as long as the nation-state paradigm prevents perception of them.

Third, the Third World is also pushing for a New International Information Order, largely because of concern that world information systems are mainly controlled by news gathering and dissemination organisations located in the industrialised countries. These organisations determine how everyone in the world (including the Third World) perceives both Third World countries and the issues in the proposed New International Economic Order. UNESCO has become the main arena of this conflict, which the United States media have for the most part ignored, except for criticism of proposals that might lead to control over the right of journalists to gather information in other countries. While such proposals are indeed reasonable subjects of concern, the fundamental problem is that newspapers and broadcasters who criticise them make little effort to inform their audience about the basic issue, which is the structure of world information systems.

Were the people of the United States informed about these systems, they might also begin to raise questions about their impact. For example, the evening half-hour TV news presented by the three commercial US broadcasting networks has tremendous impact on the way in which US people perceive and react to current world events. This image of the world is primarily shaped by what TV reporters in Washington decide is important, which is in turn affected by what the President decides is important, or what he does on that particular day. Typical of reporting is the fact that the so-called 'Iranian Hostage Crisis' was the first item on the TV evening news for month after month. Such state-centric reporting prevents the people from perceiving and putting into perspective the condition of billions of people with whom they share a common fate and some millions to whom they are directly tied by global economic and social systems. Should the US public come to really understand the issues in the proposed New International Information Order, many would find common cause with their Third World brethren.

Fourth, there is the problem of violence. Threats, insecurity, fighting and consequent suffering are the most immediate and severe of the issues. How would the direct participation of an increasing number of people, from an increasing number of smaller regions and cities, affect the likelihood of violence? The causes of such violence can be grouped into four categories, and it is clear that a more participative world society could reduce the damage done by each of them. They are: great power arms races, ethnic and nationality demands for autonomy, border disputes and rebellion among periphery peoples.

Arms races are made possible by social structures through which a small elite employ vast resources in 'solving' social problems, both domestic and external, by military power. Wider participation could, in the long term, fundamentally modify these social structures. The interests of people in each society could be projected into the world through a greater diversity of activities, using a much wider range of tools.

Demands for autonomy can only be tackled peacably if a more flexible approach is adopted, combined with a diminution of the hierarchical control of external relations by national governments. If the rigid nation-state model did not confine the thinking of national leaders, both they and the grass-roots leaders of ethnic groups would have many more options for devising external relationships for these groups that fulfil the needs of peoples desiring a greater measure of self-determination.

In the same way, border disputes could be defused. Borders in many parts of the world are now the foci for arms buildups that threaten violence. In most cases border areas have families, communities, regions and nations that are fragmented. The local people on both sides are hostages to competing interests in distant capitals. As local communities and regions develop competence for external relations that fulfil their needs, borders could become the hinges, rather than the barriers and battlegrounds of humanity.[9] More generally, periphery peoples throughout the world are rebelling against the unequal distribution of wealth and opportunity. Their fate is tragic, and it is compounded by the conversion of their struggle into a battleground for big power intervention. As the struggles develop and the foreign advisers and armies arrive, it is the lives, homes, farms and towns of the periphery people that suffer destruction. This continual pattern of disaster might be avoided as periphery people become more effective global strategists, steering away from involvement in conflicts among external centres of power, and acquiring the competence and opportunity for building politically effective relationships with other periphery peoples.

To summarise briefly, we have noted that our present world faces an array of problems that seem intractable. Instead of solving these problems, the nation-state system is producing higher and higher arms budgets, increasing arms trade, and creating ever more destructive weapons. It has been argued that the world society paradigm offers a more realistic approach to the world than approaches strongly influenced by nation-state ideology. There are widespread movements for decentralisation in the world. The world society paradigm helps us to see potential in smaller units that could make it possible for many more people to self-consciously participate in building world systems more responsive to human needs. The release of this potential could create new possibilities for dealing with world problems. Wider participation in world systems, through a diversity of avenues, would diminish emphasis on weapons of mass destruction as tools for policy implementation. The more decentralised kind of world society envisaged would also increase the competence of local people (such as those on borders and in periphery areas) to handle their own relations with world systems. They would in this way avoid involvement in big power conflicts. This would contribute to the decline of big power domination of the world and to the erosion of the ideology that declares the inevitability of this domination.

NOTES

1 A prominent exception is Galtung (1980b, p. 421) who writes: *'The basic focus of this book is the human individual, in a social setting, domestically and globally'* (Galtung's emphasis).

2 The IGO and INGO figures are taken from the *Yearbook of International Organisations* (Brussels: International Union on International Associations, 1981) p. 1981.

3 For a trenchant analysis of the 'mythical qualities' of the concept 'state' and the problems this has created for empirical analysis, see Easton (1953), pp. 106–15.

4 Lindblom (1977) has a probing analysis of these issues, concluding: 'It has been a curious feature of democratic thought that it has not faced up to the private corporation as a peculiar organisation in an ostensible democracy. . . . The large private corporation fits oddly into democratic theory and vision. Indeed, it does not fit' (p. 356).

5 One rich source for an array of viewpoints on 'a new development strategy' that takes into account 'local space, national space and global space' is *IFDA Dossier*, published by the International Foundation for Development Alternatives, Nyon, Switzerland, since 1978. See especially, Vol. 17, May/June 1980.

6 For a systematic overview of self-determination in the twentieth century, see Ronen (1979). His approach is consistent with Burton's: 'The quest for self-determination, at its core, is not a national or any other group aspiration, but the aspiration of the individual human being to the vague notions of "freedom" and "the good life"' (p. 9).

7 For a provocative treatment of these tendencies see Henderson (1981).

8 This experience is more extensively reported in Alger (1977, 1978, 1981).

9 For a provocative discussion of this point see Strassoldo and Gubert, in Strassoldo (1973). The term 'hinge' is borrowed from this work, p. 39.

9 Problem-Solving Workshops: The Role of Scholarship in Conflict Resolution

Margot Light

There is perhaps one good that has come of the increasing destructive capacity of nuclear weapons. No matter where people are located on the political spectrum, no matter to which school of international thought scholars belong or under which ideology they function, there are very few who believe that the benefits gained by nuclear conflict could outweigh the costs that would be incurred. In spite of talk of nuclear war – fighting capacity, of negotiating from strength, of launch on warning, there is this one shared value. There is also an increasing recognition of the danger of escalation from any level of international conflict, particularly when this conflict involves nuclear powers or their client states or allies. This implies general acceptance that violent conflict should be avoided and that where it exists, it should be managed in such a way that it is brought to an end as soon as possible.

There is, then, no difference of opinion about the desired end or about the optimal condition of world society: peace on earth and goodwill to all men has been a value articulated by all statesmen and women from East and West, North and South from time immemorial. It remains a dominant value. Where there are differences is in the means suggested to bring about this state of affairs, in the analysis of conflict and in the way in which it is believed that conflict can be resolved. Many scholars who adhere to the world society paradigm believe that orthodox views and methods have failed. This chapter will examine the innovative methods of resolution which have been suggested and undertaken to overcome these failures.

CHANGES IN THE INTERNATIONAL SYSTEM

The changes that have taken place in the international political system have been commented on by most of the contributors to this book. Yet the institutions of the system and the theories explaining political behaviour have, in many cases, lagged behind the changes. The mismatch between international reality and the means of dealing with it, particularly the means of managing change, is in itself a contributory cause of the conflicts which exist in the system.

In a world of monarchs and sovereigns, of armies and diplomacy, international conflicts were often based on the desire for dynastic and territorial aggrandisement. The mechanisms which were invented for producing order and handling conflicts were international law, alliances and deterrence. When the mechanisms failed, the result was war. Wars ended in peace settlements which, by imposing losses on the vanquished, produced new conflicts which led to new wars. Alliances were formed, power configurations changed, but the outlines of the system remained the same. The costs of war rose as the weapons of war were improved, but the costs that states were prepared to incur also rose. War remained the ultimate coercive instrument, a legitimate means of state policy.

Gradually rules were evolved, some tacit, others explicit, about the conduct of war. There was general acceptance that the international system worked best as a balance of power system so that there was some co-operation in preventing one state from becoming strong enough to overturn the balance. Balance of power (or of terror in the nuclear age) remains the dominant metaphor in our age. It is the model most often used for purposes of analysis but it also has concrete reality in that it is the state of affairs for which practitioners strive. The order-producing and conflict managing mechanisms of the balance of power system remain virtually unchanged. Even those institutions, like the United Nations, which were established to produce a collective security system, tend to operate on balance of power principles.

But new phenomena and new values have long existed within the international system. Industrialisation began a process of mass participation and communication which led to the politicisation of the masses. The birth of nationalism produced the belief that the state should be an instrument to serve the needs of the people rather than an institution to serve the needs of the sovereign. It became increasingly clear that these needs were not identical. As communication improved and the ideas of nationalism spread, it became necessary for sovereigns and governments to espouse at least some of the popular needs and values.

These needs have themselves undergone change. Democracy, participation and technological progress have produced demands for more democracy, more participation and more progress. There are certain individual needs which must be satisfied if society is to be just and peaceable.[1] The revolution of rising expectations is not only the hope for a better material life – it is also the demand for a more participatory life, for more autonomy and, paradoxically, for a life in which the state becomes more and more involved in what was previously considered the private domain. Communication and the growth of transactions within and between states have ensured that this revolution is universal. They have also damaged the traditional concept of a world of impenetrable billiard-ball-like states. There is a growing realisation that interactions between states occur at many levels, that states are not the only actors in the international system, that economic interdependence makes states increasingly vulnerable to conditions in other states and that the domestic politics in one state can cause conflict and affect the international system as much as its foreign policy can.

CONFLICT IN WORLD SOCIETY

These changes have had important consequences for the kinds of conflict which arise in modern society and the ways in which they need to be handled. Firstly, the changes in popular demands mean that the load on governments has increased. Policy-making becomes increasingly complex when the state has to occupy itself both with its traditional concerns of law and order and diplomacy and with attempts to meet new welfare demands. Secondly, conflicts tend to be inter-connected and complex. The result is that existing institutions are often inadequate to deal with them. Finally, since it is as much problems which originate within states which cause conflict as it is traditional inter-state relations, conflict management institutions can no longer afford to operate only at an inter-governmental level.

The traditional view of society holds that order exists within society because there is a common interest in avoiding disorder and a set of rules which explains what orderly behaviour is. In international society there is a similar common interest and an analogous set of rules (Bull, 1977). Within states governments control the means of coercion and this enables them to impose when necessary. Indeed, it is the prime function of government to ensure order and protect the security of its citizens. The rules are obeyed because of an implicit or explicit threat that infringement will be punished. The problem at the level of international society is that there is no legitimate source of coercion. This in part explains why wars occur.

Astute diplomacy often enables the adjustment of the inevitable conflicting state interests which arise when governments act 'to keep power, to increase power or to demonstrate power' (Morgenthau, 1967, p. 36), the only policy options recognised by power theorists. However, when diplomacy fails, war is the likely result. War brings conflict to an end, the outcome is decided by force of arms and the victor dictates terms which the vanquished is forced to accept. More often there is intervention by some 'third party' before total defeat, or even before the conflict has escalated to violence. This intervention may take the form of mediation, in which case bargaining takes place and a compromise is reached, or of arbitration, after which a legal solution is offered with the threat of negative sanctions in the case of non-compliance.[2] At the nuclear superpower level, conflict exists but remains non-violent because of a mutual certainty that instantaneous annihilation will follow any act which infringes the interests of the other nuclear superpower. In all cases, it is the threat or the use of coercion which terminates conflict. The fact that conflicts which are terminated in this way tend to recur can be attributed partly to the incurably, unfortunately aggressive nature of mankind, and partly to the objective nature of that kind of conflict which arises when state interests are mutually exclusive.

Adherents of the world society paradigm would object to four main premises of this argument: that order is based on the threat or the use of coercion; that power is the only motivating force of international behaviour; that legality is the basis of societal relationships; and that conflict termination by force or arms or by imposed solution is the best or the only way to manage conflict. The counter-argument is based on the main tenet of the world society paradigm – the concept of legitimacy.

LEGITIMACY

An important distinction is made in the world society paradigm between legality and legitimacy. Legal status can be obtained by force – governments which come to power by provoking civil unrest or through *coups d'état* are often accorded *de jure* recognition by other states. Even if legal status has been obtained by due process, for example through democratic elections, it is sometimes retained by explicit or implicit force. Legally elected governments which have lost the support of the majority of their citizens but remain in power are an example. It is almost certain that conflict will occur sooner or later when legal status occurs in the absence of legitimacy. Legitimised authority rests upon the support of those over whom it is exercised. It does not rely on threat or coercion. To the extent that governments reflect the values and satisfy the needs and demands of those over whom they exercise authority, they will be legitimised. Where they cease to do so and come to rely on their control over the means of coercion, they may continue to be legal, but they will no longer be legitimised. A stable and peaceful domestic polity is indicative of a legitimised regime, a society in which there are reciprocal relationships resting on an acceptance of roles. To some extent legitimacy depends upon level of participation – clearly, participating in the structures and processes of government encourages placing a value on those structures and processes. But a high level of legitimacy can be found even when there is little popular participation, if there is acceptance of the situation (Burton, 1968, pp. 40–50). This acceptance, together with the absence of knowledge or consciousness, explains the happy slave phenomenon where subordinated groups appear to accept their status with tranquillity.

A more important influence on the level of legitimacy is the ability of authorities to satisfy needs and demands and, in periods of rapid change, to respond to changes in demand arising out of changed values and circumstances. Fundamental to a high level of legitimacy is a congruence between the values of society and the values of institutions which have authority within society:

wherever there is a difference between systemic interests, on the one hand, and the goals and values of authorities, on the other, there is . . . a reduced level of social legitimisation (Burton, 1968, p. 47).

It is legitimacy which is the basis of order in society; the acceptance of roles, rather than the threat or use of coercion. A regime which relies entirely on coercion is an illegitimate regime.

At the international level, legitimacy is significant in part because domestic conflict so often spills over into international conflict. Intervening in conflict on behalf of non-legitimised authorities not only runs counter to fundamental respect for human rights, it is also likely to be unsuccessful in the long run. More importantly, international institutions and processes also have to pass the test of legitimacy. Those which do not reflect and satisfy international needs and demands will, like national institutions, no longer be legitimised. They will either cease to be used – the reluctance of states to take conflicts to the International Court of Justice is a case in point – or the solutions which they produce for handling conflict will be ineffectual or will break down. In any case, insofar as those solutions are based upon the threat or the use of coercion, the solutions themselves will not be perceived to be legitimised by those on whom they are imposed. The conflict will be settled rather than resolved.

CONFLICT RESOLUTION

It will be clear from the above that conflict settlement is defined as the imposition of solutions on the conflicting parties by coercion or by other kinds of pressure, through force of one side's arms or by the decision of a mediating party. Whether it is judicial settlement, arbitration, mediation, conciliation or face-to-face bargaining, the amount of effective participation by the parties is likely to be minimal.[3] The result is that the causes of the conflict are not dealt with adequately and that neither, or only one, of the conflicting parties are satisfied by the outcome which at best will be a compromise. To a large extent this is caused by the fact that power politics, the dominant political theory, encourages bargaining behaviour. Disputes are perceived to be conflicts of interest in which there can be only one 'winner' and the win of one side is equal to the loss of the other. This is why a settlement is likely to leave a lingering sense of grievance in one side with consequent potential for further conflict at some later stage.

The world society paradigm suggests that conflict resolution offers a more viable outcome to conflict, because it converts the conflict into a shared problem, setting up a process in which both sides participate equally in finding solutions which are acceptable to both and which, therefore, are self-sustaining. Because the solutions are agreed by both sides, there is no need for coercion from either side or from a third party – the resolution will be legitimised because it will be valued by both parties to the dispute. The difficulty in bringing about a resolution of conflict 'is the problem of transforming a situation that appears to be a power bargaining or win-lose one, into a problem-solving one in which both sides can gain' (Burton, 1972b, p. 153). It is a procedure which has been used successfully in small group disputes and in matrimonial conflict. The early attempts to apply it to international conflict came about almost by accident – a workshop between parties to a dispute and a panel of academics, intended primarily as an academic exercise with a particular and limited research purpose, seemed to suggest a technique for resolving conflict (Burton, 1969, pp. ix–xvii). This particular 'controlled communication' and other problem-solving workshops will be described in more detail below.

The methods used in conflict resolution – the bringing together of disputing parties with a panel of professional conflict analysts in a forum which does not apportion blame and which commits the parties to no more than a mutual exploration of their relations – rely on the most significant difference between a realist or power political view of international politics and the world society paradigm. It is the belief that power is no longer the most important motivating force and organising principle of politics at any level, except insofar as power politicians and theorists perceive it to be so and therefore act to make it so. It is nearly twenty years since John Burton maintained that:

There is reason to believe . . . first, that policies of power politics are ultimately destructive of security, and second, that they are self-creating in that they create the conditions which demand them (1965, p. 246).

The self-fulfilling nature of power politics has not changed. It is when world society is viewed as a complex 'cobweb' of overlapping functional systems, when the role of authorities is perceived to be the satisfaction of human needs, when it is accepted that human needs and values are more important than institutional needs and values, when it is realised that most human aspirations, and by extension, state aspirations, are for goods that exist in unlimited supply rather than for scarce resources that conflict can be resolved.

The debate about the objective or subjective nature of conflict is an integral part of the debate between realists and behaviouralists and post-behaviouralists, as well as between Marxists and non-Marxists.[4] But if, as has been argued convincingly earlier in this book (Chapter 3), reality is less important than perception, it matters little whether the conditions creating conflict are in the real world or in the mind. What is more important is understanding and correcting the misperceptions that are common in conflict situations, some of which have been described in Chapter 6. The difficulty is that it is precisely in conflict situations that disputants are most prone to believe that the problems of their opponents are subjective, while their own are objective, created by outside forces. When conflicting parties begin to recognise the subjective element in their own perception, the possibility of a solution begins to appear.[5] It is here that third parties have a positive role to play.

THE THIRD PARTY

There is nothing innovative in the involvement of intermediaries in disputes at all levels of society. The intervention may come about because one or both of the conflicting parties wishes to terminate the conflict and requires a go-between or the third party may initiate the intervention. Bilateral face-to-face contact is difficult between disputants who are pursuing acrimonious policies towards one another. The activities of an intermediary facilitates the communication which must take place if any form of settlement is to be reached.

The range of people and institutions which have intervened in international conflict is large – from prestigious individuals to international organisations like the United Nations, the International Committee of the Red Cross or the World Council of Churches (Mitchell, 1981a, pp. 280–91). It is often believed that successful mediators possess special gifts and a particular kind of personality. Mediation is thought to be an art which must succeed if recalcitrant disputants will only be 'sensible'. In historical practice, international mediators have often been representatives of governments or international organisations which have an interest in the outcome of the conflict and which possess the power to ensure that the compromise which is reached is honoured by both sides. In the theoretical studies which have been done on mediation, these characteristics are not considered salient. In a study of third parties in international crises, Young (1967, pp. 80–90) maintains that intermediaries should be independent, particularly in relation to the parties to the dispute, that they should have prestige and authority in the eyes of the disputants, that they should be knowledgeable, skilful and flexible and that they should have access to the technological resources and services necessary to be able to conduct the mediation process without relying on either party. The ideal characteristics of third parties in intra-societal conflict were described by Walton (1969, p. 293) as a high level of professional expertise about the relevant social structures and processes, low power to enforce a settlement but a high level of services and competence to assist the implementation of a solution, a high level of control over the setting and procedures, a low level of direct interest in the outcome of the conflict and moderate knowledge of the issues in dispute and of the relevant background factors. Traditional international mediators frequently fail to satisfy Walton's criteria because they are rarely disinterested in the outcome and often impose their own values and preferred outcomes on the parties.

In conflict resolution the role of the third party is neither to offer potential solutions nor to ensure that compromises will be honoured. A conflict will only be resolved if the parties themselves, equally and mutually, arrive at their own solutions. The function of the third party is to create the conditions in which the disputants can come to view their conflict as a problem. They attempt to create these conditions by acting as a catalyst, 'injecting into the talks new ideas, not about the present dispute, but scientific concepts of some generality about the basis of conflict, its origins and processes' (de Reuck, 1974, p. 69), so that this information can be used by the parties in their analysis of their dispute. The third party must therefore have specialised knowledge about conflict theory rather than about the particular conflict to be resolved. Indeed, it is believed by some groups who have used the technique that 'the less, and not the more, the third party knows in advance of the "facts" of the situation to be approached, the better. He does not then project his own viewpoints, or select data and make assessments on the basis of his own experiences and prejudices' (Burton, 1972a, p. 18).[7] Professional expertise in a field relevant to the analysis of conflict must be combined with expertise in conducting group interactions, a reputation for neutrality in respect of the conflict,[8] and the ability to respect the confidential nature of the conflict resolution process.

Third parties who possess these qualities will be legitimised in the eyes of the disputants by their expertise. They will not require access to power or the prestige of high diplomatic status. The aim of the contributions made by these professionals is the establishment of rapport and better communication between the parties and an improved understanding of the issues, the provision of a setting which promotes effective deliberation on matters of substance and, as a by-product, the learning of technical skills of communication. Their role is active and participatory, but any terms or solutions which emerge must be generated by the participants themselves (UNITAR, 1970, p. 21). One commentator has described the role of the third party as 'supportive neutrality' (Banks, forthcoming, p. 33).

PROBLEM-SOLVING WORKSHOPS[9]

On a practical level, the number of representatives from each party taking part in a problem-solving workshop needs to be kept to a minimum. The process requires intensive group interaction which is less likely to occur if the group is unwieldy. The optimum number is probably three members. It is important that the venue is neutral both in respect of geography and in respect of funding and the immediate physical location of the meetings. From a procedural point of view, seating should not be seen to favour or confer status on either of the parties, or on the panel. In practice, a long table with the chairman at the centre of one of the long sides and with panel members rather than disputants adjacent to him seems to work best.

The sessions begin with a short word of welcome and assurances from the chairman that the procedures will be confidential. Each participant is then asked to introduce him or herself and his or her field of work. This ensures that everyone has an early opportunity to talk. The chief representative of each side is then asked to present his party's view of the conflict. Panel members may follow this presentation with questions to elicit information but there is no discussion or interruption at this stage. In the next phase the panel discusses the main issues which have emerged from the presentations by the parties. The panel introduces analytic reformulations of various aspects of the conflict, using other well known conflicts to provide concrete examples of the phenomena which they are explaining. In the third stage of the workshop the parties begin to discuss substantive issues and hopefully, possible solutions begin to emerge.

Typically, the parties will address the panel in the first stage, avoiding talking or even looking at one another. In the second stage they will gradually begin to adopt analytical roles and will, from time to time, respond to one another. In the third phase 'the group attains a fitful and fragile integration, sufficient however for the parties to collaborate in joint problem-solving' (de Reuck, 1983, p. 28). It may take several weeks to reach the third stage, or it may take several workshops. Panelists who have participated in problem-solving workshops do not minimise the difficulty of reaching this stage or, having reached it, of finding practical and practicable solutions to problems which often seem intractable. However, they stress that 'analysis offers the parties not only the intellectual tools for re-interpreting the conflictual relationship between them, but also the immediate experience of joint co-operation in problem-solving' (de Reuck, 1983, p. 31).

One of the major difficulties in initiating contact between parties to an international dispute is their fear that communication with the opponent will be seen as a sign of weakness or as the granting of recognition. An equally prevalent fear is that participation in the process will commit them in advance to any compromise outcome which may result. Those who employ conflict resolution allay these anxieties by making it clear that the disputants are invited on a 'no fault' basis without any commitment except the commitment to participate in the analysis of the conflict. There can be no question of recognition or of interpretations of weakness, since the discussions are private. There is no public knowledge that they are taking place. Honouring the confidential nature of the exercise is vital to any future attempts to resolve that or any other conflict. In spite of the resulting limitations on publicity, there are a few detailed accounts of problem-solving workshops published either with the explicit consent of the participants or without mentioning who they are.[10] Called by various names and with slightly different aims, these workshops have certain important assumptions and features in common.

The goal of all problem-solving workshops is conflict resolution rather than settlement. Resolution can only take place if the participants reinterpret their conflict as a problem to be solved rather than a fight to be won. In effect, they must cease perceiving their differences in terms of a zero-sum game, in which the win of one side equals the loss of the other. Instead they must begin to view their mutual problem as a positive-sum game in which both sides can gain from collaborative problem-solving. This might involve exploring and developing superordinate goals. It certainly requires recognition of the subjective elements in the interpretations of both sides of the conflict. But resolution does not rely upon an acceptance of the 'rights' of the opponent nor upon a romantic appeal to some innate sense of justice. Resolution will come about because of self-interest, based on the realisation that the costs of continuing the conflict outweigh the benefits to be gained by finding a solution. In all problem-solving workshops it is the parties themselves that suggest solutions. The role of the third party is passive in respect of possible outcomes to the particular conflict, but active and interested in a resolution (Hill, 1982, p. 118). When communication between the parties becomes difficult, regressing to the accusatory, legalistic atmosphere which characterises initial face-to-face communication between disputants, the third party leads 'a retreat back to the analytical framework' (de Reuck, 1974, p. 67).

The problem-solving workshops which have been described in the literature have been held in neutral settings removed from the political environment of the disputants. Academic sponsorship has ensured that the third party is seen to be disinterested in particular outcomes and has fostered alternative norms of behaviour to counteract conflict norms (Kelman and Cohen, 1979, p. 289). An informal atmosphere and a relatively unstructured agenda have

been used to encourage direct communication between the conflicting parties and to give 'an impetus to move away from a rigid
reiteration of official positions and from efforts to justify their own
sides and score points . . . and instead to absorb new information,
explore new ideas, revise their perceptions, reassess their attitudes,
and engage in a process of creative problem-solving' (Kelman, 1972,
p. 177).

There are differences in the participants who have been invited to
workshops. The Fermeda workshop was attended by academics with
government approval but not representing governments (Doob,
1970, p. 13). Government representatives were sent to the first
London workshop and representatives of national groups to the
second. The Harvard group believe that the ideal participants are
'individuals who are highly influential within their respective
communities, but are not themselves in policy-making positions'
(Kelman and Cohen, 1979, p. 289). In fact, deciding whom to invite is
one of the thorniest analytical problems in setting up a workshop.
Since conflicts almost always occur at more than one level, multi-
level participation is required. However, there is an optimal size for
workshops and a limit to the number of people who can participate.
Moreover, there are often splits within parties to a conflict. Deciding
who the parties are to a conflict is, in fact, an integral part of the
analysis of the conflict. Ideally, it is the disputants themselves who
should define the parties as well as the issues.

Differences in the status of invited participants reflects differences
in the concept of the role of the workshop. The Centre for the
Analysis of Conflict envisages a closer link to international and
national political processes than the Yale Group which, like the
Harvard Group, places more stress on social interaction and the
analysis of group processes. The latter groups perceive problem-
solving workshops as a preparation for diplomatic negotiation and as
an adjunct to traditional techniques. Burton views the technique as a
replacement for conventional procedures, a response to the apparent
failure of traditional institutions. His approach is essentially
normative and he pleads for the institutionalisation of problem-
solving as a 'second track', running parallel to power policies and
procedures, 'hopefully becoming more and more significant and
finally becoming the dominant track' (Burton, 1982a, p. 107).

Since the workshops which have been reported have been
conducted by academics who have had an explicit research interest
and since the confidential nature of the exercise places limitations on
the substantive issues which can be reported, it is not surprising that

more is known about the theoretical and procedural knowledge which has been gained from these workshops than about the actual outcomes. Participants and researchers alike found that the notion that conflict is primarily subjective is supported by the workshops. The perceptual problems and distortions which were described in Chapter 6 were observed in action and were to some extent corrected in the workshop atmosphere. While there is no agreement on the ideal participants, there is general acceptance that an academic setting, unstructured discussions and a non-coercive third party make the consideration of innovative solutions possible and encourage an alternative set of behavioural norms (Hill, 1982, p. 132). It is generally believed that problem-solving workshops produce changes in attitude among the participants, but there is some disagreement on the extent to which the 're-entry' problem prevents these changes from being transferred to the policy process. Even if the changes are maintained in the participants themselves, their new perceptions and proposals might be met with hostility on their return to the real world. Burton maintains that the closer the participants are to official policy-makers, the less severe will be the re-entry problem, while Kelman claims that participants who are further removed from the locus of decision making will be more open to change and will be better able to retain the change.[11]

In spite of the scantiness of substantive conclusions which have emerged from the workshops which have dealt with international and communal conflicts, the ideas of conflict analysis and resolution appear to be gaining ground. While they have not yet achieved Burton's ideal of 'supplanting conventional policy' (1982a, p. 107), peacemaking rather than peacekeeping is being espoused by a number of political practitioners as well as by concerned laypeople and academics.[12] There are attempts to institutionalise the processes and train specialists in the techniques so as to provide a constant pool of third parties who can be approached by disputants before conflicts escalate to the level of overt violence or during a violent conflict. Two recently proposed institutions, the International Facilitating Service and the Foundation for International Conciliation, envisage international institutions free from the control of any government. The former will combine problem-solving with research and a permanent seminar in which a rotating series of scholars participate in analysing the international situation and particular international crises.

CONCLUSION

Problem-solving and conflict resolution do not imply the elimination of conflict from society. It is accepted by those who adhere to the world society paradigm that conflict is endemic to the human condition. Indeed, it is difficult to envisage how change could take place if there was no conflict. The problem is to minimise the destructive potential and maximise the constructive consequences of conflict. What is required is the management of change, not its elimination.

Problem-solving is neither a new philosophy, nor a new theory of international relations. It is based on the ideas of the world society paradigm which differs from orthodoxy only by stressing different aspects of the same world. The paradigm maintains that healthy political relations are build upon the satisfaction of human needs and legitimised relationships rather than on the knowledge that coercion will be used to enforce conformity. It is believed that participation and consensus will contribute to a sound polity. Since world society contains many systems, there are many cross-cutting conflicts within world society. These cross-cutting conflicts in some measure serve to consolidate world society. They should therefore prevent any one conflict from getting out of hand. If conflict is subjective, there is nothing in principle which makes war necessary, particularly since values like security, a frequent cause of conflict, are not in short supply. Conflict conditions have been made by the parties themselves and they can unmake them. It is a matter of policy, not of divine will nor of aggressive human nature. Conflict resolution is not based on wishful thinking or on a restructured view of human nature – it is a matter of enlightened self-interest.

NOTES

1 For a discussion of the nature of these needs, see Burton (1979, pp. 55–84).
2 For a full discussion of the termination of conflict, see Mitchell (1981b, pp. 165–217).
3 Pat Lowry, Chairman of the Advisory, Conciliation and Arbitration Service, defines *conciliation* as the process through which employers and trade unions in dispute are helped by a neutral and independent third party to reach mutually acceptable settlements. The two parties themselves are responsible for the agreements reached. *Arbitration* is the process by which one or more impartial persons are invited to make a

decision or an award which the disputing parties undertake in advance to accept. In *mediation* the independent mediator both conciliates and makes formal recommendations which, although the parties are not committed to them, may later be accepted as they provide the basis for further negotiations leading to a settlement (*The Times*, 3 December 1982, p. 13). For a taxonomy of the range of settlement outcomes in international conflict, see Mitchell (1981a, pp. 4–6).

4 See Mitchell (1981a, pp. 12–42) for a detailed discussion.

5 For the way in which assumptions about the nature of conflict influence possible outcomes, see Mitchell (1981a, pp. 5–10).

6 This may involve the intermediary in many thousands of miles of weary travel, a technique made fashionable by Kissinger in the Middle East, and repeated by Haig in his attempt to mediate between Britain and Argentina.

7 This view of the disadvantages of area specialists in conflict resolution is not universal. See UNITAR (1970, pp. 14–15).

8 The need for neutrality does not imply a belief in the ability of professional conflict analysts to be value-free. But it is essential that they make no judgements on the rightness or wrongness of either disputant or on any outcome which may be discussed.

9 I am particularly indebted to Tony de Reuck for allowing me the use of published and unpublished materials to enable me to write this section.

10 See, for example, Burton (1969; 1972a); Cohen, Kelman, Miller and Smith (1977); de Reuck (1974); Doob (1970); Doob and Stevens (1969); Kelman (1972); Kelman and Cohen (1979); Levi and Benjamin (1977). UNITAR (1970) examines two early exercises and Hill (1982) is an excellent survey and evaluation of problem-solving in international conflict.

11 For a detailed discussion of the re-entry problem see Kelman (1972, pp. 195–200) and Mitchell (1981a, pp. 144–50).

12 Amongst others, former President Carter has recently set up an institute to study conflict and the Carnegie Corporation is reported to be establishing a joint Soviet–American search for ways to avoid crises.

10 Dealing with Terrorism: Deterrence and the Search for an Alternative Model

Helen Purkitt

Since the 1960s terrorism has been widely perceived as an increasingly important international problem. There are three reasons for this. First, terrorism is a particularly odious form of political violence. Second, its impact affects all of us, by making us feel vulnerable as potential victims of both near and remote conflicts. Third, terrorist threats are diverse, which makes them difficult to understand.[1] This diversity stems from the multitude of reasons for terrorist acts, and the wide variety of groups involved. In spite of this diversity, counter-terrorist responses by governments tend to share a common logic which may be characterised as containment, control and deterrence.[2] While this logic sometimes proves satisfactory, in many critical situations it fails to solve the problem.

Containment, control and deterrence cannot always solve the problem because there are a variety of root causes, goals, means and impacts of terrorist activities, and they vary across groups, situations and conditions. By ignoring such variations, policy makers are able to apply a relatively simple rule, maximising rather than optimising.[3] This involves raising the cost to the terrorists by increasing both the risk of punishment and its severity. The main disadvantage of using this rule is that while it may put an end to an episode it does not deal with the full set of underlying issues. Application of the rule does not lead to the development of preventive policies; once the immediate threat is contained, the underlying problems are forgotten.

To understand the nature and shortcomings of containment, control and deterrence as a general response to terrorism, the issue is approached here through a threefold discussion. First, why is attention usually focused almost exclusively on the act of terrorism itself? Second, is deterrence an appropriate strategy? And third, is an alternative strategy available? Given the complexity and uncertainty of some terrorist threats, policy makers really do need to follow a flexible, adaptive and open-ended decision making mode. They also need a specific optimising strategy, although none can be recommended until better understanding is available. But it is clear that any which is adopted should rest upon three criteria for assessing its effectiveness: the response to terrorism must be *timely*, *reliable*, and *valid*. It is also clear that terrorist threats which have a political basis, reflecting widely shared perceptions of important and legitimate grievances, together with inadequate channels for redress of those grievances, are not likely to be solved over time by a deterrence strategy.

TERRORISM: THE CONVENTIONAL RESPONSE

Following Burton's (1979) insight that the conventional view of terrorism is to treat it as a special type of deviant behaviour, it can be seen that governmental response strategies for coping with terrorist challenges are similar to those used to contain, control and deter deviants at a number of levels of world society.[4] Crime, terrorism and international aggression are all conventionally viewed as abnormal, unacceptable and illegal forms of behaviour. The principal problem in coping with them is to contain the immediate threat and to deter future acts by punishing apprehended deviants. Authorities attempt to increase the risks and costs to would-be terrorists by hardening targets and when possible by administering severe and certain punishment.

This general response strategy is the same as that used by police and neighbourhood citizen groups who patrol their area in an effort to cut down crime. It is also, of course, the rationale for increased national defense expenditures and for the tactic of demonstrating national power when challenged by a would-be international aggressor. In all these cases, the goal is to control behaviour by increasing the costs and risks and by reducing the perceived benefits to would-be deviants. Thus, control, containment and deterrence are key ideas involved in authoritative responses to deviance at a number of levels in world society.

This approach, however, tends to ignore the general issue of deviance in the absence of an immediate threat. The characteristic governmental response to a terrorist threat, as with any policy crisis, focuses primary attention on the short-term problem of control and the medium-term problem of deterring future terrorist acts. Noticeably absent from the current repertoire of governmental responses is an emphasis on longer term prevention measures designed to deal with the root causes of political terrorism (Burton, 1979, pp. 3–34; Pierre, 1976). Instead, terrorism comes into focus only when it 'emerges' as a policy crisis requiring an immediate response. At this point, governments try to control the threat before them by instituting crisis management procedures.

Reliance on short-term coercive measures rather than longer term preventive measures is understandable. Political terrorism poses a fundamental challenge both to the legitimacy of authorities, and to the credibility of their claims to be able to protect their citizens. Moreover, because terrorism is intended to produce fear and intimidation by its deliberate disregard of moral and legal norms, and by its violence against symbolic and innocent targets, it produces strong pressures for coercive responses. However, the fact that many national decision makers have increasingly relied on similar coercive policies, to cope with a variety of terrorist threats in very different political contexts, suggests the need to assess their general effectiveness. Terrorism, after all, is neither new nor rare. Thus, we may consider the experience of the past decade in evaluating the effectiveness of approaches designed to control terrorism by short-term containment and longer term deterrence.

The evidence seems to indicate that short-term security measures designed to harden targets by limiting access and increasing the cost to a potential terrorist often produce immediate and positive results.[5] Thus, increased security efforts can be successful in reducing the total level of particular types of terrorism. In the case of skyjackings, mandatory, screening and surveillance procedures produced an immediate drop in the total incidence, and appear to have been a primary factor in their longer term decline. The success of target hardening measures is evident from the aggregate statistics. The effectiveness of US security measures during the 1970s illustrates the general trend in terms of hijackings. As Farrell and Edsall note (1981, pp. 130–5), from 1960 to 1967 there were only nine attempted or successful hijackings on US registered aircraft. From 1968–1972 the number jumped to 134 as hijackings became a favoured terrorist tactic. From 1973–79 the number fell to thirty-four and only one of the seventeen hijackings on US air carriers during 1978–9 was labelled terrorist. Despite the emphasis placed by some experts on other deterrence measures (for example, the sky marshall programme instituted in 1970, and various international conventions and agreements) most airport security personnel attribute the decline primarily to mandatory screenings. Worldwide, the statistics indicate that by 1975 extraordinary means were required to seize an aircraft at most airports.

However, aggregate statistics (Jenkins, 1980) also indicate that terrorists have been adept at shifting targets and tactics in response to the increase in security measures and the hardening of targets. For example, since the mid-1970s there has been an increase in embassy stormings, especially at the embassies of states already prone to other forms of terrorist incident: the USA, United Kingdom, West Germany, and France. Although extensive security precautions were taken at these embassies, they did not prevent the takeover of the American embassy in Tehran in 1979, or the Dominican Republic embassy in Bogata and the Iranian embassy in London in 1980.

While target hardening measures, then, can be successful in limiting the total level of particular terrorist incidents, there is no evidence that the highly committed political terrorist will be deterred by such measures. Thus, target hardening does have the advantage of increasing the risk and thereby driving out the less committed terrorists. But it also has the disadvantage of holding out the false promise of being an effective counterfoil to terrorism in general. Moreover, the cost of hardening all targets, like the cost of hardening entire neighbourhoods against burglaries, is prohibitive.

Since target hardening is only a partial solution, a number of other deterrent measures have also been adopted by states. Typical containment measures adopted over the past decade include: increased anti-terrorist tactical and intelligence capabilities; expanded scope and jurisdiction of anti-terrorist legislation; and increased legal sanctions designed to delegitimise terrorism by focussing public attention on the criminal nature of terrorist activities. Deterrence thinking has also been the primary rationale underlying increasingly hardline, no-concession government policies in incidents involving hostages. Efforts to ensure punishment of apprehended terrorists have also been stepped up, even though the aggregate statistics do not support the proposition that such an approach necessarily serves as a deterrent in either the short or the long term for the committed terrorist.[6]

Governmental efforts to control terrorism, like efforts to control crime, appear to vary widely in effectiveness at different times and in different circumstances.[7] Many empirical studies of the impact of terrorism suggest that the success of governmental anti-terrorist activities in containing terrorism is mediated by a variety of factors related to internal political factors.[8] In the medium-to-long run, success appears to depend on the perceptions of the general public and in particular of the perceived reference group(s) of the terrorists.[9] While generalisations are difficult, it appears that efforts at control must be seen as *timely*, *reliable*, and *valid* by significant groups in the public, including the perceived reference group of the terrorists, in order for the policies to succeed. Both empirical evidence of the importance of political factors in determining the success of specific governmental anti-terrorist programmes, and a large body of sociological literature, have indicated that the deterrent value of severe and certain punishment is highly variable across specific types of crimes and social situations. Despite this, authorities generally continue to rely on analogies to the control of crime, and to the success of military deterrence, to justify their anti-terrorist policies.

This tendency is understandable since the proposition that a threat of severe and certain punishment is both a necessary and sufficient condition for successful deterrence is a generally accepted proposition at all levels of world society (Burton, 1979, pp. 85–9; Morgan, 1977, pp. 17–24). Within nation-states, this logic is reflected in the law-and-order proposition that crime can be deterred by increasing both the severity and certainty of punishment for criminals. In international relations this proposition is expressed as a deterrent model which predicts successful deterrence if defenders can persuade a would-be aggressor with a high degree of certainty that the costs and risks of intended actions are greater than the perceived benefits (George and Smoke, 1974, pp. 48–60).

Superpower conflict represents the simplest form of deterrence, involving the smallest degree of uncertainty about the probability of punishment. It is the 'purest' form of contingent threat since it involves the 'worst case' of total nuclear war. Deterrence at this level is an explicit, well-developed theory which has been the basis for many national defence policies. Because the theory has been applied with apparent success to prevent the escalation of strategic superpower conflicts, there is a tendency to generalise the necessary and sufficient conditions for successful strategic deterrence to conflicts at other levels of world society (George and Smoke, 1974, pp. 48–60; Burton, 1979, p. 88).

But the logic of superpower strategic deterrence is based on certain simplifying assumptions and conditions which may not be applicable to conflicts at other levels of world society. It assumes a simple conflict between two roughly equal national powers. Threats to the status quo can only arise from a single identifiable adversary. It is assumed that both actors use a similar rational decision making calculus in order to maximise expected costs, benefits and risks, and that both parties accept common well-defined limits on the extent to which either side will attempt to maximise unilateral gains.

These assumptions are usually identified as the prerequisites for successful strategic deterrence. However, they describe a set of unique conditions associated with the hypothetical worst case of all-out nuclear war. The high levels of cost, risk, and certainty of a mutually undesirable outcome for all parties all decrease dramatically as one moves downward through conventional wars, limited conflicts, and international crises to the lower levels of conflict such as terrorism (George and Smoke, 1974; Kahn, 1965).

While there is widespread recognition of certain problems involved in generalising deterrence theory to more complex conflict situations, the fact remains that many of the propositions from this body of theory, especially the proposition of severe and certain punishment, are used by authorities at all levels of world society. Terrorism is only one of several types of deviant behaviour for which authorities appear to use a deterrent strategy. This use of deterrence at all levels of world society suggests the existence of a common problem-solving logic among decision makers.

DETERRENCE AS A PROBLEM-SOLVING LOGIC AND STRATEGY

Once the immediate terrorist crisis is over, there is an important constraint on any possible shift from a security-maximising approach (deterrence) to a more flexible approach which would maximise other values. It consists of the mental process by which people deal with complex problems under conditions of uncertainty. The fundamental problem is that individuals 'don't have the wits to optimise' (Simon, 1976, p. xxviii), because of their cognitive limitations. Two of these are cognitive constraints and cognitive conceit. Cognitive constraints limit our abilities to process large amounts of information; we experience difficulty in selecting the relevant items, in comparing them properly, and in dealing with discrepancies. Cognitive conceit, in contrast, leads us to have a greater faith in our processing abilities than is warranted: often we wrongly assume that we have systematically reviewed all the evidence and appropriately weighed it against the relevant criteria. The results are biases, failures in learning from past experience, and difficulty in improving our ability to predict outcomes in uncertain situations.[10]

The information-processing literature indicates that people have evolved a method to compensate for their various cognitive limitations, which is the use of informal heuristics. Heuristics are simplifying 'rules of thumb' which delineate problems and help to infer causation, estimate risks, and choose a 'best' solution for handling uncertain situations (Newell and Simon, 1972). Heuristics play a central connective role in providing rules for decision in information search and processing, and eventually in exercising a choice (Skjei, 1973). Even the reappraisal stage, after an action has been decided upon and implemented, is still subject to the same process, as the heuristic provides reinforcement of the view that past choices were correct (Carroll and Payne, 1976, pp. 17–20).

A recognition that there are significant patterns in the way that people structure and process information is now widespread among social scientists.[11] The general role played by individual beliefs, cognitive schema, thought models or images has been stressed in many studies (for example, Boulding, 1956; Jervis, 1970; Steinbruner, 1974; Axelrod, 1976; Bonham and Shapiro, 1977; George, 1979). Specifically, problems arise from the use of intuitive heuristics when they contain large and persistent biases (Slovic and Lichtenstein, 1971; Kahneman and Tversky, 1972, 1973). The most common bias is to avoid risks, a tendency which is reinforced by organisational norms and procedures (George, 1974; Lindblom, 1959; Janis and Mann, 1977). This cognitive advantage for status quo perceptions creates a status quo bias in policy, one which is highly resistant to the processing of discrepant information.[12] Thus, a steady increase in terrorist incidents is rarely viewed as a warning sign of the need to shift to alternative problem solving approaches in order to focus on the fundamental problems that give rise to terrorism.

Initially, a terrorist incident confronts authorities with a two-pronged challenge – an immediate threat and a contingent threat of future actions (Hutchinson, 1982, pp. 383–5). While the evidence is still impressionistic on this issue, a general tendency appears to emerge. This is to identify and select relevant information related to the immediate task of determining a tactical response, which in turn controls and minimises future risks (see Kupperman, 1979, pp. 379–441). There is no indication that decision makers focus either on the long-term implications, or on the hidden costs of pursuing an approach designed to maximise short term security. Still less is there evidence that they consider solutions which address the root causes of terrorism. The general definition of the threat and its implications appear to be similar whether the threat stems·from international terrorism, from small fringe groups or from indigent minorities (see Lodge, 1981).

The suggestion, then, is that decision makers using a general problem-solving logic such as deterrence will tend to concentrate on certain aspects of events which are perceived to be similar: crime, terrorism, and deviant acts in general. Attention is focussed on two aspects of the problem: the need for an immediate response involving punishment and an estimation of the risk of future terrorist acts.

By redefining deterrence theory as an overarching problem-solving heuristic, we are able to grapple with the problems caused by reliance on a single *a priori* and categorical device. The fundamental criticism made in this analysis is not that deterrence fails, but rather that it is used in practice to manage, rather than solve, problems. And by its use, deviance, crime, terrorism and war, in all their complexities, are collapsed into a single oversimplified category.

SUMMARY AND SUGGESTIONS FOR AN ALTERNATIVE APPROACH

The conventional wisdom is essentially to ignore terrorism – until and unless a threat is posed. Once confronted with a threat the typical response is to apply deterrence strategy under a crisis-management decisional system. The objective of deterrence is to control, contain and to preserve the capability to administer severe and certain punishment. Explanation of motivations and root causes are shunted aside. After the crisis subsides, programmes are implemented to harder targets and to punish apprehended deviants. This is done in spite of a plethora of evidence, from research both on crime and on international conflict, suggesting that deterrence and security pre-paredness are inadequate strategies. This unwillingness to grapple with all facets of the problem is short-sighted and difficult to understand. However, research on information processing offers an explanation for the persistence of this 'satisficing' approach to decision making.

Terrorist threats confront decision makers with a complicated set of problems within a dynamic political context. If the intuitive deterrence heuristic is not adequate for handling them, what is? Clearly, there is a general implication that decision making should be more structured, more systematic and contained within a logically clear sequence of stages. Beyond this, the information-processing literature suggests that an optimising heuristic would distinguish the full opportunity of each alternative response, long-term as well as short-term, to a given threat.

Such a framework would have to include the *political* as well as the legal and security dimensions of the challenge posed by terrorists.

While attacks by committed deviants cannot always be deterred, the nature of the threat can be reduced, contained and thus controlled if, and only if, the attackers can be detached from their potential constituency. As in counter-insurgency warfare, the authorities are faced with the dual challenge of winning both the battles *and* the 'hearts and minds of the people'. The variable effectiveness of governmental terrorist programmes shows that a variety of internal political considerations are important factors in determining whether authorities are successful in gaining public support for their definition of terrorists as common criminals and outlaws, rather than political freedom fighters who enjoy at least the passive support of significant portions of the population. Counter-terrorist efforts must therefore be perceived as *timely*, *reliable*, and *valid*, by significant groups of the public, including the perceived reference group of the terrorists, in order for governmental control and containment policies to succeed.

For a government response to be *timely*, it must be perceived as 'appropriate' at a particular time by politically significant groups in society. The key is not whether a hard or soft line is adopted but rather whether 'the punishment fits the crime' in the judgement of a significant proportion of the population. In highly polarised societies, extreme factions will never accept governmental policies. However, a response which is relevant, balanced, and perceived to be appropriate for meeting the challenge, is essential if the government is to gain the active support of the moderates in a conflict situation.

Reliability or consistency in policies across time and groups, such as ethnic factions or economic classes, is a second precondition for governmental legitimacy. This is a widely recognised criterion of acceptability in other policy areas, and counter-terrorism is no exception. All deviants must be treated alike, all the time. For example, a government cannot crack down on left wing groups while ignoring right wing groups and still expect the support of leftist partisans.

Finally, *validity* refers to the extent to which policies are perceived as coping with the 'real' issues underlying the terrorist challenge. In societies where there is little or no sense of historical grievance among the potential constituency of the terrorists, the official labelling of the terrorists as common criminals will meet with widespread acceptance. However, the larger the number of citizens or groups within the society who feel that terrorist challenges are symptomatic of real but unmet problems, the more difficulty governments will have in selling the credibility of their counter-terrorist campaigns.

There are certain problems with this proposed alternative to the deterrence heuristic. First, it is an ideal standard, because widespread agreement on the meaning of the three criteria will always be difficult to obtain. Deciding just who constitutes the significant reference group for a newly announced 'liberation army' is a difficult and controversial task. Second, these criteria describe a set of conditions which are nearly impossible to implement – particularly in the face of a widespread and intense campaign of violence. Even discussing this heuristic indicates the real dilemma facing modern governments: *all three* criteria must be implemented *simultaneously*. This is because the failure to meet any of the three criteria may cause the control efforts of the government, rather than the terrorist actions, to be perceived as the source of the problem. Finally, those governments which are not particularly concerned with legitimacy or with the longer term implications of their actions can, and do, ignore one or more of the criteria. Consequently, many will simply reject them as unrealistic.

However, it is argued here that these three criteria can and should serve as a useful alternative formal heuristic both in formulating, and subsequently re-evaluating the impact of, governmental efforts at control.[13] It would be better than continued reliance on the maximising logic of deterrence, especially in situations where traditional policies have failed to deter, or where governmental actions are increasingly viewed as the crux of the problem. The deterrence heuristic is short term, limited, and inadequate for coping with certain deviants at all levels of society, especially after deterrence has broken down. Since the reliance on intuitive heuristics, reinforced by cognitive biases, limits our ability to move to more adequate coping strategies, a need exists to incorporate this threefold heuristic explicitly into all phases of government decision making. Such a practice may encourage a broader focus on the implications of various response strategies in both the short and the long term, help to keep attention focussed on problems in between the phases of crisis, and direct attention to the long-term benefits of a more enlightened approach. The prospect of steadily increasing deviance in the future of world society calls for positive strategies of prevention, not for a repeated matching of terrorist violence with official counter-violence.

NOTES

1 Political terrorism is violence which is directed toward creating a general climate of fear in order to influence political events. It is generally considered to be an especially odious form of political violence, using 'extraordinary' and 'abnormal' techniques in order to manipulate or coerce relevant targets and events. Frequently, innocent victims are attacked. The violence is designed to influence certain indirect targets, including the perceived constituency of the terrorist group, and a political adversary such as a legal authority. Beyond this sort of general definition there is little agreement. Past efforts have attempted to classify political terrorism into categories by asking such questions as: is it interstate or state terrorism? Is it international or domestic? Is it purposive or nihilistic? Is the operative group separatist, nationalist, ethnic, class-based? For further discussion of such typologies, see Mickolus (1980) and Russell *et al.* (1979). In this chapter, no distinctions are drawn between groups because the argument focusses on common patterns in government responses to terrorism. From a governmental perspective, the terrorist action, rather than the group behind it, presents the challenge to be met.

2 Deterrence is an attempt to induce another party to refrain from doing something by threatening a penalty, such as the use of force, legal sanctions or incarceration, for noncompliance. Manipulation via threats of retribution, punishment or denial captures the essence of it (Morgan, 1977, pp. 9–20). The intent is to convince another party not to undertake a given course of action because the costs and risks of that course outweigh the benefits (George and Smoke, 1974, pp. 597–613). It is a primitive but pervasive control strategy used in interpersonal, societal and international relationships when other means, such as persuasion, will not work. This root meaning of the term is used throughout this chapter. See Burton (1979, pp. 85–9); George and Smoke (1974, pp. 48–60); Morgan (1977, pp. 9–20); and Schelling (1966) for a further discussion of these points.

3 The concept of optimality requires that decision makers (1) gather and use all relevant information, (2) use a number of factors which must be maximised and/or minimised simultaneously, (3) recognise that at a particular time *the* optimum may not be discoverable, and (4) develop and use formal heuristics such as an algorithm. We assume in this paper that although there is no global optimum (unique) solution to the problem of coping with terrorism, the typical problem solving approach of policy makers may preclude finding the set of optimum solutions. See Simon (1976) and Lindblom (1959) for further discussion of these points.

4 Most conventional definitions of terrorism distinguish it from other forms of political violence (revolution, war, and so on) because the use of force against symbolic or indirect targets violates certain social, legal and political norms of acceptable behaviour. However, there is no universally

agreed definition of terrorism because the act of so labelling certain actions is a normative and controversial exercise, implying acceptance of the status quo in a conflict situation. As Jenkins (1974, p. 1) notes, 'terrorism is what the "bad guys" do'. Burton (1979, pp. 180–92) has observed that the conventional view of terrorism and deviant behaviour as a departure from prevailing social and legal norms is based on an acceptance of a set of fundamental assumptions. These concern the consensual nature of society, the legitimate use of force by authorities, and the existence of alternative channels of grievance redress and meaningful social change. These criticisms are useful for understanding the current lack of progress in developing widely accepted analytical concepts for studying terrorism.

5 For a review of the literature on specific governmental response strategies for coping with recent terrorist threats see Kupperman (1979, pp. 379–441); and Lodge (1981). For a comprehensive bibliography of recent publications on terrorism see Mickolus (1980).

6 For example, hard-line, no-concession policy has been the official US stance since the Nixon administration. The basic logic is that such a strategy is necessary to decrease terrorist incidents and save human lives, not only in the long run but in the short run as well (Evans, 1979, p. 80). Refusing to give in to blackmail has been deemed necessary to deter future kidnappings. However, the effectiveness of such a strategy both in the short and long term is questionable in view of comparative data for terrorist kidnappings of US, West German, and Japanese citizens between 1970 and 1975. During this period both Germany and Japan made concessions and neither lost a life. The total number of hostage incidents directed against them (fifteen) was less than half of those (thirty-four) directed against the US. In twenty-one of the American hostage situations where the targets were government personages, five were killed. In eleven of the thirteen other cases, which were directed against private individuals, the demands were completely met by business or personal sources (Evans, 1979, pp. 86–90). A CIA study published in 1978 reported that 35 per cent of the political hostage situations from 1971–7 involved American nationals (Farrell and Edsall, 1981, pp. 130–5). These statistics suggests that such a policy has not had a deterrent effect in either the short or long run.

7 Despite the analogy of the usefulness of capital punishment as a deterrent for would-be terrorists there is no clear evidence from a vast amount of empirical research for a significant effect of the death penalty, present or absent, on civil homicide rates. Similarly, there is no evidence of a direct relationship between severe and certain punishment and other types of crime. Instead, threats of legal punishment appear to be an extremely effective deterrent for many 'marginal' deviants 'some of the time'. The general conclusion from the sociological literature is that there is no direct relationship between threats of legal punishment and effective social control of deviants. The relationship, if real, appears to be highly

variable and contingent upon other complex factors related to characteristics of the individual (such as the potential impact of social disapproval
and internalised norms); the type of crime (for example, use of drugs
versus murder); and a host of complex environmental factors. See, for
example, Gibbs (1977, pp. 408–23) and Geerken and Grove (1977, pp.
424–47).

8 This general conclusion emerges from both macroanalytical studies of
terrorism (Gurr, 1977) and from case studies of terrorism in specific
countries (Lodge, 1981), Wainstein (1977); and Krahenbuhl (1977).

9 As Krahenbuhl (1977, p. 102) notes, 'if the local terrorists are a small,
isolated force with a narrow base and shallow depth of support in the
country, removing the current leadership and breaking up the organisation
may terminate the terrorist threat. However, if the terrorists represent
significant (in number and/or political influence) social or cultural
groups who have grievances against the government, a policy of
repression will be effective only in the short term. In such cases, terrorist
activities may escalate into general political unrest and even civil war, or
they may simply persist as a chronic but manageable problem.'

10 The importance of cognitive constraints in public decision making is
discussed in detail by George (1980). For discussion of uncertainty
avoidance and sources of status quo biases in organisations see March
and Simon (1958). The impact of organisational routines and bureaucratic
politics in foreign policy decision making is discussed in Allison (1971),
and in Allison and Szanton (1976). See also Farrell and Edsall (1981) for
discussion of the organisational problems involved in formulating an
effective counter-terrorist strategy.

11 See Janis and Mann (1977) and Carroll and Payne (1976) for a discussion
at the individual and group level; Simon (1976) and George (1980) for a
discussion of the use of information for decision making within
organisations.

12 For a discussion of the use of uncertainty as a principal factor seized by
decision makers to gain latitude in making choices and to justify policies
see Schroeder, Driver and Strenfert (1967), and Carroll and Payne (1976).

13 The theoretical importance of these criteria derives from the fact that, in
information processing terms, people generally evaluate information in
terms of timeliness, reliability and validity (Dyson, 1980). These criteria
thus provide a universal heuristic which people use to understand politics
and to evaluate public policies. Given the problems, in past research on
terrorism, in developing analytically useful concepts, these criteria may
provide a useful framework for evaluating the effectiveness of counter-
terrorist programmes both across countries and over time.

11   Implications of the World Society Perspective for National Foreign Policies

Christopher Hill

The concern of this chapter is to consider the implications for policy of the assumptions which are made by those sympathetic to the way of looking at the world developed and articulated by John Burton. This means taking on two endeavours often distasteful to theorists of international relations: soiling one's hands with the problem of implementing values or aspirations, and (even worse) thinking about how the state and national foreign policies should respond to what are often highly generalised desiderata pitched at the level of global society – for states and national communities are undoubtedly the raw materials, the actual decision-making centres, with which we have to work.

Before embarking upon this difficult task, it is worth noting the extra problems caused by some basic points of obscurity and imprecision about the premises from which we are starting. First is the sheer eclecticism of the world society paradigm, which tends to dull its definitional edge. Pacifism, liberalism, Kantian idealism, anti-imperialism, democratic socialism, and even extreme individualism or Friedmanite economics can all variously be seen as consonant with the values of the Burton perspective. This is fine up to a point: the very aim is to demonstrate how people of very different persuasions in fact do share common interests, and there is a respectable case to be made for placing all the above intellectual positions in their common heritage – predominantly of European history. Yet such catholicism also weakens the argument by robbing the world society perspective of both clear normative grounding and some explanatory power.

It is here that the second major difficulty arises. When discussing how policy-makers should take into account the ideas of the world society school, what is it that is really being said? Is it that we must re-cast our ideas of how the world works and wake up to realities? Or is it that we should accept the moral force of the description being offered of a better world, *and its feasibility as an option*, and thereby change our criteria of action from those derived from past ideals which have proved inappropriate? Are we, in short, working at the descriptive or prescriptive level? Of course, as always, both are relevant and each affects the other. They should still be kept analytically separate, however, and will be outlined as such below.

THE PARADIGM AND ITS RELEVANCE

In its descriptive aspect, the world society paradigm essentially down-plays the role of the state in determining events and their structure. From its very language it is clear that politics on the surface of the earth are seen as an integrated process, operating in a single community. States constitute an important sub-system in this overall community but they are not the only or even the principal actors. The constituents of world society are the individual human beings who inhabit the globe, and who are seen as continually forming and reforming groups for self-expression, whether states, nations, religions, trades unions or professional associations. The basic source of problems, but also of progress, in this global system, is conflict, which takes place at many and various levels and may involve different combinations of the units just mentioned. Destructive conflict – that is, that which imposes more costs than gains (the criteria for which are not always clear) – is by and large the result of people attempting to fulfil their basic values without seeing that this does not need to involve the over-riding of other groups with their own separate goals.

It is at this point that Burton's analysis begins to shade over into the prescriptive. It is his view that there exist such things as basic 'human needs', which are universal and can be discovered by scientific enquiry. He argues that when we have both identified these needs and commenced strategies for fulfilling them, we shall be well on the way to the securing of positive peace, that is a state of tranquillity and co-operation beyond the mere absence of war. The 'solving' of conflicts which this involves will come specifically from the parties concerned recognising that each other's views are all equally legitimate and that, with professional help, it is possible for both sides to redraw a problem so that each benefits rather than loses. These points are certainly important, and they may turn out to be correct, but even a sympathetic commentator cannot classify them as anything more than shrewd opinions and predictions.

These, in brief, are the main elements of the world society paradigm which John Burton has set up for us. They constitute a distinctive perspective partly because of the very duality that we have identified. Very few writers on international affairs have combined a wideranging description of the way the world is, and where it is going, with a highly practical series of suggestions about *processes* (not laws, or institutions), for putting it right. Burton gives us the paradox that only the people involved in conflict can truly resolve it, yet at the same time they are in urgent need of specialised, dispassionate, advice about how to get themselves on the right tracks. Burton largely eschews philosophy, and states positivistically that people have many different and equally justifiable ways of satisfying their basic needs, whether they are material (hunger), psychological (identity), or sociobiological (participation). Politics is about resolving the inevitable clashes between these different routes to salvation, not the definition of a single way of living. Least of all is it about the imposition of one set of values on everyone via a single political structure.

FOREIGN POLICY IN A WORLD SOCIETY

Let us now examine what those of us concerned with foreign policy analysis can get out of the different sides of the world society paradigm, beginning with its descriptive qualities. What are the implications of the approach for the conduct and future of national foreign policies? If we assume that Burton's view of the world is broadly correct, then there are few choices open to the state considering its external relations: the force of constant change will prove impossible for it to control and will produce new realities to which a government will only be able to react. Leaders will have to recognise that their power is limited, inside and outside the state, that they are only one among many types of actor involved in managing events, and that the accretion of power is largely self-defeating.

An example of the kind of national strategy which in the Burton view will become anachronistic, if practised at all, would be that of isolation or autarky. As the population of the globe is now bound together in a cobweb of interwoven activities, the product of two centuries of industrial expansion, it is barely possible to opt out of modernity, let alone to sustain it singlehanded. So far, so conventional: J.M. Keynes and Jean Monnet have said such things before,[1] and the counter-factual examples of China, Tanzania and Burma seem to bear them out. In this respect the world society paradigm can be fitted without too much distortion into any reasonably sophisticated description of the external environment in which modern states conduct their foreign policies. Partly leaning on the academic transnational relations school, most observers of contemporary foreign policy would wish to stress that states now have to cope as much with markets, ideas, and social movements, most of which have been created by external and non-governmental forces, as with the consequences of formal diplomacy.

To this picture of an external environment which is simply more complex and interdependent, however, John Burton has added a gloss which is worth attention. His image of world society is an all-embracing one, and subsumes transnationalism, a planet-earth style ecology, and, crucially, functionalism. Functionalism is important in this context because to the extent that it occurs it is impossible for states to perform all the tasks which their citizens expect. In an expanded version of the theory of comparative advantage it is stressed not only that specialisation is inevitable in the modern world economy, but also that states are virtually irrelevant as the units of this specialisation. National decision makers will therefore have to face the fact that they should actually encourage groups to penetrate boundaries and to build constructive bridges to other societies, by-passing governments if necessary. Since the latter's role as gatekeepers is doomed to failure, they should participate in the process of creating multiple linkages between communities.

Another basic element of the world society perspective, although certainly not unique to it, is its attack on the power politics approach. The pursuit of power in an open-ended sense, as by Napoleon or Hitler, would be regarded as impossible as well as undesirable by most practitioners already; Burton hardly bothers with such points. Where he is more controversial is in his extension of the criticism to the point where power as simply the useful and inevitable currency of interstate relations, is still seen as beside the point, even counter-productive.[2] This is not a matter of cheerfully casting prudence to the winds. Rather, the world society paradigm suggests that power intrinsically involves some form of dictation, even in its most defensive guises, and dictation does nothing to reconcile the differences at the level of values which are the source of most conflicts. (This is as true of collective security as of *machtpolitik*.) Indeed, acts of compulsion are likely to exacerbate disputes because they will breed new resentments or humiliations, and teach the lesson that change can only be achieved by force. The dicta of power politics will inevitably lead to successes of a most seductive kind, but at great costs and containing the seeds of their own destruction.

This slant on power politics is naturally one which some perceptive makers of foreign policy have already arrived at and by experience rather than a full-blown theory of world society. Commonsense (and the likes of Edward Gibbon) has taught them that even Roman Empires crumble, that power alone is nothing, and that one's opponents should always be treated with respect rather than ground down as a matter of course. Among others, Iain Macleod, Willy Brandt and John Kennedy have all shown signs of appreciating these points. But not enough statesmen or women share the perspective, except perhaps as dimly perceived truths at the back of their consciousness. We only have to look at the sad deterioration of détente, after less than a decade of civilised relationships between the superpowers, to see that the dominant wisdom on each side is that power only respects power, and that a great state is almost bound to have an interest in the difficulties of another. Equally, in the Middle East, Israel's insistence that her security can only be achieved by demonstrable military superiority, plus a *cordon sanitaire* of subordinate territories, is as self-defeating as the PLO's previous re-iteration of the need to destroy Israel and replace it by a triumphant Palestine. Conflicts will probably only be sharpened by a mentality in which power is seen as the principal means of benefiting 'us', while 'they' become a dehumanised outgroup. The fundamental causes of a grievance have to be addressed – by all sides.

The other side of this coin is that, in order to be successful, an action in foreign policy has to be seen as *legitimate*. Whereas a conventional approach to evaluating success might refer to the rational process of achieving one's aims by relating them closely to means and likely costs, Burton would say that this begs the question of what the ends of foreign policy should be, and leaves it open for the most short-sighted acts of national selfishness if circumstances permit. Foreign policy cannot be simply whatever you can get away with. We naturally recoil from the moral implications of such a strategy, and also sense that the more advantage one is able to take in the short run, the harder the ultimate reckoning is likely to be.

Coercion in a world of separate communities is unlikely ever to be seen as legitimate by its objects, even when the force might be imposed according to international law. Nonetheless the profound need for legitimacy, as a fact more than a mere label, remains, for when an action is regarded consensually as legitimate it means that it has been found fully acceptable – not just for tactical or temporising reasons, but because it meets the essence of the needs of the parties concerned. Moreover, in the world of foreign policy, those accepting authority are in the same category as those exercising it; therefore agreements are consensual and positive-sum, or they are nothing. By extension, the only way to remove grievances is to involve *all* the aggrieved in any negotiations for a settlement (even if they are not states) and to use as fundamental criteria the perceived primary needs (not necessarily wants) of all parties. The implications for the Middle East, for Poland, for the Horn of Africa, for the Gulf War, for the war in the Western Sahara and for many other sores of international diplomacy are clear enough.

If isolation and the attempt to rely on commanding power are both 'self-defeating strategies', what sensible posture is open to the modern state in its external relations? It is clear that Burton is not enamoured of the state as such, and that he does not see a great future for it, although as we shall stress again later, it is not at all clear as to what alternative structures of government in world affairs he does conceive of, or approve. On the other hand his attitude is not to be mistaken for utopianism, and not even for an ivory tower unrealism. Burton's work is that of an eminently practical man, interested in immersing himself in the real world and tinkering with its mechanics. He may make mistakes in his diagnoses and preferred solutions, but he does attempt to grapple with the applied side of his subject and to suggest procedures which might be used in the here and now.

BLOCS AND INTERNATIONAL ORGANISATIONS

To this end, Burton accepts that states form a powerful element of the status quo, and he attempts to nudge responsible decision makers in directions which are more in tune with the needs of contemporary conditions. In particular, he warns against the tendency to find salvation in blocs in international relations. The solution to the increasing ineffectuality of even the most powerful states is not simply to increase the scale of the unit by banding together with the like-minded or similarly placed. This is to repeat the errors of the power politics approach, even if it does buy a certain amount of time. Furthermore it is bound to increase fears among other members of the world community. Whether the bloc is military (NATO, or the Warsaw Treaty Organisation) or economic (the EEC, OPEC), the only possible response of the excluded can be to organise themselves in some form of adverserial posture. The subsequent squaring up of the separate groups of states to each other, constitutes a new set of problems on top of the substantive issues the groups were formed to deal with. The world society paradigm, therefore, does not lead one down the road of regionalism, let alone world government. While the individual state, as a mechanism for satisfying needs, is undoubtedly being pulled in opposite directions by both decentralising and internationalising forces, the Burton view is that states should, as it were, relax and enjoy it. Such deep-rooted processes cannot be withstood and any attempt to do so will only cause more trouble.

Those responsible for foreign policy should not take their stand on a rigid and ultimately untenable obsession with sovereignty, but should accept, for example, that where a distinct community within their society is set on self-government, they should be allowed to do so. Burton (1972b, p. 99 and p. 157) was in favour of Biafra's right to secede from Nigeria, and saw no future in Greece or Turkey intervening to 'resolve' the Cyprus problem. Less dramatically, states should encourage co-operation through international institutions, particularly those of a functional type where experts, pressure-groups and so on are as likely to be involved as governments. For only when those people who are most closely concerned with an issue are able to participate will some appropriate strategy emerge. This will mean accepting multiple membership in international groupings, with many separate strands to one's foreign policy.

THE ROLE OF NONALIGNMENT

The alternative to exclusive reliance on membership of one group of states is therefore something akin to the movement for which John Burton was so enthusiastic in the 1960s – nonalignment. Although some might see nonalignment as an opting out of world society, a more polite form of isolationism, this corresponds neither to the reality nor its place in the kind of functionalist paradigm we have been discussing. Historically, nonaligned states like Egypt, India and Yugoslavia have been extremely active in trying to promote both détente and development, and have often proved an embarrassment to the great powers. In Burtonian terms (1966, p. 98) nonalignment is important because it has been a way 'to devalue power'; it has shown that high scores on conventional indicators of strength are not always necessary either to survive in international relations or even to take positive initiatives to promote change.[3]

Nonalignment has clearly changed considerably over the last twenty years, perhaps weakened by détente, perhaps tainted by being dragged into the revival of the cold war towards the end of the 1970s and certainly cut across by the North–South debate. Nonetheless, so long as exaggerated expectations are laid aside, there are two good reasons for continuing to stress its value in the evolving contemporary international system, and as a principle, not simply a particular historical movement.

Firstly, assuming we do wish to settle international disputes on some more orderly basis than that of *force majeure*, nonalignment can provide us with a model or starting point. Nonaligned states make a virtue of necessity in the sense that they often have a limited capacity for military self-defence, but they also tend to be convinced of the dangers which alliances and deterrence policies themselves generate. They therefore take the position that 'a non-power relationship is possible in the settlement of disputes', a view that Yugoslavia, at least, has also acted upon. By virtue of not using threat as the basis of *achieving change*, and of not being tied into some formidable military alliance, a nonaligned state must concentrate its actions at the diplomatic level, and be more flexible, even lateral, in its thinking about disputes.

Unfortunately, and Anwar Sadat's trip to Jerusalem notwithstanding, both Egypt and India have also displayed a conventional propensity to use force. This only proves the inconvenient complexity of international affairs and the entanglement of different traditions of thought and types of goals in any one state's foreign policy. It does not invalidate the point made by nonaligners that the dichotomy between taking sides in a dispute and remaining entirely passive is a false one. States have a more creative strategy open to them. They should participate actively, so as to mediate, conciliate, and in the original terms which Burton has given us, attempt to redefine the problem through breaking down conventional ways of thinking.[4]

The second good reason for taking nonalignment seriously as a foreign policy strategy is the way in which, in Burton's interpretation at least, it suggests a way of linking internal to external needs. Too much prescription about foreign policy is couched in the terms of diplomatic manoeuvres or world roles, with reference only to the state's place in the global pattern of things. To the extent that domestic criteria are taken into account, they tend to be concerned with accountability and available resources. In recent decades, however, it has become clear that governments cannot divorce welfare goals from foreign policy, as domestic pressures increase and many forms of welfare (for example, employment) come to depend on developments outside the state's boundaries. The problem then moves beyond that of a mere trade-off between competing demands: it becomes a question of how to give oneself sufficient room to work towards the kind of society that seems desirable in the circumstances, and by extension, of what kind of a world is most consonant both with the freedom of its component communities and the values that the particular state is concerned to protect.

The rub, as has often been pointed out, lies in the clash between irreconcilable values which is almost bound to result. Where the theory of nonalignment is attractive is precisely at this point. On the one hand it stands for independence and a certain relativism of values. While many powerful states pay lip-service to the sanctity of sovereignty but in practice work towards exporting their political system as widely as possible, nonalignment starts from the right of society to take responsibility for its own destiny, and goes on to stress the benefits which will flow from variety in the international system. On the other, it emphasises a developmental approach at both internal and external levels. If a state enjoys many but varied contacts in the world, but is not cramped by devotion to a particular bloc, it should be able to keep at arms length an individual suitor whose attentions become claustrophobic (as India has just managed to do with the Soviet Union) and be free to support initiatives to solve major international problems on their merits, rather than on the basis of a reflex solidarity with allies. Such groupings as are joined can be loose, functional, and non-exclusive. Burton praised the Commonwealth in this connection (1969, pp. 101–2); and might equally approve of the Lomé agreements between the EEC Ten and sixty-three African, Caribbean, and Pacific States.

THE SIGNIFICANCE OF DECISION MAKING

The final important implication for foreign policy-making which follows from assuming the truth of the world society paradigm, relates to the nature of decision making itself. It can be argued, and supported from Burton's earlier work, that the whole problem-solving approach rests on the assumption that it is what individual people, acting politically, *do* that determines change, not some collective, impersonal determinism. On the other hand, there is a strong element of determinism about the world society paradigm, mixing as it does description with prediction. Much of its analysis gives the marked impression that an understanding is being presented not just of the immediate past or the frozen present, but of a process of *becoming*, whose future evolution will be very much of a part with the essential reality the paradigm identifies. It is in the nature of a process of becoming, of course, that it is only susceptible to subjective interpretation, and so we may be forgiven for not accepting the characterisation of a burgeoning world society, with states reduced to mere shells, as absolutely given.

It is, nonetheless, an interesting dual paradox that Burton regards decision making as of central importance while at the same time leaning towards a deterministic macro-level interpretation of world politics, in which state decision makers seem to play only minor parts. The paradox is partly worked out by Burton's tendency to lose interest in decision making explanations in his later work, and to emphasise world society, but there remains the awkward problem that if problem-solving is so vital a procedure (a breakthrough of 'historic importance', Michael Banks called it (1979, p. 262)) then a good deal hinges on the problem-solvers and their capabilities. Although Burton is at pains to emphasise that most major conflicts are inter-communal and can only be dealt with by the communities themselves, whose structures may not coincide with state boundaries, the fact remains that in all his favourite cases (Cyprus, Nigeria/Biafra, the Horn of Africa, Northern Ireland, Kashmir, Indonesia) nothing of significance can be achieved without reconstructing the views of state decision makers. Burton recognised the basic paradox early on, and confronted it squarely (1968, p. 63):

even the limited range of choices that exists at a particular time is responsible over long periods of time for systemic changes, and for resistances by states to systemic changes that ultimately lead to conflict between them. If States finally become irrelevant to world society, if supranational authorities are created or disarmament occurs, this will no less be due to decision making processes – to limited choices made at many points of time. For these reasons the details of decision making – trivial matters in comparison with the great movements of history – are of particular interest in the study of international politics and conflict.

Practical men of affairs and 'realist' students of international relations alike will recognise the dilemmas contained here, even if they disagree with the drift of Burton's conclusions. It is folly to concentrate our explanations of international politics at one level alone, macro or micro. Only an appreciation of the interplay between individual decisions and the nature of structure can give us any sort of understanding of what sort of political change is occurring in the world, let alone of its primary causes.

It is hardly possible here to do more than catalogue some of the elements of the decision making process which Burton has high-lighted as being crucial in determining how well communities adapt to change. The details are well set out in several of his books.[5] But three points are important to single out, because they illustrate how the functionalist approach of the world society school sees decision making in a different light from the more power-oriented analysts of bureaucratic politics, interest-group pluralism or executive leadership, who these days tend to dominate the academic study of foreign policy, at least as it comes into contact with practitioners themselves.

First is the stress on perceptions. The world society paradigm tends to lead naturally to an interest in how the many different parties to disputes see themselves and their adversaries. There is no obvious solution discoverable by rationality; the actors have to rethink their problems creatively and to examine whether or not they can satisfy their needs by other means than those to which they have become attached. They should also scrutinise the images they hold of others, and ask whether these are accurate or instead reflect prejudice, wishful thinking, anachronistic expectations or the impact of sheer stress (scapegoating, over-simplification). To the extent that barriers to acceptance of the truth can be discovered, so do opportunities open up for improving the rationality of decision making. Others have subsequently explored these matters in greater depth,[6] but Burton and his colleagues have been unique in their integration of a decision making approach with a wider systems theory treatment of the whole international environment, and ultimately, with a concern for conflict resolution.

Second is the interest in cybernetics, taken to mean the operation of control systems in organisms and processes. Burton is at pains to argue that decision makers cannot expect to operate on the basis of grand strategies, or hope to impose their preferred solutions on complex problems by force, or power of will. The best that they can hope for is to 'steer' accurately through the minefields which events will lay for them. This is an empirical approach which involves constant adjustment and flexibility as circumstances inevitably change in unforeseen ways, and in particular a sensitivity to the importance of feedback, that is the way in which actions return to affect an actor in the form of changes in the environment on which it has had an impact.

Up to a point this is a formal statement of what most intelligent people do by second nature, and indeed British diplomats might claim that it corresponds to their famous style of 'pragmatism', but an important difference lies in the emphasis which the academic approach places on the handling of information.[7] If decision making is seen as a system of information flows in which inputs and outputs are being processed simultaneously, it is easy to see that routines rapidly emerge which will make it difficult to spot the significant new developments and which may not be able to cope with conditions of overload. British officials were made painfully aware of both these points during the Falklands crisis of 1982, and they are probably relevant to an exploration of the Soviet Union's shooting down of a Korean airliner in September 1983. Practitioners would do well to reflect on their working milieu as a system of communication in which the nature of information and the conclusions derived therefrom is a delicate business, requiring constant monitoring and critical self-awareness.

The third and last face of Burton's approach to decision making is his attitude towards professional expertise. Put simply, it is his view that diplomacy as it has historically been practised has been woefully lacking in any real understanding of how the international system functions, and has been tragically incompetent as a result. His remedy for this state of affairs is disarmingly confident: scholars with a proper understanding, professionally trained, should be listened to a great deal more. Graduates with qualifications in international relations should be recruits of choice for the diplomatic services of the world, and not regarded as intrinsically suspect. Practitioners should deliberately seek out theoretical approaches so as to enable them to see the wood as well as the trees. 'Foreign policy decision making can now be transformed from an art into an applied science' (1968, p. 214).

It is this last kind of overstatement which has made actual decision makers (and many academics) shy away from theoreticians like Burton, but there can also be no doubt that they have been looking for the slightest excuse to do so. Although things have slowly begun to change, it is still the case in Britain that practising diplomats have little time or inclination to read works of theory.[8] To their credit, the members of the world society school have been one of the very few groups to continue proselytising the value of theory while also not being afraid to tackle real conflicts. There is a real case to be heard about the value to foreign ministries of the academic approach to international relations, in terms of both casting light on decision making and negotiations, and creating an awareness of values, assumptions, and causation. John Burton has been vigorously making his version of the case for more than two decades.

CRITICISMS

Most of this chapter has been concerned with the implications for national foreign policies of assuming that the world society paradigm provides us with a true picture of how international relations are being transformed. Many may wish to challenge the premise, however, and argue that the paradigm is not accurate in its descriptive aspect. Without diverging too much from our main purpose, it is important to consider the charge.

As with any general framework for thinking about a large subject, it is difficult to know whether disagreement occurs at the level of fundamental beliefs, or at that of the observation of facts. Either way, it is clear that there is room for scepticism about the world society image on the grounds of its attack on power politics. Although Burton has usually been far more circumspect in his statements than he is given credit for, his whole work is based on a reaction against the notion that power is the dominant motive of peoples and the best guarantee of success for state policy. He stresses, by contrast, the importance of changing perceptions as a means of resolving conflict and achieving peace. It takes little thought, however, to imagine the kind of formidable case that can be made in favour of realism, based not only on the careers of Richelieu, Palmerston or Bismarck, but also the modern experiences of Trotsky and Stalin, Chamberlain and Churchill, Nasser and Sadat. These pairs of men did differ between themselves in their perceptions of foreign policy, but where one failed and the other succeeded, it was probably because of a superior appreciation of the realities of external pressure – in a word, power.

The corollary of the view of power as anachronistic is, of course, the elevation of functionalism as a major factor in international relations, and this is another point of vulnerability for the world society paradigm. The idea that cooperation is steadily being built up through the compelling need for joint action in increasing numbers of technical spheres is undermined by any close analysis of international organisations, especially those for which such high hopes were held, like the EEC, UNESCO, and the World Bank. Most have become primarily fora for traditional diplomacy, even if it is true that they have each added some new constraints and procedures to interstate politics. The saga of the UN Law of the Sea Conference is a classic demonstration of how states need to come together in some particular area, but find it intensely difficult to do so and can even create new barriers to understanding in the attempt.

The identification of transnational relations as the filigrees of the cobweb model, in contradistinction to the billiard-ball image associated with power politics, might also be looked at sceptically. The fashions of international studies, especially those initiated in the United States, tend to follow on from developments in the world of international politics itself, and the emphasis on non-state actors (for which Burton was hardly alone responsible) flowed from the great expansion of world trade in the 1960s and the expectations of continued world-wide economic growth on a laisser-faire basis. The Middle East war of 1973 was the first marker of a changed tide and the last decade has seen recession, signs of protectionism, and the distinct revival of the state as the perceived main actor in the system – even if via such unhappy events as Afghanistan, the Gulf War, and Poland. Academic fashion will doubtless soon be catching up with these developments.

The changing role of the state – the heart of the matter – is naturally contentious. On the other hand, it cannot be denied that Burton's descriptions have at times had strong elements of wishful thinking contained within them. His picture of the state's permeability, for instance, ignored what was happening in the Chinese Cultural Revolution, or in Albania, Israel, Libya and other such examples. The combination, especially in socialist states, of a 'progressive' ideology with a determined use of the state to resist contamination from outside, poses the world society model a problem it has not yet resolved. In 1965 (p. 198) Burton saw socialism and 'neoneutralism' as the twin foundations of a fluid middle way between capitalism and communism: 'Socialism, underdevelopment and nonalignment are likely to be found simultaneously in the one environment', but by 1979 (p. 199) he had become dismissive:

The historical process is a search not for a structural 'ism', but for one that concentrates on processes by which structures can change and evolve in the quest for the fulfilment of needs: process and needs are the ingredients of the ideal 'ism'.

There is a good deal in this view, which again elevates cybernetics over structures, but it does beg the question of whether some processes (for example, unfettered private enterprise or neo-colonial influences from other societies) actually threaten needs, and can only be resisted by resort to the power of the state and the barriers it alone can erect. Values may at times need to be reinforced by symbolic and practical action.

WORLD SOCIETY, THE STATE, AND INTERNATIONAL THEORY

This brings us to the concern of the last section of this chapter. To what extent do the flaws in the empirical basis of the world society paradigm really matter? Are the criticisms serious enough to invalidate the predictive and prescriptive aspects of the model? It is on the question of the role of the state that this bears most sharply. If it is factually undeniable that many states remain highly effective gatekeepers against the outside world, it is also likely that in many others people will continue to look to national, governmental action as providing them with their only source of protection in the 'global system' – which Burton is quite right to insist on. This will be true for groups as diverse as Icelandic fishermen, American steelworkers threatened with unemployment, Falkland Islanders, Jewish settlers on the Golan Heights, Amazonian Indians threatened by pollution, and French intellectuals concerned about Franglais. The fact that these people may also be threatened by their own state, or that in the long run they may be fighting a losing battle, does not undermine the basic argument that they will feel the need for assistance, and have a right to it. The institution on which they ultimately depend (and can be ruined by), is the state, which is also the only body they can hope to hold to account.

The world society view is simply not clear on what will and should happen to 'authorities' in a global system where states become decreasingly capable of delivering the collective goods. Are different sets of authorities to emerge in parallel, as with the uneasy division of powers in the EEC between states and the Commission? If so, what happens when differences of opinion (at the least) emerge, as they inevitably will? The result, if the EEC is a guide, is paralysis and/or the loss of legitimacy by the *supra*national institutions, as the states resist attempts to impose uniform strategies and are able to do so through their monopoly of the sinews of power. The points Hobbes made over three hundred years ago about 'covenants without the sword' being 'but words', and about the logical impossibility of dividing sovereignty, should not be taken lightly. For the question of sovereignty is not, as Burton thinks, beside the point. Men and women still desire governments they can identify with, who are responsible for particular, demarcated, communities on a human scale. This, more than mere nationalism, leads them to be attached to their states.

If this is not so, the issue is the scope, level and philosophical foundation of the government we choose to live with. If the state is no longer appropriate then we need to be furnished by intellectuals with alternative models of government which will satisfy the needs of efficiency *and* democracy better. It is not enough to say that problem-solving does this, by stressing the need for legitimate parties and solutions. In a system where there are no accepted channels of participation or institutions of responsibility (whether at the level of the nation-state, supranationalism or even devolved autonomy), groups will have little option but to insist on protecting themselves, if necessary up to and including the use of force. It is exceedingly dangerous to undermine the legitimacy of one policy without being clear on how to move into an improved structure, as the recent history of both Northern Ireland and the Lebanon demonstrates so vividly. The corollary of recognising that disputes like that in the Middle East will not be solved by ignoring key parties like the Palestinians, is *not* to encourage direct involvement on the world scene by all non-state actors. Rather, it is to clarify the demarcation of responsibilities between states and international organisations, such as, say the European Court of Human Rights, or the International Atomic Energy Agency, and to find ways in which states can open themselves up to regular procedures of cooperation, mediation, and standard-setting, without feeling threatened. The dangerous implication of the world society paradigm, and one that Burton and his colleagues would obviously deplore, is that as the state becomes enmeshed in the cobweb, so the spiders will fight destructively over the prey.

Fundamental to this issue is the neglect of moral philosophy by proponents of the world society paradigm. The blurring of 'is' and 'ought' damages the credibility of the explanatory aspect of the paradigm, but it is more unsatisfactory in the way it slides over the issue of which imperatives should be followed in international affairs. 'Human needs' will not do as a criterion. They too are vague and impossible to 'discover' empirically, as Burton hopes (1979, p. 63). What is needed is the working out, at an *a priori*, philosophical level, of the values which human society should serve and why, and of the conditions which will best allow individuals to fulfil their own needs, whatever these may be. This has been the self-imposed task of political theorists over the centuries, but they seem to be beyond the pale so far as the world society paradigm goes. This is a shame, for one can distil from the relevant writings a set of values which could be placed in front of foreign policy decision makers as a pure statement of the basis of which outsiders should be dealt with. Among these (a full analysis would require a separate book) would be such concerns as legitimacy, participation, peace, empathy, creativity, tolerance, differentiation, empiricism, and a recognition that individual rights simultaneously derive from the meaning of humanity as well as from mere state structures. It can easily be seen how these values develop classical traditions of western liberalism, as much as they are consistent with the spirit of the world society paradigm. What is most crucial in this context is to appreciate the latter's relative neglect of 'international theory', that is, that branch of political theory which deals with relations between states, or between people across state borders, however it may be formulated. John Burton has highlighted certain values of the highest importance, and shown how they are far from being served by present arrangements. What he has not yet done is to indicate more specifically how they may act as criteria for action in the world, and (the rub) *for whom*. When it comes to serious concrete problems, like poverty, or apartheid, we need guidance on what sort of justice we should seek, and on whom the obligations devolve.[9]

It is interesting that Burton neglects the actual substance of the dilemmas which face decision makers, and indeed all of us, in formulating attitudes to the major problems of the day. Even though there is real force in his likely response – that the whole point of a problem-solving approach is to allow the engaged parties to discover solutions themselves, not to present prepackaged schemes – it does expose the world society paradigm to the charge that it is intrinsically incompatible with practical advice to those responsible for national foreign policies, once they prove resistant to attempts to inveigle them into problem-solving – as they do. Problem-solving as a workshop technique is almost bound to fail when confronting such great conflicts as those which dominate our newspapers daily. Its success is likely to be long-term and imperceptible, in the sense that those involved in negotiations may painfully come to realise the truth behind many of John Burton's admonitions. For the present moment however, it has too relativistic a quality, too dry an emphasis on process rather than the substance of the values which win hearts and minds, to transform international relations in the way that we might hope.

All these criticisms are serious. But they are the compliment paid by commentary to originality. Very few men and women have had the knowledge, scope and nerve to attempt a general analysis of that seething universe we know as international relations. John Burton has been one of them, and his ideas will outlive the foreign policy-makers of today to be discussed and learnt from when scholars look back to images of the 'world society' in the late twentieth century. And even if the practitioners of the 1980s have some difficulty distinguishing the 'is' from 'ought' in Burton's work, they should pay careful attention to it, for his 'is' may not be far from the mark, and his 'ought' adds up to a compassionate and far-sighted view of human relations.

NOTES

1 This is the thrust of Keynes' essay (1931), in which he takes 'mankind' as the unit of analysis and predicts continuing sustained growth. He also makes a distinction between absolute and relative human needs. See also Monnet (1978) especially pp. 428–30.
2 The metaphor of power as the 'currency' of international relations was given extended treatment in Modelski's work (1962), which was interesting both for itself and because it never caught the imagination of succeeding generations of writers on foreign policy.
3 Burton's view of nonalignment can, of course, be contested, and a recent book which does take issue with it is by Willetts (1978). He regards nonalignment as a non-military alliance, often serving to provide its members with consistency in their foreign policy. Burton's writings on nonalignment extend beyond his edited book of that title (1966) to part V of his general textbook (1965) and passages of both his (1968) and (1972b) works.
4 In making this point (1966, p. 24) Burton himself was quoting from Cohn (1939), who said: 'The system of war-prevention should be a development of the neutrality policies of the countries at peace, and not of the war policies of the great military Power' (p. 340, cited by Burton). Burton's originality consists in adding the notion of problem-solving to that of active 'neo-neutrality'.
5 Especially Burton (1968) and (1972b).
6 See, for example, Axelrod (1976) and Jervis (1976).
7 Burton regularly refers to Deutsch (1963). An important later work (Steinbruner, 1974) dealt with similar problems.
8 See, for example, the revealing exchange between Sir James Cable (1981) and Joseph Frankel (1981).
9 These nettles are difficult to grasp even in a work of real political philosophy, as admitted by Linklater (1982).

12 Practitioners and Academics: Towards a Happier Relationship?

A.J.R. Groom

Practical men, who believe themselves to be quite exempt from any intellectual influences, are usually the slaves of some defunct economist. Madmen in authority, who hear voices in the air, are distilling their frenzy from some academic scribbler of a few years back. I am sure that the power of vested interests is vastly exaggerated compared with the gradual encroachment of ideas. Not, indeed, immediately, but after a certain interval – for in the field of economic and political philosophy there are not many who are influenced by new theories after they are 25 or 30 years of age, so that the ideas which civil servants and politicians and even agitators apply to current events are not likely to be the newest (J.M. Keynes).

The relationship between 'practical men' and 'academic scribblers' is not easy, especially in international relations. While there is nothing as practical as a good theory, the problem is finding good theories, making them operational in the context of a decision making process and getting practitioners to recognise and adopt them. Moreover, academics and practitioners each have a false image of what the other does. Academics lust after the possibilities of pulling the levers of power, yet practitioners say that they do not make decisions. They rightly claim that all they can do is to nudge along a process which they do not in any real sense control. This is particularly true in international relations. The illusion of practitioners is that academia is all peace, calm, reflection and high thought in the ivory tower.

Don Price has identified four 'estates' which, although separate, do overlap in a way that makes the relationship between academics and practitioners difficult (Price, 1965). The scientific estate concerns itself principally with pure science, while the professional estate is in the business of applied science. The administrative estate has the duty to relate both the scientific and professional estates to that of the political estate. The administrative estate is manned by civil servants who aid the political estate in identifying the good society and the means to attain it. The purpose of the political estate is to promote a particular set of values. Frequently these estates are at odds in their needs, *modus operandi*, and paradigms, yet they cannot operate to their full potential except in reasonable concord with each other. Hence the love–hate relationship between academics, who dominate the scientific and professional estates, and practitioners, who control the administrative and political estates.

International relations, however, is unusual in that there has been a degree of unity between academics and practitioners who have often shared the same paradigm – power politics. Thus little communication between them was necessary since their paradigmatic unity was so strong that they could go their separate ways safe in the knowledge that their work was compatible. At most they traded data.

When academics challenged the dominant paradigm of power politics in a sustained way and social science as a whole became methodologically and epistemologically more sophisticated, then they felt that communication with practitioners was necessary. But it was also difficult for there was no longer paradigmatic harmony. Ironically, John Burton, after having been one of those who brought about this disharmony is now, and equally controversially, promoting a new harmony between the four estates.

Burton has been active in all four estates. As a conceptual thinker his work is recognised throughout the world,[1] while as a professional he developed the technique of 'controlled communication' or 'problem solving' on the basis of his conceptual analysis (Burton, 1969; 1982a). To his enviable academic credentials must be added his salience as a practitioner. While permanent head of the Australian Ministry of External Affairs he participated significantly in building the United Nations system. Only in the political estate did Burton fail to make a lasting mark although, characteristically, he did 'make waves'.

Burton was in the forefront of those academics who broke the spell of unspoken harmony between academic and practitioner in international relations. Burton was not only critical of the tautological, self-fulfilling and self-defeating aspects of the power politics paradigm, he also evolved an alternative paradigm – that of world society (Burton, 1968; 1972b; 1979; 1982a). Neither the attack on the paradigm in the scientists' estate, nor its translation in the form of 'controlled communication' into the professional estate is the end of the matter, for in the administrative estate Burton also took nonalignment seriously in his External Affairs days. More generally, the cumulative effect of the conceptual and methodological innovations of Burton and others gave rise to a case of severely strained relations between academics and practitioners in international relations putting it four square with other social sciences. Burton's present position could heal the rift since he feels that social scientists can now aspire to speaking truth to power.

ON SPEAKING TRUTH TO POWER

Academic-practitioner relationships are far from being a mere matter of speaking truth to power since academics can only aspire to a version of 'truth' and practitioners have but a tenuous hold on 'power'. Moreover, the language and form of communication is anything but easy. In short, the relationship is much more complex and subtle.

The academic is in search of some highly probable statements about the ways of the world which have stood the test of an appropriate measure of verification. The practitioner cannot ignore such findings; indeed he would be stupid to do so. His purpose is to achieve success in the world according to some set of value preferences or, as a minimum, an acceptable form of survival according to the same values (Rothstein, 1972, p. 127). Such differences are not an unbridgeable gulf since both academic and practitioner work within a paradigm. What the academic has to say about that paradigm, its anomalies and alternatives is crucial for the practitioner in the recognition of his problem. The academic may also have much to say about the relative effectiveness of means for addressing the problem as well as information about it. However, 'the knowledge necessary to make a decision about an issue is different from the knowledge necessary to diagnose a case. Decisional knowledge is specific, up-to-date, and applicable only at a moment in time; cognitive knowledge is abstract, generalised, and applicable whenever or wherever the necessary conditions hold' (Rothstein, 1972, p. 139). The practitioner is satisfied with success but the academic seeks to explain and predict. Therefore it is not enough for him that things *seem* to work. Furthermore, the academic puzzles over problems, but the practitioner turns 'problems' into 'puzzles'; while it is not known whether a 'problem' can have an answer, a 'puzzle' must by definition have an answer. Since a practitioner has to have an answer, even if he is confronted with a genuine 'problem', he perforce turns it into a 'puzzle' in order to arrive at an answer. An academic, however, can afford to puzzle over his 'problem'. In contrast, the practitioner is only likely to meet his criterion of success if he makes the correct 'puzzle' of a 'problem'. Thus, the academic's effort to elucidate a 'problem' is vital for the practitioner.

By turning a 'problem' into a 'puzzle' an academic can lead a practitioner to ask the right question, to choose the right means and to have on hand the relevant information. Academic research can provide the practitioner with 'enlightenment' thereby sensitising him to problems. Even if such general enlightenment tells him little about how to answer a difficult cable, it is no less potent for that. Gunnar Myrdal, like Keynes and Burton a distinguished academic and practitioner, has said,

> Our kind of power, which I have called influence, is most of the time only feebly related to the politics of the day; but if historical research lifted its eyes above the political constellations and machinations and sought the sources of the ideas out of which social change comes, it would be led to books and their authors (Myrdal, 1958, pp. 24–5).

Academics pursuing pure research in the scientific estate, as well as those in the professional (applied science) and administrative (social engineering) estates have something to offer. In the scientific estate it is about problems and turning problems into puzzles; in the professional estate it is about 'doing' (solving) puzzles; and in the administrative estate it is about applying the solution. But the 'something to offer' has to be made palatable to the practitioner not only in substance but also in a form that is relevant for his role in the decision making process. General influences of a paradigmatic nature are easy to identify; specific influences are seldom obvious. Social science is rarely so conclusive at the practitioner's level to close an argument, but the academic input can have some specific influences.

An academic contribution may bring greater consistency to a programme by making explicit the values and rationale that underlie it. The provision of information may elucidate some obscurities. However, consistency, a clear rationale and fuller information can sharpen conflicts rather than precipitate harmony by banishing a convenient muddle or misapprehension: it may enable parties to argue their differences more effectively and bring to the fore competing paradigms.[2] If research is following policy by being primarily located in the professional and administrative estates, then the parameters of policy may give it a specificity. However, this will be an element in the practitioner's hoped-for success only if those parameters are themselves valid. This suggests again the crucial, if not immediately obvious, specific or utilisable nature of research on paradigms. Such research is not only effective and important when it leads to the casting aside of one paradigm, such as power politics, and the adoption of a new one, such as world society. It also fills out an existing paradigm (Rein, 1976, p. 117). But whether in questioning or filling our paradigms, or in the tactics of social engineering, the product of the social scientist must have authority. Authority can come from tending to confirm conventional wisdom even if the scientific standing of the finding is somewhat open to question. But the greatest potential authority lies in any statement that can claim high scientific standing in an 'objective' social science. While the achievement of such a standing is a vain hope, for there can be no objective social science in the sense of it being value-free, value-controlled statements of a high degree of probability are a reasonable aspiration. They merit such authority and therefore salience and relevance as this world permits.

The fashion for 'barefoot empiricism' has now largely passed in social science. An empirical description cannot in practice include everything: something, no matter how minute, is almost inevitably left out. This implies a criterion for inclusion and exclusion which constitutes an embryonic theory. Thus, it is impossible to describe, still less think, without a theory. Facts do not speak for themselves: they tell us what we make them tell us. C. Wright Mills pointed out that 'Social research of any kind is advanced by ideas; it is only disciplined by fact' (Mills, 1959, p. 71) – a sentiment that Burton would share. But the 'discipline of fact' is crucial in promoting or safeguarding the authority of the academic's contribution to the decision making process and is a touchstone of the degree of 'truth' which aspires to speak to 'power'. Ideas – hypotheses – must therefore be tested in as scientific a way as possible by attempting to falsify them. An example of an hypothesis in action is useful, since it demonstrates that the hypothesis is worth pursuing. However, the real test comes from the attempt to demonstrate that the hypothesis does not hold, for that will indicate not merely the *possibility* of the hypothesis being 'true', but the degree of *probability* of the statement. If it cannot be falsified then it has a very high probability and can be taken as 'true'. While the probabilities of international relations do not reach those of much of so-called 'hard' science, the differences are of degree, not kind.

Even if findings in international relations had a high degree of probability then the relationship between academic and practitioner would still not run smooth. The academic is dealing with probabilities in relationships and explanation and prediction relating to those probabilities. The practitioner is concerned with the desirability of ends and means. The academic can point to consequences of particular choices but he cannot tell the practitioner what he should choose. The choice depends on the values of the judge the worth of which is not amenable to a scientific analysis which will tell the practitioner 'right' from 'wrong'. Can the academic therefore only help the practitioner with the likely functionality of means? Perhaps. No empirical or descriptive analysis can be value-free, but it can be as 'value-controlled' as humanly possible through the specification of the values involved in every stage of the research process. Can the academic thereby go further and make an academic contribution towards 'ought' statements? Burton argues that this is a false dilemma since there are clear imperatives that can be deduced from his empirical analysis. If his position is sustainable, then truth really *can* speak to power with compelling authority. However, pending an assessment of his position we are left with several possibilities.

The first of these is the positivistic one that social science should be as value-free or value-controlled as possible and recognise the gulf between 'is' and 'ought' statements. In this case, while the academic may help the practitioner with means, he can say nothing about ends; even his discussion of means is circumscribed because they are permeated by value premises. At the other end of the scale there is the view that social science should be 'value-promoting'. The academic, through his research, should join with the practitioner in promoting a particular set of values. But which values? Burton claims to have arrived at a satisfactory scientific explanation of the values to be promoted although usually advocates of this position suggest a version of Marxism. As Rein describes this position 'Facts organise values' and 'As reality unfolds in history it provides the ultimate source of authority for our values, because it informs us about what is "true" and hence what is "legitimate" ' (Rein, 1976, p. 252). This view can also be embraced by conservatives as it has been by Morgenthau and the power politics school. They claim to see from history that the struggle to dominate is universal in time and place.

Between the two extremes of 'value-controlled' and 'value-promoting' research lies what Rein calls a 'value-critical' approach in which the academic has something to offer the practitioner on 'ought' questions. Rein argues thus:

A value-critical position treats values not merely as the accepted aims of policy but as a subject for debate and analysis . . . Even our first principles become subject to further analysis when we subscribe to a number . . . that are mutually contradictory . . . We need an examination of goal concepts in their own terms but this task is difficult because there are no final solutions and no self-evident criteria against which to judge progress . . . Policy analysis involves the use of social science tools that produce inherently uncertain and incomplete findings, and these doubtful findings are then brought forward in an attempt to understand goals which are ambiguous and conflicting and where the elusive question of priorities is always dominant . . . The analyst who works within this framework may yearn for the self-assurance that the rigours of science or the faith of ideology can provide. But he cannot be tempted by these false idols, nor can he possibly undertake his work without method and belief. This tension provides the basis for creative work and informs the value-critical posture towards questions of policy (Rein, 1976, pp. 72, 73, 74, 79).

But is Rein merely offering a dubious pie-in-the-sky because he cannot bear either to be relatively separate from practitioners or to be fused with them? Is this a genuine case of trying sensibly to make the best of an impossible job in the higher interests of academics, practitioners and publics? Certainly a rigour in the exposure and definition of values together with their analysis in terms of consequences in the real world are called for from all points of view – value-controlled, value-promoting and value-critical. However, for Burton the 'is-ought' problem is a false one. The discussion turns on his views which, if correct, will lead to a much closer relationship between academic and practitioner.

BURTON'S POSITION[3]

There is no logically deduced truth or law that states that there can be no objective assessment of public policy. The syllogism – public policy concerns subjective values, subjective values are not subject to scientific evaluation, therefore public policy is not subject to scientific evaluation – is based on what could be a false premise. Public policy could concern subjective values while, at the same time, being concerned also with over-riding behavioural traits that are constant and scientifically determined. That subjective values must be the basis of authoritative decision making is itself a subjective judgement that may be false (Burton, 1982a, pp. 21–2).

Burton recognises that his position is challenging since it dismisses the seemingly important debate that has just been sketched.

We are asserting that if there were to be discovered a definite set of human needs on the basis of which societies could be harmonious, major methodological problems in behavioural sciences and in policy-making would be avoided. If there were agreement as to human needs then there would be a logical starting point of behavioural analysis for there would be a scientific basis for determining goals (Burton, 1979, p. 63).

It is a view shared by others. The starting point is that the individual is adopted as the basic unit of analysis for all of social science from individual psychology to the study of world society. While institutions of all types at all levels and in all dimensions have a considerable effect, outcomes, it is argued, are significantly related to individuals acting as individuals out of role and in nature. In the hoary argument over whether nature or nurture 'maketh man', Burton comes down heavily in favour of nature. Moreover, since individual behaviour is fundamentally grounded in an unchanging nature then social science knowledge can be objective and constitute a set of navigation points for practitioners.

Burton, along with others, points to the 'genetic drive to learn' (1982a, p. 34) about a set of universal basic human needs 'such as stimulus, security, identity, consistency of response and the need for control by the person of his/her environment as a means of pursuing these needs' (1982a, p. 16). Since these drives are of a genetic origin then they will be pursued come what may. The only constraints are 'values attached to relationships' (1982a, p. 16). If institutions obstruct the fulfilment of such needs then conflict will result and the individual will prevail for even if one or many are crushed others will (because they will have to) pursue similar goods. However, conflict is not inevitable because the needs being pursued are not necessarily in short supply.

Everyone can be stimulated, secure, have a sense of identity and the like, although there is no guarantee of this in practice. Security, for example, can be defined so that it is thought by others to engender insecurity for them whereupon conflict will ensue. But it can also be defined in such a way that it does not threaten others. The same can be said of identity, participation, development and other similar basic needs. Indeed, it is the job of the practitioner to ensure that basic needs are fulfilled in such a manner that conflict does not ensue and Burton suggests the process of problem-solving to ensure that dysfunctional policies are changed.

Basing himself on a number of needs theorists Burton stresses Sites' notion that 'The individual's most fundamental drive [is] . . . to attempt to control his environment in order to meet his needs' (Burton, 1982a, p. 35) whether by societally acceptable means or otherwise. If society is not able to offer the individual acceptable relationships, then there will be no constraints on the forms of the pursuit of needs. If society offers relationships cherished by the individual he will not prejudice them by anti-societal behaviour. The individual and his needs therefore provide 'objectively determined guides to policy – bases on which goals and policies could be assessed and predictions made as to success or self-defeating consequences' (Burton, 1982a, p. 36). Reflecting on where his thought has taken him Burton has pointed out that,

At no point have we entered the arena of values. Whether needs are promoted or frustrated as a matter of neglect or of deliberate public policy is a value matter. What has been argued is that needs lead to behavioural patterns that cannot be suppressed permanently, that are supportive or destructive of systems. Institutions either promote the pursuit of needs or are subject to destruction. It is a value matter how much destruction can be tolerated, how much coercion is acceptable, in the preservation of a system. The needs approach to public policy is *not* necessarily promoted by a humanistic interest in the individual. The proposition is that for a society to be harmonious and stable certain needs have to be promoted. However, such an approach undoubtedly highlights value considerations and the costs of frustrating the pursuit of needs if structures are maintained that are incompatible with the pursuit of needs. Furthermore, such a theory helps to legitimise protest movements, minority struggles for recognition, terrorism and other acts of rebellion. Such an approach, therefore, will be resisted, not only at the public level but also within centres of learning (Burton, 1982b).

This will be particularly the case when individuals are engaged in defence of privileges which they feel can be rendered secure in the short term. But society, and especially world society in a nuclear age, may thereby find itself jeopardised in the long term in a possible clash between the inexorable pursuit of individual needs and a tenacious role defence in a world vulnerable to breakdown. How convincing is the line that Burton and others are espousing to both academics and practitioners?

The academic will wish to examine the assertion of genetically based universal needs. While some needs theorists have offered some empirical data Burton quotes Sites to the effect that such hard empirical data is unnecessary:

In using the need concept we must ever be conscious that we are operating at an abstract conceptual level and that in the last analysis the actual basis of the need is tied up with certain psycho-physiological processes which are in interaction with the environment and which are not at this point in our scientific development directly observable. The fact that these processes are not directly observable, however, should not prevent us from working with the need concept if it allows us better to understand and to explain human activity. (The atom was conceptualised long before it was 'observed'.) That is, if we observe certain kinds of activity (or lack of activity) in behaviour which we need to account for, and can do so with the use of certain concepts which do not do violence to other things we know and which are consistent with other data which cause us to think in the same direction, there is no reason why we should not do so. We can always admit we are wrong (Sites quoted in Burton, 1979, pp. 66–7).

Positivists will despair at this. Nevertheless, Popper has suggested, in line with his argument that all observation is based on prior theory, that inborn 'expectations' or needs lead to problem-solving forming the basis of learning and an explanation of development – which is also Burton's position (Magee, 1973, pp. 56–7). But Burton does not start from an hypothesis the determination of which is essentially a private matter and then proceed to falsification. He follows Peirce in arguing that the hypothesis is an end in itself: it is the hypothesis, the process through which it is derived (abduction or retroduction) that is all-important rather than its falsification.

In short, we are back to wisdom, to deduction, to prescription and to the proof-of-the-pudding test. If an hypothesis works to the best of our knowledge after due care in application and observation, we will accept it as a basis for explanation and prescription. And if it works others will accept it too. But there will be feedback, for wisdom is not immutable. In the absence of wisdom, conventional wisdom changes: Morgenthau's theory of power politics was deduced from the assertion of a basic need to dominate but that basic need has been rejected by Burton and others in favour of a different set of basic needs that are more richly explanatory and helpfully predictive. Perhaps the basic needs currently in fashion are not universal: it matters little if they give the analyst a rich explanatory and predictory tool enabling him thereby blithely to treat them as a paradigm on which 'normal science' for practitioners can be based. Nevertheless, not all problems can be so easily put aside.

In embracing so whole-heartedly the cause of 'nature', Burton and needs theorists may well have overly down-played the role of 'nurture'. Even if there are basic universal human needs genetically implanted which act as the motor for learning and an explanation of behaviour, their expression takes place in a social environment. The social environment differs for each individual and the experience of the search for the fulfilment of basic needs feeds back into a specific environment – that of each individual and group. Even if society cannot, in the last resort, mould man so as to turn him from his basic needs, it can engage in a dialogue with an individual and influence substantially the way in which those needs will manifest themselves. Moreover, society is not homogeneous. Basic needs therefore are mediated by culture – *different* cultures. The process of mediation may make the end result significantly different in terms of concrete expression. Thus, even if the starting point point is universality, the end point is heterogeneity. This makes things difficult for the practitioner for he is dealing with the heterogeneous concrete manifestation of basic universal human needs. For him it is no great consolation to know that there was universality before culture and nurture got to work to present him with his daily fare of very different looking problems. Difficulties in the operationalisation of the needs approach therefore face the practitioner. Here, however, Burton has been especially innovative in his development of 'controlled communication' and 'problem-solving'. This is a vital part of his contribution to the amelioration of the academic–practitioner relationship. Through problem-solving techniques the cultural factors can receive their proper due.[4]

POWER HARNESSING TRUTH

While 'truth may speak to power', there are problems for 'power' in harnessing 'truth' which academics too frequently and wrongly dismiss as inconsequential or easily removable if only practitioners would exert the will to do so. Moreover, in many cases 'it is social scientists, rather than social science *per se*, that play the most prominent role in policy making' (Rein, 1976, p. 33). In playing politics in such a way an academic 'may ignore [power] . . . ; he may subordinate some of his autonomy to power; or he may have an independent base of power won by his own prestige' (Rein, 1976, p. 125). But what is meant by 'power'? A politician? A civil servant? A process?

Practitioners, even those in a high political or administrative position, often deny that they make decisions since they are largely circumscribed by their role in a continuous process. Their decision latitude varied from issue to issue and over time. While they may be able to generate enough political and administrative steam to move the administrative machine significantly on a particular issue and even against its grain, it is a time-consuming and tiring effort. In the meantime the drift of daily bureaucratic output continues 'rationally' but mindlessly in the general direction dictated by consensual values and the conventional wisdom of the dominant groups of society. Occasionally the drift gets out of step with the operating environment and disaster looms. At this point crisis decision making by top political leaders, officials and other relevant actors usually puts it back on the rails. The leaders then move on to the next crisis.

To the extent that this conception of a lumbering bureaucratic monster is accurate, power is unlikely to be able to harness truth. Practitioners do not make decisions: they help to move a process along, a process which has its internal micro rationality but one which is only with difficulty susceptible to control and reason at the macro level. While academics can influence this process at the micro level where the element of rationality enables power to harness truth to a limited degree, their greatest influence lies in contributing to the formation of the value consensus and conventional wisdom that underlies the societal drift. They do this through teaching and writing, although their influence is not immediate. After they 'programme' young people their ideas are diluted by time and institutionalised socialisation processes. It may take literally a lifetime, from professor to student to senior executive, for there to be any semblance of a significant paradigm shift, unless a looming catastrophe perchance speeds up the process.

In the meantime there is much room for a working relationship at the micro level in different parts of the decision-making process, although such academic-practitioner relationships have not always been easy. Weiss has suggested some

reasons for the disjunction between research and decisions: research does not examine all the relevant variables, research rarely fits the exact circumstances within which decisions are made, research is not ready on time for decisions, research conclusions are not clear or authoritative enough to provide trustworthy guidance, research reports do not reach the right audience, decision makers do not understand or trust research findings or understand how to interpret and apply them, the lessons from research are outweighed by competing considerations of agency self-interest and individual career advancement (Weiss, 1980, p. 170; pp. 16–23).

Furthermore, practitioners are often unwilling to rely on research inconsistent with their values. Moreover, they frequently look only at the results and not the argument, which may be more important if it enhances the practitioner's capacity for judgement on that and other issues. Requests for research are often ill-conceived, but equally academics sometimes ignore a specific request without good reason by doing what they want not what has been asked of them. While practitioners sometimes think that by throwing facts at a problem they can resolve it, academics ignore that their work is but one element in a continuous process.

Weiss found that what practitioners were looking for in her case studies of research was: relevance; technical quality, objectivity and cogency; plausibility in terms of prior knowledge, values and experience; explicit guidance for feasible implementation; and, surprisingly, a challenge to existing assumptions, practice and arrangements (Weiss, 1980, p. 250). The challenge, although not immediate in its effect, was a valued source of stimulation and enlightenment which practitioners found forced them to think more cogently about future general directions. However, what practitioners are looking for is not exactly the same as the uses they make of the academic input.

The academic's and practitioner's dream is research that directly solves a specific problem. This is rare since such research must be timely, new and overwhelmingly convincing as well as being the product of a close consensus on values, ends and means between the academic and the practitioner. In Weiss's 'knowledge driven model', 'Research can be used for policy making not so much because there is an issue pending that requires elucidation as because research has thrown up an opportunity that can be capitalised upon' (Weiss, 1977, p. 13). In the 'interactive model' research is only one part of a complicated process that also uses experience, political insight, pressure, social technologies and judgement (Weiss, 1977, p. 14). Research is also used as political ammunition in the morass of bureaucratic politics. Finally, there is the encouraging finding that research can be used to gain conceptual perspective, even to the extent of giving a retrospective rationale to past decisions, which becomes part of a learning process.

Some nefarious uses of research are the price paid by academics in attempting to influence practitioners and the decision making process. For some that price may be too high; others may like the political game, or may feel that the potential positive gains are worth the risk. After all, social science can enrich and clarify intuition and experience and thereby change expectations in order to form a new conventional wisdom.

THE GAP BETWEEN THEORY AND PRACTICE

Burton's work as a practitioner has been in the field of diplomacy: as an academic his field is international relations broadly defined as the political sociology of world society. While much of it has been conceptual, the problem solving exercises are important and meritorious efforts to put conceptual thinking to work in a policy context. Burton has bridged the gap between theory and practice. How have others fared?

Foreign Offices, at least in developed Western countries, tend to cultivate either the lawyer or the generalist. Experts are kept on 'tap not on top'. Thus, 'the higher the level of authority, the lower the level of knowledge' (Rothstein, 1972, p. 40), as the generalist holds sway basing himself on an outdated conventional wisdom. However, most countries have established a 'planning staff' capable in some cases of introducing a theoretical leavening to this generalist experience. In Britain policy-planning staffs have been small (usually five members) and, although membership has often been a step in a successful career in the FCO and Diplomatic Service, the group itself, as in most countries, has not had commensurate influence.

Planning staffs need direct access to the top. Otherwise they will be subverted, willy-nilly, by geographical and functional departments (whose work on no account should be duplicated in an attempt to gain influence or salience). Planning staffs need to think critically, and ahead, and they should not be afraid of controversy. Moreover, they can serve an important purpose by acting as a lookout and worrying about problems that are *not* on the agenda of other people. Planners have a difficult time since Foreign Offices usually think in terms of tactical flexibility in the short term rather than undertaking a long term analysis, a delineation of goals and a commitment to their achievement. Rothstein alludes to the Foreign Office mind 'which uses assumptions of unpredictability to justify an exclusive pre-occupation with the present' (1972, p. 83). What then can planning staffs do?

Clearly, if they are to act as a conduit between the academic world and the decision–making process, and for their own good, they need to be concerned with both ends and means. Indeed they must challenge the dominant paradigm and conventional wisdom of the day. An adversary role would probably be dysfunctional since it could be discounted as the 'paid opposition', so the function needs to be more that of an independent 'discussant'. This 'discussant' needs access at all levels, especially to the top, but organisationally it might be better outside a Foreign Office (to remove the temptation to meddle in day-to-day affairs). Geographical and functional depart-ments require their own 'in-house' planning, organic to their operations. 'In house' departmental planning operates in the shorter term and also involves coordination with other departments and with the 'discussants'. While 'in house' planning is time-bound, the discussant's' role is not, and its contribution, as Rothstein notes, 'is intellectual and not operational. Its primary commitment must be to ideas and assumptions, not programmes' (1972, p. 93). It is thus most concerned with theory and not with the area specialists of the academic world who feed more directly into the geographical departments.[5]

Planning staffs of several western Foreign Offices, when asked, have professed to thinking with detachment beyond the usual hand-to-mouth situation; to analytical thinking about what the problem is; and to future-oriented thinking beyond the in-basket (Bloomfield, 1977, pp. 816–22). But these comments appear to be more *desiderata* than an accurate description. Most Foreign Office planning staffs appear to have a paltry influence for a number of reasons: their members may subconsciously bear in mind that they will be going back to operational tasks; their academic training is frequently not in social science; they have been subject to intense institutional socialisation processes; and, as in the British case, they often feel a (reciprocated) antipathy and superiority towards the academic world. Above all, they rarely feel willing (and able) to challenge basic premises. To this degree they have abdicated an important part of their functions.

There are two alternatives to 'in-house' planning which may facilitate academic–practitioner relationships. The first of these is the outside 'discussant' formula which gives access to, but organisational separation from, the practitioners. The discussant's role is to facilitate the infusion of ideas and the questioning of basic parameters. The second facilitating procedure is the secondment of Foreign Office personnel to academic institutions. Part of the time such personnel should do what they see fit, but part of the time their sojourn should be guided by academics. In the other direction internships for students or junior staff would give them a feel for the policy process which would stand them in good stead later, be they either academics or practitioners. Thus, face-to-face academic–practitioner contacts are important because practitioners seem to prefer talking to reading. Moreover, personal contact provides instant feedback which may help to overcome communication difficulties.

CONCLUSION

Burton has argued that the problem lies not in an absolute lack of knowledge but in an increasing knowledge gap between what is known and the actual knowledge of administrators and politicians.[6] Burton elaborates further:

The role of the political and social scientist is to place contemporary changes in their longer-term perspective and thus to remove some of the fear element. Society is not necessarily endangered by change; change is demanded frequently to preserve and to enhance it . . . It is processes that social sciences have to offer – not ready-made solutions. The processes offered include, as a main ingredient, an analysis, hypothesis, a probable 'solution', an input of pieces of theory, much of which has the support of tests at one behavioural level or another. The actual solution is for the parties to determine. Their decisions are the final test of the scholars' analysis and tentative 'solution' (Burton, 1979, pp. 30, 38).

Burton's approach avoids another problem for academics. If the academic is primarily offering perspective, paradigmatic thinking and processes rather than prescription of a day-to-day nature, then he avoids a loyalty problem in dealing with 'power'. If the academic deals with processes and paradigms rather than daily prescription then he does not have to restrict himself to one practitioner. He is open and available to all since he hopes to be offering a universal commodity – 'truth' – something without which no government, body or group can ultimately survive. In turn, he preserves his academic freedom, which, although at times inconvenient, is in his long-term interest to protect.

If, like Burton, the academic claims to know how the world is, and, moreover, how it must be, then there is no value problem since there is no choice. The academic is only concerned with helping practitioners to avoid self-defeating policies in the short run. He is providing a short cut to the world as it will be in the long run, whether the practitioner likes it or not, or whatever he does about it. Burton's proposal of navigation points for practitioners, based on a growing literature of needs theorists, and a process of problem-solving and controlled communication for safe steering, offers a possibility of a happier relationship between academics and practitioners. But first academics and practitioners alike have to be convinced by this novel approach. *Prima facie* the case is a cogent and a practical one.

NOTES

1 For example, D.Sc London University, works published in Japanese and Spanish, leading figure in ISA, subject of a Ph.D. dissertation at IMEMO, Moscow.
2 See Paul Streeten's introduction in Myrdal (1958, pp. xvi–xvii).
3 This is summarised on pp. 130–2 of Burton (1982a).
4 This process is described in chapters 6, 7, 8 and 9.
5 A similar suggestion is made in Bloomfield (1978, pp. 388–9).
6 Burton (1982a, p. 18). This is a view shared by James Mullin, Chairman of the Committee for Scientific and Technological Research (Mullin, 1979).

Bibliography

Alger, Chadwick F. (1977), 'Foreign Policies of U.S. Publics', *International Studies Quarterly*, 21, 2 (June), pp. 277–318.

Alger, Chadwick F. and David C. Hoovler (1978), *You and Your Community in the World*, Columbus, OH: Consortium for International Studies Education, Ohio State University.

Alger, Chadwick F. (1981), 'Creating Participatory Global Cultures', *Alternatives*, 4, 4 (Spring), pp. 575–90.

Allison, Graham T. (1971), *Essence of Decision*, Boston: Little, Brown & Co.

Allison, Graham T. and Peter L. Szanton (1976), *Remaking Foreign Policy: the Organizational Connection*, New York: Basic Books.

Almond, Gabriel A. and Stephen J. Genco (1977), 'Clouds, Clocks and the Study of Politics', *World Politics*, 29, 4 (July), pp. 489–522.

Ashley, Richard K. (1980), *The Political Economy of War and Peace*, London: Frances Pinter; New York: Nichols.

Ashley, Richard K. (1981), 'Political Realism and Human Interests', *International Studies Quarterly*, 25, 2 (June), pp. 204–36.

Axelrod, Robert (ed.) (1976), *The Structure of Decision: the Cognitive Maps of Political Elites*, Princeton, NJ: Princeton University Press.

Banks, Michael H. (1978), 'Ways of Viewing the World Society', pp. 195–215 in A.J.R. Groom and C.R. Mitchell (eds), *International Relations Theory: A Bibliography*, London: Frances Pinter; New York: St Martin's.

Banks, Michael H. (1979), 'General Theory in International Relations: New Directions', *Millennium: Journal of International Studies*, 8, 1 (Winter), pp. 252–66.

Banks, Michael H. (forthcoming), *Resolution of Conflict: a Manual on the Problem-Solving Approach*.

Barkun, Michael (1970), *Law Without Sanctions*, Princeton, NJ: Princeton University Press.

Bateson, Gregory (1979), *Mind and Nature: a Necessary Unity*, New York: E.P. Dutton.

Beitz, Charles R. (1979), *Political Theory and International Relations*, Guildford, Surrey and Princeton, NJ: Princeton University Press.

Bernstein, Richard J. (1976), *The Restructuring of Social and Political Theory*, Oxford: Basil Blackwell; New York: Harcourt Brace Jovanovich.

Bertalanffy, Ludwig von (1968), *General System Theory: Foundations, Development, Applications*, New York: George Braziller.

Blalock, Jr., Hubert M. (1964), *Causal Inferences in Nonexperimental Research*, Chapel Hill, NC: University of North Carolina Press.

Blau, Peter M. (1964), *Exchange and Power in Social Life*, New York: Wiley.

Bloomfield, Lincoln P. (1977), 'Policy Planning Redefined: What the Planners Really Think', *International Journal*, 32, 4 (Autumn), pp. 813–28.

Bloomfield, Lincoln P. (1978), 'Planning Foreign Policy', *Political Science Quarterly*, 93, 3 (Fall), pp. 369–91.

Bonham, Matthew G. and Michael J. Shapiro (eds) (1977), *Thought and Action in Foreign Policy*, Basel: Berkhauser.

Boulding, Elise (1982), 'Education for Peace', *Bulletin of Atomic Scientists*, 38, pp. 59–62.

Boulding, Kenneth E. (1956), *The Image: Knowledge in Life and Society*, Ann Arbor, MI: University of Michigan Press.

Boulding, Kenneth E. (1962), *Conflict and Defense: a General Theory*, New York: Harper & Row.

Bowie, Norman E. and Robert L. Simon (1977), *The Individual and the Political Order*, Englewood Cliffs, NJ: Prentice-Hall.

Brandt Commission (1980), *North-South: a Programme for Survival*, London: Pan; Cambridge, MA: MIT Press.

Brecher, Michael (ed.) (1978), *Studies in Crisis Behavior*, New Brunswick, NJ: Transaction Books.

Bull, Hedley (1977), *The Anarchical Society*, London: Macmilian; New York: Columbia University Press.

Bundy, McGeorge, George F. Kennan and Gerard Smith (1982), 'Nuclear Weapons and the Atlantic Alliance', *Foreign Affairs*, 60, 4 (Spring), pp. 753–68.

Burton, John W. (1965), *International Relations: a General Theory*, London and New York: Cambridge University Press.

Burton, John W. (1966), *Non-Alignment*, London: André Deutsch.

Burton, John W. (1968), *Systems, States, Diplomacy and Rules*, London and New York: Cambridge University Press.

Burton, John W. (1969), *Conflict and Communication: the Use of Controlled Communication in International Relations*, London: Macmillan; New York: Free Press.

Burton, John W. (1972a), 'The Resolution of Conflict', *International Studies Quarterly*, 16, 1 (March), pp. 5–29.

Burton, John W. (1972b), *World Society*, London and New York: Cambridge University Press.

Burton, John W., A.J.R. Groom, C.R. Mitchell and Anthony V.S. de Reuck (1974), *The Study of World Society: a London Perspective*, Pittsburgh, PA: International Studies Association (occasional paper, no. 1).

Burton, John W. (1979), *Deviance, Terrorism and War: the Process of Solving Unsolved Social and Political Problems*, Oxford: Martin Robertson; New York: St Martin's.

Burton, John W. (1980), 'Universal Needs and Public Policies: the End of Ideologies', unpublished paper, International Congress of Arts and Sciences, Harvard University.

Burton, John W. (1982a), *Dear Survivors*, London: Frances Pinter; Boulder, CO: Westview.

Burton, John W. (1982b), 'Unpublished Documents on Problem Solving as a Means of Conflict Resolution, 1978–1982', Canterbury: Centre for the Analysis of Conflict, University of Kent (April).

Cable, Sir James (1981), 'The Useful Art of International Relations', *International Affairs*, 57, 2 (Spring), pp. 301–14.

Cannon, W. B. (1939), *The Wisdom of the Body*, rev. ed. New York: Norton.

Capra, Fritjof (1977), *The Tao of Physics*, New York: Bantam Books.

Carr, Edward H. (1939), *The Twenty Years Crisis, 1919–1939*, London: Macmillan; New York: Harper & Row.

Carroll, John S. and John W. Payne (1976), *Cognition and Social Behavior*, Hillsdale, NJ: Laurence Erlbaum.

Chambliss, William J. and Robert B. Seidman (1975), *Law, Order and Power*, London and Reading, MA: Addison-Wesley.

Chein, Isidore (1972), *The Science of Behavior and the Image of Man*, New York: Basic Books.

Choucri, Nazli (1980), 'International Political Economy: a Theoretical Perspective', in Ole R. Holsti, Randolph M. Siverson and Alexander George, (eds), *Change in the International System*, Boulder, CO: Westview Press.

Christensen, Cheryl and Robert Butterworth (1976), 'An Appraisal of the Philosophy of Science of the Inter-Nation Simulation

Project', in Dina A. Zinnes and Francis W. Hoole (eds), *Quantitative International Politics: an Appraisal*, New York: Praeger.

Claude, Inis L. (1962), *Power and International Relations*, New York: Random House.

Claude, Inis L. (1964), *Swords into Plowshares*, New York: Random House.

Cohen, Stephen P., Herbert C. Kelman, Frederick D. Miller and Bruce L. Smith (1977), 'Evolving Intergroup Techniques for Conflict Resolution: an Israeli–Palestinian Pilot Workshop', *Journal of Social Issues*, 33, 1, pp. 165–89.

Cohn, George (1939), *Neo-Neutrality*, New York: Columbia University Press.

Common Security: a Blueprint for Survival (1982), Report of the Independent Commission on Disarmament and Security Issues (Palme Commission), London: Pan; New York: Simon and Schuster.

Compton, Arthur H. (1935), *The Freedom of Man*, New Haven, CT: Yale University Press.

Coser, Lewis (1954), *The Functions of Social Conflict*, London: Routledge and Kegan Paul; New York: Free Press.

Cox, Robert (1981), 'Social Forces, States and World Orders: Beyond International Relations Theory', *Millennium: Journal of International Studies*, 10, 2 (Summer), pp. 126–55.

Cronbach, Lee J. (1975), 'Beyond Two Disciplines of Scientific Psychology', *American Psychologist*, 30, 2, pp. 116–27.

Dahl, Robert A. (1956), *A Preface to Democratic Theory*, Chicago: University of Chicago Press.

Dahl, Robert A. (1965), 'Cause and Effect in the Study of Politics', in Daniel Lerner (ed.), *Cause and Effect*, New York: Free Press.

Dahl, Robert A. (1970), *Modern Political Analysis*, Englewood Cliffs, NJ: Prentice-Hall.

Dedring, Juergen (1976), *Recent Advances in Peace and Conflict Research*, London and Beverly Hills, CA: Sage.

de Reuck, Anthony V.S. (1974), 'Controlled Communication: Rationale and Dynamics', *The Human Context*, 6, 1 (Spring), pp. 64–80.

de Reuck, Anthony V.S. (1983), 'A Theory of Conflict Resolution by Problem Solving', *Man, Environment, Space and Time*, 3, 1 (Spring), pp. 27–36.

de Rivera, Joseph (1968), *The Psychological Dimension of Foreign Policy*, Columbus, OH: C.E. Merrill.

Deutsch, Karl W. (1963), *The Nerves of Government*, New York: Free Press.

Deutsch, Karl W. (1981), 'Coping with the Risks of Peace: a Look at Some Prospects', *Millennium: Journal of International Studies*, 10, 2 (Summer), pp. 156–69.

Deutsch, Morton (1973), *The Resolution of Conflict*, London and New Haven, CT: Yale University Press.

Deutsch, Morton (1982), 'Preventing World War III: a Psychological Perspective', Presidential Address, Fifth Annual Scientific Meeting of the International Society of Political Psychology.

Donelan, Michael (ed.) (1978), *The Reason of States*, London and Winchester, MA: George Allen & Unwin.

Doob, Leonard W. and Robert B. Stevens (1969), 'The Fermeda Workshop: a Different Approach to Border Conflicts in Eastern Africa', *Journal of Psychology*, 73, 2, pp. 249–66.

Doob, Leonard W. (ed.) (1970), *Resolving Conflict in Africa: the Fermeda Workshop*, London and New Haven, CT: Yale University Press.

Dougherty, James E. and Robert L. Pfaltzgraff, Jr. (1981), *Contending Theories of International Relations*, 2nd ed. New York: Harper & Row.

Dyson, James (1980), 'Information Processing and Choice', unpublished ms., Florida State University.

Easton, David (1953), *The Political System*, New York: Alfred A. Knopf.

Edmead, Frank (1971), *Analysis and Prediction in International Mediation*, New York: UNITAR.

Einstein, Albert (1936), 'On Physical Reality', *Franklin Institute Journal*, 221, pp. 349 ff.

Erickson, John (1981), 'Barbarossa: the Night Russia Can't Forget', *The Sunday Times* (London), 21 June, p. 16.

Evans, Ernest (1979), *Calling a Truce to Terror*, Westport, CT: Greenwood Press.

Farrell, William R. and B.G. Edsall (1981), 'An Organizational Perspective on the U.S. Government's Effort to Counter Transnational Terrorism, 1972–1980', Newport, RI: Naval War College, June.

Festinger, Leon (1962), *A Theory of Cognitive Dissonance*, Stanford, CA: Stanford University Press.

Fisher, Roger (1969), *International Conflict for Beginners*, London: Allen Lane, the Penguin Press, 1971 (retitled *Basic Negotiating Strategy*); New York: Harper & Row.

Forgas, Joseph P. (1981), *Social Cognition*, London: Academic Press.

Frank, Philipp (1961), *Modern Science and Its Philosophy*, New York: Collier Books.

Frankel, Joseph (1973), *Contemporary International Theory and the Behaviour of States*, London and New York: Oxford University Press.

Frankel, Joseph (1981), 'Conventional and Theorising Diplomats', *International Affairs*, 57, 4 (Autumn), pp. 537–48.

Frohock, Fred M. (1967), *The Nature of Political Inquiry*, Homewood, IL: Dorsey Press.

Galtung, Johan (1980a), 'A Structural Theory of Imperialism: Ten Years Later', *Millennium: Journal of International Studies*, 9, 3 (Winter), pp. 183–96.

Galtung, Johan (1980b), *The True Worlds*, New York: Free Press.

Geerkin, M. and W.R. Grove (1977), 'Deterrence and Incapacitation: an Empirical Evaluation', *Social Forces*, 56, 2 (December), pp. 424–47.

'Generals for Peace' (1982), *Christian Science Monitor*, 30 June, p. 24.

George, Alexander L. (1974), 'Adaptation to Stress in Political Decision Making: the Individual, Small Group, and Organizational Context', in George V. Coelho, David A. Hamburg and John E. Adams (eds), *Coping and Adaptation*, New York: Basic Books.

George, Alexander L. (1979a), 'Case Studies and Theory Development: the Method of Structured, Focused Comparison', in Paul G. Lauren (ed.), *Diplomacy: New Approaches in History, Theory and Policy*, London: Collier Macmillan; New York: Free Press.

George, Alexander L. (1979b), 'The Causal Nexus between Cognitive Beliefs and Decision-Making Behavior: the "Operational Code" Belief', in Lawrence S. Falkowski (ed.), *Psychological Models in International Politics*, Boulder, CO: Westview Press.

George, Alexander L. (1980), *Presidential Decisionmaking in Foreign Policy: the Effective Use of Information and Advice*, Boulder, CO: Westview Press.

George, Alexander L. and Richard Smoke (1974), *Deterrence in American Foreign Policy: Theory and Practice*, New York: Columbia University Press.

Gibbs, J.P. (1977), 'Social Control, Deterrence and Perspectives on Social Order', *Social Forces*, 56, 2 (December), pp. 408–23.

Gilpin, Robert (1975), *U.S. Power and the Multinational Corporation: the Political Economy of Foreign Direct Investment*, New York: Basic Books.

Gouldner, Alvin W. (1955), *Wildcat Strike*, New York: Harper & Row.

Groom, A.J.R. (1975), 'Conflict Analysis and the Arab–Israeli Conflict', pp. 28–58 in James Barber, *et al.* (eds), *International Politics and Foreign Policy,* Block 4, Milton Keynes: Open University Press.

Gurr, Theodore Robert (1977), 'Some Characteristics of Political Terrorism in the 1960s', Paper prepared for the Southwestern Social Science Association Annual Convention, Dallas, Texas (March).

Habermas, Jürgen (1971), *Knowledge and Human Interests*, Boston: Beacon Press.

Halle, Louis (1960), *American Foreign Policy*, London: Geroge Allen & Unwin.

Heisenberg, Werner (1930), *The Physical Principles of the Quantum Theory*, New York: Dover Publications.

Heisenberg, Werner (1958), *The Physicist's Conception of Nature*, New York: Harcourt, Brace.

Henderson, Hazel (1981), *Politics of the Solar Age: Alternatives to Economics*, Garden City, NY: Anchor Press.

Hermann, Charles F. (ed.) (1972), *International Crises*, London: Haigh & Hochland; New York: Free Press.

Herz, John (1981), 'Political Realism Revisited', *International Studies Quarterly*, 25, 2 (June), pp. 182–97.

Hesse, Mary (1980), *Revolutions and Reconstructions in the Philosophy of Science*, Brighton: Harvester Press; Bloomington, IN: Indiana University Press.

Hilgard, E.R., R.C. Atkinson and R.L. Atkinson (1971), *Introduction to Psychology*, 5th ed. New York: Harcourt Brace Jovanovich.

Hill, Barbara J. (1982), 'An Analysis of Conflict Resolution Techniques: from Problem Solving Workshops to Theory', *Journal of Conflict Resolution*, 26, 1 (March), pp. 109–38.

Hilton, Gordon (1976), 'An Appraisal of the Philosophy of Science and Research Design Involved in the Dimensionality of Nations Project', in Dina A. Zinnes and Francis W. Hoole (eds), *Quantitative International Politics: an Appraisal*, New York: Praeger.

Hinsley, Francis Harry (1963), *Power and the Pursuit of Peace*, Cambridge: Cambridge University Press.

Hobson, John A. (1915), *Towards International Government*, London: George Allen & Unwin; New York: Macmillan.

Hoffmann, Stanley (1977), 'An American Social Science: International Relations', *Daedalus*, 106, 3 (Summer), pp. 41–60.

Holsti, Kalevi J. (1983), *International Politics: a Framework for*

Analysis, 4th ed. London: Prentice-Hall International; Englewood Cliffs, NJ: Prentice-Hall.

Holsti, Ole R. (1967), 'Cognitive Dynamics and Images of the Enemy', in David J. Finlay, Ole R. Holsti and Richard R. Fagen, *Enemies in Politics*, Chicago: Rand McNally.

Holsti, Ole R. (1971), *Crisis, Escalation, War*, London: Haigh & Hochland; Montreal: McGill-Queens University Press.

Hutchinson, Martha C. (1982), 'The Concept of Revolutionary Terrorism', *Journal of Conflict Resolution*, 26, 3 (September), pp. 383–96.

Inkeles, Alex (1975), 'The Emerging Social Structure of the World', *World Politics*, 27, 4 (July), pp. 467–95.

Janis, Irving L. (1973), *Victims of Groupthink*, New York: Houghton Mifflin.

Janis, Irving L. and Leon Mann (1977), *Decision Making*, New York: Free Press.

Jenkins, Brian M. (1974), 'International Terrorism: a New Kind of Warfare', Santa Monica, CA: Rand Corp., P-5216.

Jenkins, Brian M. (1980), *Embassies Under Siege: a Review of 48 Embassy Takeovers, 1971–1980*, Santa Monica, CA: Rand Corp., R-2651-RC.

Jervis, Robert (1970), *The Logic of Images in International Relations*, Guildford, Surrey and Princeton, NJ: Princeton University Press.

Jervis, Robert (1971), 'Hypotheses on Misperception', in George H. Quester (ed.), *Power, Action and Interaction*, Boston: Little, Brown & Co.

Jervis, Robert (1976), *Perception and Misperception in International Politics*, Guildford, Surrey and Princeton, NJ: Princeton University Press.

Jervis, Robert (1980), 'Political Decision-Making: Recent Contributions', *Political Psychology*, 2, 2 (Summer), pp. 86–101.

Jones, Susan D. and J. David Singer (1972), *Beyond Conjecture in International Politics*, Itasca, IL: F.E. Peacock.

Kahn, Herman (1965), *On Thermonuclear War*, New York: Praeger.

Kahneman, Daniel and Amos Tversky (1972), 'Subjective Probability: a Judgement of Representativeness', *Cognitive Psychology*, 3, 3, pp. 430–54.

Kahneman, Daniel and Amos Tversky (1973), 'On the Psychology of Prediction', *Psychological Review*, 80, 4 (July), pp. 237–51.

Kahneman, Daniel, Paul Slovic and Amos Tversky (1982), *Judgement under Uncertainty: Heuristics and Biases*, London and New York: Cambridge University Press.

Kaplan, Abraham (1964), *The Conduct of Inquiry: Methodology for Behavioral Science*, New York: Harper & Row.

Kelly, George A. (1953), 'Man's Construction of His Alternatives', in Gardner Lindzey (ed.), *Assessment of Human Motives*, New York: Rinehart & Co.

Kelman, Herbert C. (1972), 'The Problem-Solving Workshop in Conflict Resolution', pp. 168–204 in Richard L. Merritt (ed.), *Communication in International Politics*, London & Chicago: University of Chicago Press.

Kelman, Herbert C. and Stephen P. Cohen (1979), 'Reduction of International Conflict: an Interactional Approach', pp. 288–303 in W.G. Austin and S. Worchel (eds), *The Social Psychology of Intergroup Relations*, Monterey, CA: Brooks-Cole.

Kennan, George F. (1952), *American Diplomacy 1900–1950*, New York: Mentor.

Kennan, George F. (1981), 'A Proposal for International Disarmament', presented following acceptance of Albert Einstein Peace Prize, Washington, D.C., 19 May.

Kent, Randolph C. and Gunnar P. Nielsson (eds) (1980), *The Study and Teaching of International Relations*, London: Frances Pinter; New York: Nichols.

Keohane, Robert O. and Joseph Nye, Jr. (eds) (1971), *Transnational Relations and World Politics*, Cambridge, MA: Harvard University Press.

Keohane, Robert O. and Joseph Nye, Jr. (1977), *Power and Interdependence: World Politics in Transition*, Boston: Little, Brown & Co.

Keynes, John Maynard (1931), 'Economic Possibilities for Our Grandchildren', in *Essays in Persuasion*, London: Macmillan.

Knorr, Klaus and James N. Rosenau (eds) (1969), *Contending Approaches to International Politics*, Princeton, NJ: Princeton University Press.

Korzybski, Alfred (1933), *Science and Sanity: an Introduction to Non-Artistotelian Systems and General Semantics*, Lancaster, PA: The Science Press Co.

Krahenbuhl, M. (1977), 'Political Kidnappings in Turkey, 1971–1972', Santa Monica, CA: Rand Corp.

Krasner, Stephen D. (1978), *Defending the National Interest: Raw Materials Investments and U.S. Foreign Policy*, Princeton, NJ: Princeton University Press.

Krasner, Stephen D. (ed.) (1983), *International Regimes*, London and Ithaca, NY: Cornell University Press.

Kuhn, Thomas S. (1970), *The Structure of Scientific Revolutions*, 2nd ed. Chicago: University of Chicago Press.

Kupperman, Robert H. (1979), 'Facing Tomorrow's Terrorist Incident Today', pp. 379–441 in Augustus R. Norton and Martin H. Greenberg (eds), *Studies in Nuclear Terrorism*, Boston, MA: G.K. Hall.

Lakatos, Imre (1970), 'Methodology of Scientific Research Programmes', in Imre Lakatos and Alan Musgrave, *Criticism and the Growth of Knowledge*, Cambridge and New York: Cambridge University Press.

Latham, Earl (1965), *The Group Basis of Politics*, New York: Octagon.

Levi, A. M. and A. Benjamin (1977), 'Focus and Flexibility in a Model of Conflict Resolution', *Journal of Conflict Resolution*, 21, 3 (September), pp. 405–25.

Lijphart, Arend (1974), 'The Structure of the Theoretical Revolution in International Relations', *International Studies Quarterly*, 18, 1 (March), pp. 41–74.

Lijphart, Arend (1981), 'Karl W. Deutsch and the New Paradigm in International Relations', pp. 233–51 in Richard L. Merritt and Bruce M. Russett (eds), *From National Development to Global Community*, London and Boston: George Allen & Unwin.

Lindblom, Charles E. (1959), 'The Science of "Muddling Through"', *Public Administration Review*, 19 (Spring), pp. 79–88.

Lindblom, Charles E. (1977), *Politics and Markets: the World's Political Economic Systems*, New York: Basic Books.

Linklater, Andrew (1982), *Men and Citizens in the Theory of International Relations*, London and New York: Macmillan.

Lipscomb, William N. (1981), 'Our Schools Stifle Creative Thought in Science', *U.S. News and World Report*, 20 April, p. 85.

Little, Richard (1981), 'Ideology and Change', pp. 30–45 in Barry Buzan and R.J. Barry Jones (eds), *Change and the Study of International Relations*, London: Frances Pinter.

Lloyd-Bostock, Sally M.A. (1979), 'Explaining Compliance with Imposed Law', pp. 9–24 in Sandra B. Burman and Barbara E. Harrell-Bond (eds), *The Imposition of Law*, New York: Academic Press.

Lodge, Juliet (ed.) (1981), *Terrorism: a Challenge to the State*, Oxford: Martin Robertson; New York: St Martin's Press.

Lorenz, Konrad (1967), *On Aggression*, New York: Bantam Books.

Lowi, Theodore J. (1968), *The End of Liberalism*, New York: W. Norton & Co.

Magee, Bryan (1973), *Popper*, London: Fontana.

Maghroori, Ray and Bennett Ramberg (eds) (1983), *Globalism Versus Realism: International Relations' Third Debate*, Boulder, CO: Westview Press.

Malinowski, B. (1922), *Argonauts of the Western Pacific*, New York: E.P. Dutton.

Mansbach, Richard W., Yale H. Ferguson and Donald E. Lampert (1976), *The Web of World Politics: Nonstate Actors in the Global System*, London: Prentice-Hall International; Englewood Cliffs, NJ: Prentice-Hall.

Mansbach, Richard W. and John A. Vasquez (1981), *In Search of Theory: a New Paradigm for Global Politics*, Guildford, Surrey and New York: Columbia University Press.

Maoz, Zeev (1981), 'The Decision to Raid Entebbe: Decision Analysis Applied to Crisis Behavior', *Journal of Conflict Resolution*, 25, 4 (December), pp. 677–707.

March, James G. and Johan P. Olsen (1976), *Ambiguity and Choice in Organizations*, Bergen: Universitetsforlaget.

March James G. and Herbert A. Simon (1958), *Organizations*. London and New York: Wiley.

Marcuse, Herbert (1969), *An Essay on Liberation*, Boston: Beacon Press.

Maslow, Abraham (1968), *Toward a Psychology of Being*, 2nd ed. New York: Van Nostrand.

Mathiesen, Thomas (1980), *Law, Society and Political Action*, New York: Academic Press.

Mayall, James (ed.) (1983), *The Community of States*, London and Winchester, MA: George Allen & Unwin.

McClelland, Charles A. (1961), 'The Acute International Crisis', *World Politics*, 14, 1 (October), pp. 182–204.

McClelland, Charles (1972), 'On the Fourth Wave: Past and Future in the Study of International Systems', in James N. Rosenau, V. Davis and M.A. East (eds), *The Analysis of International Politics*, New York: Free Press.

Meade, Robert H. (1978), *Physics for Poets*, 2nd ed. New York: McGraw-Hill.

Meehl, Paul E. (1967), 'Theory-Testing in Psychology and Physics: a Methodological Paradox', *Philosophy of Science*, 34, 2 (June), pp. 103–14.

Merton, Robert K. (1968), *Social Theory and Social Structure*, 3rd ed. New York: Free Press.

Merton, Robert K. and Robert A. Nisbet (1961), *Contemporary Social Problems*, New York: Harcourt Brace.

Mickolus, Edward F. (1980), *The Literature of Terrorism: a Selectively Annotated Bibliography*, Westport, CT: Greenwood Press.

Miller, George A., Eugene Galanter and Karl Pribram (1960), *Plans and the Structure of Human Behavior*, New York: Henry Holt.

Mills, C. Wright (1959), *The Sociological Imagination*, London and New York: Oxford University Press.

Mitchell, Christopher R. (1981a), *Peacemaking and the Consultant's Role*, Farnborough, Hants: Gower; New York: Nichols.

Mitchell, Christopher R. (1981b), *The Structure of International Conflict*, London: Macmillan; New York: St Martin's Press.

Mitrany, David (1966), *A Working Peace System*, Chicago: Quadrangle Books.

Modelski, George (1962), *A Theory of Foreign Policy*, London: Pall Mall.

Monnet, Jean (1978), *Memoirs*, London: Collins.

Morgan, Patrick M. (1977), *Deterrence: a Conceptual Analysis*, London and Beverly Hills, CA: Sage.

Morgan, Patrick M. (1981), *Theories and Approaches to International Relations: What Are We to Think?*, 3rd ed. London and New Brunswick, NJ: Transaction Books.

Morgenthau, Hans J. (1948; 4th ed., rev., 1967), *Politics Among Nations: the Struggle for Power and Peace*, New York: Alfred A. Knopf.

Morse, Edward L. (1976), *Modernisation and the Transformation of International Relations*, London: Collier Macmillan; New York: Free Press.

Mullin, James (1979), Introduction by the Chairman of the Committee for Scientific and Technological Research, *OECD: Social Sciences in Policy Making*, Paris: OECD.

Myrdal, Gunnar (1958), *Value in Social Theory*, New York: Harper & Row.

Newell, Allen and Herbert A. Simon (1972), *Human Problem Solving*, Englewood Cliffs, NJ: Prentice-Hall.

Nicholson, Michael (1983), *The Scientific Analysis of Social Behaviour*, London: Frances Pinter.

North, Robert G., Ole R. Holsti and Nazli Choucri (1976), 'A Reevaluation of the Research Program of the Stanford Studies in International Conflict and Integration', in Dina A. Zinnes and Frances W. Hoole, (eds), *Quantitative International Politics: an Appraisal*, New York: Praeger.

Olson, Mancur (1965), *The Logic of Collective Action*, Cambridge, MA: Harvard University Press.

Oppenheimer, J. Robert (1954), *Science and the Common Understanding*, New York: Oxford University Press.

Paige, Glenn D. (1978), 'The Primacy of Politics', in Paul G. Lewis and David C. Potter (eds), *The Practice of Comparative Politics*, London: Longman.

Pettman, Ralph (1979), *State and Class: a Sociology of International Affairs*, London: Croom Helm.

Phillips, Warren R. (1974), 'Where Have All the Theories Gone?', *World Politics*, 26, 2 (January), pp. 155–88.

Pierre, Andrew J. (1976), 'The Politics of International Terrorism', *Orbis*, 19, 4 (Winter), pp. 1251–69.

Popper, Karl R. (1972), *Objective Knowledge: an Evolutionary Approach*, Oxford: Clarendon Press.

Presidential Commission on Foreign Language and International Studies (1979), *Strength Through Wisdom: a Critique of U.S. Capability*, Washington, D.C.: U.S. Government Printing Office.

Price, Don (1965), *The Scientific Estate*, Cambridge, MA: Harvard University Press.

Pruitt, Dean G. (1969), *Theory and Research on the Causes of War*, London and Englewood Cliffs, NJ: Prentice-Hall.

Pruitt, Dean G. (1981), *Negotiation Behavior*, New York: Academic Press.

Purnell, Robert (1978), 'Theoretical Approaches to International Relations: the Contribution of the Graeco-Romano World', pp. 19–31 in Trevor Taylor (ed.), *Approaches and Theory in International Relations*, London: Longman.

Rapoport, Anatol (1970), 'Modern Systems Theory: an Outlook for Coping with Change', *General Systems: Yearbook of the Society for General Systems Research*, 15, pp. 17–18.

Rein, Martin (1976), *Social Science and Public Policy*, Harmondsworth: Penguin.

Ronen, Dov (1979), *The Quest for Self-Determination*, London and New York: Yale University Press.

Rosenau, James N. (ed.) (1969), *Linkage Politics*, New York: Free Press.

Rosenau, James N. (1973), *International Studies and the Social Sciences: Problems, Priorities and Prospects in the United States*, London and Beverly Hills, CA: Sage.

Rosenau, James N. (ed.) (1976), *In Search of Global Patterns*, London: Collier Macmillan; New York: Free Press.

Rosenau, James N., *et al.* (1977), 'Of Syllabi, Texts, Students and Scholarship in International Relations', *World Politics*, 29, 2 (January), pp. 263–340.

Rosenau, James N. (1983), 'Order and Disorder in the Study of World Politics', pp. 1–7 in Ray Maghroori and Bennett Ramberg (eds), *Globalism Versus Realism*, Boulder, CO: Westview Press.

Ross, Edward A. (1920), *The Principles of Sociology*, New York: Century.

Rothstein, Robert (1972), *Planning, Prediction and Policymaking in Foreign Affairs*, Boston: Little, Brown & Co.

Runciman, W. G. (1966), *Relative Deprivation and Social Justice*, London: Routledge & Kegan Paul.

Russell, Charles A., L. J. Banker Jr., and Bowman H. Miller (1979), 'Out-Inventing the Terrorist', in Yonah Alexander, David Carlton and Paul Wilkinson (eds), *Terrorism: Theory and Practice*, Boulder, CO: Westview Press.

Samuelson, Paul A. (1970), *Economics*, 8th ed. New York: McGraw Hill.

Schattschneider, E. E. (1960), *The Semi-Sovereign People*, New York: Harcourt.

Schelling, Thomas C. (1966), *Arms and Influence*, New Haven, CT: Yale University Press.

Schrodinger, Erwin (1956), *What is Life? And Other Scientific Essays*, Garden City, NY: Doubleday.

Schroeder, H.M., D.M. Driver and S. Strenfert (1967), *Human Information Processing*, New York: Holt, Rinehart & Winston.

Scott, Andrew M. (1965), *The Revolution in Statecraft: Informal Penetration*, New York: Random House; rev. ed. (1982), Durham, NC: Duke University Press.

Simon, Herbert A. (1976), *Administrative Behavior*, 3rd ed. New York: Free Press.

Singer, J. David (1961), 'The Level of Analysis Problem in International Relations', pp. 72–92 in Klaus Knorr and Sydney Verba (eds), *The International System: Theoretical Essays*, Guildford, Surrey and Princeton, NJ: Princeton University Press.

Singer, J. David and Associates (1979), *Explaining War: Selected Papers from the Correlates of War Project*, London and Beverly Hills, CA: Sage.

Sites, Paul (1973), *Control: the Basis of Social Order*, New York: Dunellen.

Sivard, Ruth L. (1981), *World Military and Social Expenditures 1981*, Leesburg, VA: World Priorities.

Skjei, Stephen S. (1973), *Information for Collective Action*, Lexington, MA: D.C. Heath.

Slovic, Paul and Sarah Lichtenstein (1971), 'Comparison of Bayesian and Regression Approaches to the Study of Information Processing in Judgement', *Organisational Behavior and Human Performance*, 6, pp. 649–744.

Smith, Michael, Richard Little and Michael Shackleton (eds) (1981), *Perspectives on World Politics*, London: Croom Helm.

Snyder, Glenn H. and Paul Diesing (1977), *Conflict Among Nations*, Guildford, Surrey and Princeton, NJ: Princeton University Press.

Snyder, Mark (1982), 'Self-fulfilling Stereotypes', *Psychology Today*, 16, (July), pp. 60–8.

Stapp, Henry (1972), 'The Copenhagen Interpretation and the Nature of Space-Time', *American Journal of Physics*, 40, pp. 1098 ff.

Steinbruner, John D. (1974), *The Cybernetic Theory of Decision*, Guildford, Surrey and Princeton, NJ: Princeton University Press.

Stinchcombe, A.L. (1968), *Constructing Social Theories*, New York: Harcourt.

Strassoldo, Raimondo and Renzo Gubert (1973), 'The Boundary: an Overview of its Current Theoretical Status', in Raimondo Strassoldo (ed.), *Boundaries and Regions: Explorations in the Growth and Peace Potential of the Peripheries*, Trieste: Edizioni Lint.

Sullivan, Michael P. (1976), *International Relations: Theories and Evidence*, London and Englewood Cliffs, NJ: Prentice-Hall.

Sullivan, Michael P. (1978), 'Competing Frameworks and the Study of Contemporary International Politics', *Millennium: Journal of International Studies*, 7, 2 (Autumn), pp. 93–110.

Taylor, Trevor (ed.) (1978), *Approaches and Theory in International Relations*, London and New York: Longman.

Thompson, John W. (1964), 'Prediction in Physics and the Social Sciences', *General Systems: Yearbook of the Society for General Systems Research*, 9, pp. 15–23.

Thompson, William R. (ed.) (1983), *Contending Approaches in World System Analysis*, London and Beverly Hills, CA: Sage.

To Establish the United States Academy of Peace (1981), Report of the Commission on Proposals for the National Academy of Peace and Conflict Resolution, Washington D.C.: U.S. Government Printing Office.

Torney, Judith V., Abraham N. Oppenheim and Russell F. Farnen (1975), *Civic Education in Ten Countries*, New York: Wiley.

Tucker, Robert W. (1977), *The Inequality of Nations*, Oxford: Martin Robertson: New York: Basic Books.

UNITAR (1970), 'Social Psychological Techniques and the Peaceful Settlement of International Disputes', UNITAR Research Reports, No. 1, New York: UNITAR.

University for Peace: Basic Documents (1981), Presidential Commission for the University for Peace, San Jose, Costa Rica.

Vasquez, John A. (1979), 'Colouring it Morgenthau: New Evidence for an Old Thesis on Quantitative International Politics', *British Journal of International Studies*, 5, 3 (October), pp. 210–29.

Vasquez, John A. (1983), *The Power of Power Politics: a Critique*, London: Frances Pinter; New Brunswick, NJ: Rutgers University Press.

Wainstein, E.J. (1977), 'The Cross and Laporte Kidnappings, Montreal, October 1970', Santa Monica, CA: Rand Corp.

Wallerstein, Immanuel (1976), *The Modern World System*, vol. 1., London and New York: Academic Press.

Wallerstein, Immanuel (1980), *The Modern World System*, vol. 2., London and New York: Academic Press.

Walton, Richard E. (1969), *Interpersonal Peacemaking*, London and Reading, MA: Addison-Wesley.

Waltz, Kenneth N. (1979), *Theory of International Politics*, London and Reading, MA: Addison-Wesley.

Ward, Benjamin (1979), *The Ideal Worlds of Economics: Liberal, Radical and Conservative Economic Views*, London: Macmillan.

Wedge, Bryan and Dennis J.D. Sandole (1982), 'Conflict Management: a New Venture into Professionalization', *Peace and Change: a Journal of Peace Research*, 8, 3 (Summer), pp. 129–38.

Weiss, Carol H. (ed.) (1977), *Using Social Science Research in Public Policy Making*, Lexington, MA: Lexington Books.

Weiss, Carol H. with Michael J. Bucuvalas (1980), *Social Science Research and Decision-Making*, Guildford, Surrey and New York: Columbia University Press.

Whaley, Barton (1973), *Stratagem: Deception and Surprise in War*, rev. ed. New York: Praeger.

White, Ralph (1982), Presentation at a discussion of *Perception and Misperception* by Robert Jervis, The Fifth Annual Scientific Meeting of the International Society of Political Psychology, Washington D.C., 24–7 June.

Wight, Martin (1966), 'Why Is There No International Theory?', pp. 17–34 in Herbert Butterfield and Martin Wight (eds),

Diplomatic Investigations, London: George Allen & Unwin; Cambridge, MA: Harvard University Press.

Wight, Martin (1977), *Systems of States*, Leicester: Leicester University Press.

Wight, Martin (1978), *Power Politics*, Harmondsworth: Penguin Books; New York: Holmes & Meier.

Willetts, Peter (1978), *The Non-Aligned Movement*, London: Frances Pinter; New York: Nichols.

Wilson, Edward O. (1975), *Sociobiology: The New Synthesis*, London and Cambridge, MA: The Belknap Press of Harvard University Press.

Wilson, Edward O. (1978), *On Human Nature*, London and Cambridge, MA: Harvard University Press.

Wilson, Edward O. and Charles J. Lumsden (1981), *Genes, Mind and Culture: the Co-evolutionary Process*, London and Cambridge, MA: Harvard University Press.

Wolfers, Arnold (1959), 'The Actors in International Politics', pp. 83–106 in W.T.R. Fox (ed.), *Theoretical Aspects of International Relations*, South Bend, IN: University of Notre Dame Press.

Wright, Quincy (1965), *A Study of War*, 2nd ed. London and Chicago: University of Chicago Press.

Yearbook of International Organisations (1981), Brussels: International Union of International Associations.

Young, Oran R. (1964), 'A Survey of General Systems Theory', and 'The Impact of General Systems Theory in Political Science', *General Systems: Yearbook of the Society of General Systems Research*, 9, pp. 61–80, pp. 242–3.

Young, Oran R. (1967), *The Intermediaries: Third Parties in International Crises*, Guildford, Surrey and Princeton, NJ: Princeton University Press.

Young, Oran R. (1969), 'Interdependencies in World Politics', *International Journal*, 24, 3 (Autumn), pp. 726–50.

Author Index

Subject Index